My

...and wha

Find Kellie Jo Holly

Verbal Abuse Journals at http://www.VerbalAbuseJournals.com
Facebook at https://www.facebook.com/VerbalAbuseJournals
Twitter at https://twitter.com/abuse_journals
YouTube at http://www.youtube.com/user/verbalabusejournal
Amazon.com at http://www.amazon.com/Kellie-Jo-Holly/e/B009UYGMIG

Copyright © 2014 Kellie Jo Holly, Verbal Abuse Journals

All rights reserved worldwide. You not replicate, redistribute or give away any part of this publication in any form without the prior written consent of the author. The author designed this publication to provide accurate and authoritative information concerning the subject matter covered. If legal advice or other expert assistance is required, seek the services of a professional.

Dedication

This book goes out to every abuse sufferer, present and past, who stay in an abusive relationship because the abuse seems more manageable than leaving and creating a new life. I hope you use my experiences to calm your fears and come to believe that you are strong enough, courageous enough and wise enough to create the life of your dreams.

Table of Contents

Prologue 1
   No Surprise 2
   My Heart Is Failing 4
Part I: ... and the aftermath of leaving 6
   Ex Parte 7
   I Left Twice 8
   Don't Worry 23
   Thank You 25
   Events of the Day 27
   Slippery 29
   Emergency Money 32
   Laughing 33
   Red to Blue 34
   Am I Happy He Is Gone? 36
   Potty Talk 40
   Emergency Plan = Emotional Pain 41
   What Would You Do With Omnipotence? 44
   A Necessary Evil 48
   This One, I'll Address above Board 53
   Adding To It 56
   Apology at the End 61
   Conflicting Thoughts 64
   Tired and Weak 65
   Half Life 66
   Army of Snot 68

Part II: ... and the living begins 71
    Transition Title 72
    Too Soon 73
    Semantics.. 75
    Change is Stability... 78
    In the Way.. 79
    Fixing It 81
    Rules 84
    Liar Liar 85
    Wasted Time... 88
    20 Minutes 90
    I Love Who I Am Becoming 92
    Top 8 Signs It's Time to Leave Your Marriage............................... 93
    I Want to Lie to You 94
    Of Guardians and Demons.. 103
    Seek and Ye Shall Find.. 107
    Murder Suicide 111
    Running Away.. 112
    Letting Go 112
    Wrong... 114
    Fix and Please 121
    Choose 122
    Will I Survive This? 126
    I Was Happy... 129
    Fantasy 131
    Justice vs. Right... 132
    Paradigm Shift 135
    Chocolate Bon Bons 137
    Missing Time.. 139
    Damaged But Not Broken 140
    How Did I Get Here? 141
    Resisting Temptation 143
    Why Did I Stay in My Abusive Marriage?................................... 147
    Looking for Work 150
    Residue... 153
    18th Anniversary... 159
    Not Over Yet.. 163
    There is No Good God 167

Mediation	171
The Boys	172
Wishbone	175
Write Something Good	177
From Them	179
Conflicted	182
Still a Knot	184
Churning but Less So	187
Dependent	192
This is Me, That is Him	200
Time Reports	202
Envisioned	203
All Right	207
New House New House New House New House!	209
Checking In	211
Daybreak	214
My Job	219
Loneliness	221
Calm and Crazy	224
Tomatoes for Lunch	226
Secrets	227
Got a Raise	230
Some Guy off the Street	231
Luxury	235
In the End	237
Searching	239
I'm Not That Person…Yet	241
Verbal Abuse Revisited	245
Dear Erin	246
Hold and Release	248
DreamScapes	252
In Isolation	255
Fairy Tale	260
My Real World	261
Leaving But Not Free	262
Bouncy Ball	265
What to Say	267
Last Year	270

- The Moonlight Dance 271
- Part III...and the second year arrives 276
  - I'm Doing It! 277
  - Courage 278
  - Anniversary Anxiety 281
  - If I Were Married To Will Today 283
  - Dream World 284
  - Spiraling 285
  - Poets and Knights 287
  - Promise Me a Rose Garden 290
  - Pride Revisited 293
  - I Appreciate You 296
  - Shutting Up 297
  - Exorcising Demons 299
  - Verbal Abuse Teen Style 302
  - Treatment 305
  - Free to Follow My Dream 306
  - Taboo 307
  - Stranglehold 310
  - God, I Promise You 312
  - What I Want 313
  - Nurturing Myself to Death 315
  - Marc & Amy 317
  - Whoomp! There It Is! Verbal Abuse Strikes Again 319
  - Missing Link 320
  - Begging for It 320
  - Old Guilt 322
  - Denial Springs Everlasting 324
  - Voicemails From the Day I Left 325
  - An Anniversary Worth Celebrating 328
- Appendix i
  - About the Author ii
  - Bibliography iii
  - Recommended Websites v
  - End Notes vi

Prologue

No Surprise
January 21, 2010
1 day until freedom

Last night, I tried to make Will mad because I was angry with him. I was angry with him because, over dinner with his father, Will began laying it on thick and heavy about how society thinks pills are the answer to everything and weak people go to therapy because they don't know how to deal with reality. I mean, he was practically yelling it and looking directly at Marc as he said it. This went on for about three minutes at least.

Finally, I reminded him that I take anti-depressants and I am glad I do. I had hoped he would calm down a bit because he promised not to undermine me in front of the kids, and that was precisely what he was doing. He implied to Marc and Eddie that I was weak because I took pills and went to therapy.

He ignored me and kept ranting. I knew that if I pressed the issue, we would end up fighting in front of his father. I could *not* let it go internally. I was *so mad*.

A little later, I found myself taking digs at Will. For example, I said that Will was a flip-flopper (says one thing when convenient, and then changes to the other later). I know I said something else that got no reaction from him, but I cannot remember for the life of me what it was. Probably can't remember it because it didn't work. But the flip-flopper thing didn't work either. I mean, Will acted ticked, but he didn't take the bait.

Round about this point, I realized that I was trying to control his anger - to control *him*. The more terrible thing about it was that I didn't know *why* I wanted to make him angry. In hindsight, I wanted my own anger validated by seeing him angry. I wanted to make him feel the same pinched way I felt - wanting to say something but being constrained.

He said, to his father, "She's trying to dig at me," and I got angrier.

Why is it okay for him to undermine and dig at me over important issues? Why, when I do it, does he ignore it?

Oh, shit. I just figured it out. He did it on purpose to get a rise out of me, calculating that, in the end, I would look like the idiot. Whether I fought back or not, he got his way.

I was wrong for what I did. It exemplifies classic codependency because I sought validation by coercing a mirror response from Will. I was wrong because I tried to control him, control his reaction. I came up short. He was successful in controlling himself.

My challenge is to ... What is my challenge? Yes, I must not try to control him passive-aggressively, but there is more to it than that. I must learn *not* to react habitually when he steps on my toes. The next time I feel that way, I could walk out. Or, I could speak up and then walk out. Or, I could speak up, not walk out but deflect the rest of the conversation away from my heart. I could try not to react to the anger I feel when he undermines me, and later, I will take the opportunity to speak my mind when I am not so angry.

This morning, I told him that I had tried to make him mad last night and said I was sorry. I told him that it was something I wanted to overcome, and I did not plan to act that way again. You can imagine how the following *discussion* went. If you guessed that he took the opportunity to tell me how *twisted I am* and how *I am twisting our sons* the same way, then you are correct.

I did not react. I didn't take his bait. Good for me.

My Heart Is Failing
January 22, 2010
Last day of captivity

Will came into the office and asked me to show him how to clean the stove. He doesn't want to know how to clean the stove; he wants me to clean it. Now.

I told him that I didn't want to show him right now, and lied that I would clean it later. He went back to the couch muttering something about my fucked up priorities. I wish I could have responded in some constructive way, because I really wanted to say *something*. But I didn't. I ignored him. Despite my frustration, ignoring him felt like the best thing to do.

Since coming home from the Army deployment, Will has been on my ass every moment of every day. He told me he feels embarrassed because his whole family knows I am on the brink of leaving him. He tells me that I am twisted and sick, and that I am doing the same thing to our boys. He told me I am selfish because I won't listen to his family (not one person in his family has spoken to me, only to him) and because no one matters to me *except* me.

He sits on the couch muttering now. I cannot hear his words, but they sound hostile. My heart beats quickly because I recognize the signs of what is to come, but there is no way to get out from under them. We are here. Together. Alone while the boys sleep.

He is saying that I am like *all* women and do not appreciate how hard he works for me to have this roof over my head. He says that I am ready to leave and I want the house, the kids and everything he slaves to create. He told me that he despises talking to me when I am calm because he doesn't believe me. He believes my anger only, and he works hard tonight to elicit it.

Now he threatens the cats with his snapping belt.

I wish I was already gone and had not promised to be patient. I wish I felt capable enough to support myself. I wish I didn't feel like I somehow deserve to be treated like a second-class piece of shit because I am not happy with whatever *he* deems I am unhappy with, not what I tell him I'm unhappy about.

I wish I did not fear going to bed. Doing so requires me to walk past him. I'm dreading trying to sleep while he quietly sneaks through the house looking for things that piss him off, things that I haven't done because my priorities are fucked up. I ignore my thought *this isn't fair* because I am here, refusing to leave.

I am afraid it would be easier to play the part of the adoring wife than to continue being me, because being me is scaring the shit out of him in some manner that I cannot comprehend. I can judge by his words and actions that he wishes I were not here. He wishes I would disappear. Life would be so much easier for him if I were dead and gone.

I am afraid dying is easier than living, but I know that I will continue to do the hard thing because the easy thing abandons the children I love. Yet I feel sad that my children are my only reason for living because it shows me that I haven't really come too far at all, and all the work I did simply left me in the exact same place I was before writing this blog.

My heart is failing, and I must be the one to save it. I am unsure that I can do even that.

He smacks the belt in the other room. Smack. Smack. Smack.

Part I: … and the aftermath of leaving

"When you cannot bear the sound of his footsteps, it is time to hear those footsteps no more."

~Big Me, the part connected directly to All

Ex Parte
January 23, 2010
1 day of freedom

Did it happen only last night? It seems like forever ago that Will verbally harassed and intimidated me as I wrote that post. My anxiety level shot through the roof. Almost immediately after writing, "Smack Smack Smack," in reference to the belt he snapped in the next room, I stood up from my computer, went to my room, put on my boots, grabbed a pillow and a blanket and left the house.

I returned when I thought he had passed out, but he surprised me at the door. Eventually he forced himself into the bedroom where I hid and put his hands on me while yelling nasty things.

I called the cops. There were no marks on me, so they could not remove him from the house. I decided that I would leave.

For the remainder of the night through early morning, I pressed charges and requested an ex parte order, which the judge granted temporarily, until January 28. I went to the social services on post and filled them in on what happened. They notified his unit and his command issued a 72-hour no contact type order.

Finally, in the evening, the sheriff delivered the court issued ex-parte, which required Will to pack his clothes, toiletries and then leave the house. The cop (who was rude and uncommunicative with me) arrested Will in front of our boys and put him into the car with handcuffs on his wrists.

Will must stay away from our home, our children, our pets, my car and me. He may have no contact with any of us, period. We go to court on January 28.

For now, we are safe and I am holding up well. I alternate

between relief and regret, but the regret has nothing to do with the actions I took after the violence in the bedroom.

I am sad and feel like I will simply fall down and die at times.

I Left Twice
January 24, 2010
2 days of freedom

On January 22, I sat here at my desk, writing in fear when I remembered something: It is *not* okay or reasonable for me to stay in a place where I am afraid because the one who scares me once promised to love, honor and cherish me. He promised that he would almost 18 years ago. The time between then and now is full of proof that he didn't mean it.

After I finished the blog post, I realized that the anxiety, angst and fear were my cue to get the hell out of here. I logged off my computer and silently walked past him and down the hall to our bedroom. I put on my boots, my coat, and grabbed a small blanket.

He said, "Are you going somewhere?"

"Yes. I'll be back when I feel safer," I responded quickly. I grabbed my purse and left.

I drove to a safe place, previously scouted and parked the car. I shook the tension out of my body the best I could. I allowed a tear to fall. Will called my phone repeatedly, but I let his calls go to voicemail. I did not want to hear the phone ring, so I called my sister, Erin. We talked for almost two hours.

Eventually, Will stopped calling. I waited another 45 minutes or so, and then the silence convinced me that he must have passed out from drinking all night. I decided to go home and go to bed. I thought that in the morning he would pretend to forget what happened. When I pulled up in the drive, everything looked normal. The living room light and television were on, and I did not see Will's shadow roaming about the house snapping a belt. I thought he was asleep. It was about 2 AM.

I unlocked the side door in the dark and pushed it, stepping inside. Suddenly, as if shot up from out of the floor, Will stood in my way.

He said, "Give me your keys and driver's license and get out."

I assume he meant for me to give him all *except* my keys and driver's license. He was drunk and stunk of whisky. In a perfect world, with a perfect emergency plan, I would have turned away *immediately* with *all* of my needed things and left for a hotel, but that isn't what happened.

I did not have a bag in the car, and his sudden appearance threw me off balance mentally and physically. Funny thing about emergencies - they never happen when I'm expecting them, and even if I am expecting *something* it is never the worst something possible. So, out of habit, I put my purse in its spot by the door while sidestepping the man blocking my way. He later claimed to the police that I *shoulder bumped him* to gain entry to *his* home.

I walked to my room as quickly and quietly as I could. Will yelled at me that he woke the boys to tell them that I abandoned them to go "fuck a nigger" and wasn't living here anymore. He added with greater volume, "Even a *whore* doesn't abandon her children!" I heard his footsteps getting closer. I locked the bedroom door behind me. I went to the master bathroom to pee.

Will hit the bedroom door with his fist. He bellowed, "Unlock this fucking door or I'm gonna kick it in!"

I said, "If you kick in that door, I'm calling the cops." It came out of my mouth more calmly than I thought it would.

As I listened to his threats and obscenities, I repeated what I would do if he kicked in the door. I heard him walk away, watched his shadow disappear from under the door. He yelled something, and I thought the boys must be awake by now (they were in their rooms across the hall). I exited the bathroom, entered the bedroom and pushed my dresser in front of the door to buy some time. Part of me thought he wouldn't come back. I hoped that he would carry on his rant in the other rooms and not try to come in the bedroom.

He yelled at me to leave his house, reminding me that it was, in fact, *his* house because he paid for it and everything in it. The boys were *his* too - they didn't deserve a whore for a mother and he planned to take them from me.

It got quiet for a few seconds. I contemplated whether I should pack a bag or if I should crawl into bed and pretend nothing was happening (or rather, pretend that nothing could happen). His shadow appeared in the crack under the door. I heard the tickling sound of metal on metal as he unlocked the door. He tried to throw the door open but was surprised to find the dresser blocking the door. I heard more yelling and cursing.

He pushed hard on the door and the dresser slid, pressing into the wall behind the door, puncturing a hole in the wall where the top edge of the dresser cut into it. I turned to the window and tried to raise it. The damn window was freaking *stuck*. It would not budge. I looked around for something to break the glass when I saw his red face pushing into the room through the small opening. He smirked at me, yelled something, then repeatedly hit the door with his shoulder to gain entry to the room.

He didn't take his eyes off me as he squeezed into the bedroom. The door pressed against him and I remember hoping the doorknob would snap back and hit him in the balls. I had nowhere to go. I couldn't think. He was yelling at me to leave, to get out; I was not wanted here because I was a whore and a traitor and, of course, unappreciative of all he did for me.

When he finally made it into the room, I tried to slide past him to the door. He kept telling me to get out, and I *wanted* to get out. But when I moved toward the door, he pushed me on my chest hard. I lost my footing and fell backward onto the bed. My fear and the bouncy mattress put me back on my feet almost immediately. I sidestepped him once, attempting to get to the door, saying, "Then let me leave!"

He grabbed my arms and shook me violently. He said, "No! It's too late for that!" He shook me violently and my head snapped back hard again and again. He pushed me backward, but I didn't fall this time. He turned his back to me and stood between the door and me. I called out to Marc to bring me my phone. I could not believe the boys could be sleeping still. Will glanced at me over his shoulder before throwing his arm out to hit me across my throat. I coughed, got my voice back and started yelling for Marc to bring me my phone or call the police.

Will said, "Why are you going to bother calling them? You ain't gonna have no marks that show!" and he did a weird little spinning dance with his hands in the air singing, "You have no proof!"

"There's a hole in the wall!" I said.

"What? That hole?" he replied, "That has been there for months!"

Then, and this is possibly the worst part of the entire night, Marc finally poked his head through the crack in in the door and said, "Mom, stop!" Then Marc said, "If you respect me at all, you'll just leave!"

I was hurt, but I remembered that Will had woke them up to tell them lies. I said, "He put his hands on me!" and Marc stared at me blankly.

I looked at Will. Will stood there with his arms crossed, smiling at his son. Will was pleased, very pleased, and he certainly was *not* going to touch me in front of Marc.

I said, "Fine, Marc, I'll leave, but you have to get out of the way so I can get out of here."

Marc moved, I squeezed through the door, then went straight for my phone and called the police. I stayed on the line with the 911 operator until the policeman got there. At one point, Will flipped out his knife to *open a piece of gum*. He flipped the knife like a pro killer while looking at *me*, not at the gum.

The cops arrived and handcuffed Will for acting belligerent and because Will would not tell where he hid his knife. As the handcuffs snapped into place, I begged Marc to go to his brother's room and he did.

I walked away from Will to talk to one of the policemen. He said that because there were no marks on me (yet), they could not remove Will from the home. I knew I couldn't stay tonight, not after all that happened, not without protection. I packed a bag.

Remarkably, Eddie still slept. Marc sat beside his bed. I asked Marc if he wanted to go with me and Marc said there was no sense in waking up Eddie. He promised to put him on the bus in the morning. I left without my children.

Will was pleased. He thought the police forced me to go.

Comments from Readers

GoQuietly says - I am sorry this has been your life. I am so sorry.

Your last post about emergency plans hit home with me. I do not have family support that I can trust 100%. That is part of why I am still where I am. Your last post made me realize I need an even more serious plan than I already have. I would like to think that my husband would have more self-restraint. Thinking back on one of our last arguments when he said, "Don't try to make me hit you," I realize how fine that line is and how easy it would be for him to cross it.

Right now, he tells me he is trying and wants me to stay because I am wonderful. I don't have anywhere to go, so I am trying to stay. This is Dr. Jekyll. But already I see cracks in the control and self-restraint. I wonder what would happen if he lost his job or mistook something I said as "starting that shit" again?

I am not fooled enough to think that everything will be okay. I am not even hopeful. I am buying time. I hope your kids feel safe soon. I would not take Marc's defense of his father as any indication of his feelings for you or even his belief in what his dad had said about you. Watching your father beat your mother is sure to raise a self-protective instinct. I am sure he did not know what to do. If he helped you, his father's anger and hate would have turned onto him. He is a kid after all. I hope peace is with you and you are well.

> **PrincessLuceval says** - My heart was in my throat reading that. My God. I see my husband in some of that too, like QuietOne, and he doesn't drink either. I am so glad you're in a more peaceful spot now.

Ramona Vickers says - *This is a scary story. I watched your video and you stated that couples counselling did not work for you. You stated that your spouse was charming and manipulated the therapist. Why do you think there is a degree required? Therapists train to wade through the manipulative garbage of both parties and form an objective opinion. It is not personal. It is their job. Having experienced an abusive relationship myself, I can tell you, that if you do not look at yourself, no amount of blame will make you healthy or happy.*

As far as your blogs, why not use your true name. We all know who you are. (You posted your picture.) It makes you seem manipulative to those who actually know anything about the situation. As far as people who know you not believing that "Will" could be verbally abusive, you are dead wrong. He will be the first person to say he is an asshole. He has not changed since you met him. He is the same person and you know how to push his buttons, you always have. If you want your marriage go back to the therapist and listen to what they are truly saying, do not walk away because it is not what you want to hear. It's the hardest thing you will ever do!

Someone who loves you!

> **Kellie Jo says** - *And you are? I don't know a Ramona Vickers. The "we" you refer to must be Will's family.*
>
> *Yes, therapists do wade through manipulative garbage, and it is easy for them to do when they get more than two sessions. Unfortunately, none of our therapists have gotten to see us more than twice because Will refuses to return as soon as it is time to take responsibility for some behaviors.*

Being an asshole is not an excuse to abuse your wife or children - or anyone.

Is this blog manipulative? Well, opinions are like Will ... everyone has one.

If you have been in an abusive situation, then I suggest counseling for you. It has been invaluable for me, and has helped me open my eyes to so many things I once ignored and thought were normal. It is highly judgmental for you to tell me I haven't listened to what the therapist(s) were saying. Will and I were the only ones there, and we never visited a therapist named Ramona Vickers.

In addition, there is a book on How to Keep People from Pushing Your Buttons *by Albert Ellis and Arthur Lange. Perhaps you could recommend it to Will - he wouldn't read or acknowledge any of the literature I proposed to him. There's another great book called* Why Does He Do That: Inside the Minds of Angry and Controlling Men *by Lundy Bancroft. If you look on page 61, question number 4 reads, "Why does he say that I am the one abusing him?" You will find the answer informative.*

Also, page 68 of that book, question number 5 reads, "How Come Everyone Else Thinks He's Wonderful?" and the answer there will describe how he's manipulated you into believing his lies, distortions and confabulations.

Because you said that you were in an abusive situation in the past, I wonder if you have received the proper counseling and education to guard against it in the future. Whatever you did to help yourself is apparently fruitless to protect you from further abuse from members of your own family (or friend).

Thank you for posting, I will continue to publish your comments. You are giving me needed reminders of why I am leaving Will, in addition to subject matter for future posts.

Sincerely,

Kellie Jo (You Know Who)

RandomlyK says - *Double thumbs up for Kellie Jo!*

Erin says - *This comment goes out to Ramona Vickers. All I can say is that if you think Kellie is in the wrong and her husband is right, you have blinders on. There is a huge difference between being an asshole and being abusive. If you have been in an abusive relationship, like you said you have been, then you would know this. I am assuming you already know my phone number. Please call! I would love to hear what you have to say to me, the sister of the woman you are bashing. To the sister of the woman I watched be verbally and emotionally abused for 18 years. I would love to hear from you so you can tell the sister of this abused woman that watching her decline over the years was because of her own doing. Don't bother replying to this post. Call me. You obviously don't have a clue.*

And while Kellie didn't tell you, I will. She didn't use her real last name because her husband requested she didn't.

Like I said before - take your blinders off. There is so much more that went on in that marriage that you have no idea about. I didn't only hear about it - I witnessed it.

Ramona Vickers says - *No blinders here Erin. I am being as objective as possible. I do care about your sister.*

As for you Kellie, "we" is everyone who reads this stuff you post, "Will's" family included. You do not know me as a therapist, you know me from life. And as having been in an abusive relationship, I have been in counselling and it has been life changing for me. I learned there is not always a blame sticker to put on things that happen. I have also learned to take responsibility for my part in things, in order to move forward. I did not mean to sound accusing or judgmental, especially not manipulative. Obviously, I did judging by your response. As someone who loves you, "Will" and the boys it is extremely difficult to watch.

> ***Kellie Jo says*** *- So don't watch. You can turn off this channel anytime you please, Ramona. Stick with Will. He needs you.*

Ramona Vickers says *- I refuse to stick with either of you. I love you both and for that reason, I can't turn away.*

> ***EagleWolfeSpirit says*** *- I realize that each of us have our own opinions and are entitled to such, so I would like to offer mine. Please keep in mind that the following is only an expression of my opinion, not intended for any other purpose.*
>
> *Ramona Vickers says, "No amount of blame will make you happy or healthy." This is very true for every one of us. However, there is also* accountability *and* emotional maturity *that each of us need to develop to be well-adjusted members of society. In your words, Ramona, it appears you assume that Kellie Jo blames her spouse. I have been a reader of her blog for some time now, and although I won't say there has never been a hint of blame in any of her written words, I will say that Kellie tries very hard to accept her responsibility and gives responsibility of Will's behavior to him.*

I read the words of a woman who has deeply loved a man and has tried for many years to do what is right, in the name of that love. She writes her experience, her feelings, her emotions, and does so with an eloquence of a gifted writer. What you may perceive as blame in Kellie's writing is perhaps her documentation of real time events. This is actuality, not blame. Blame happens when one holds another person accountable for the actions that they themselves do! Kellie does not blame Will for what she does She also acknowledges her emotions over the events, not laying blame.

Ramona Vickers says, "As far as your blogs, why not use your true name. We all know who you are. (You posted your picture) It makes you seem manipulative to those who actually know anything about the situation."

In this comment, I sense an attack on this blogger, which would have been perhaps better suited to a private email, or perhaps as Erin says below a phone call. Even better, why make a moot point? It is personal why Kellie chose not to do or do anything, not an act for others to judge, nor should it be seen as an opportunity to imply she is wrong. You state it makes her "seem manipulative." This is Kellie's work, her choice, her decisions. I am unable to see how any of the above situation implies she is manipulative.

I do sense however a direct manipulation in your words by telling her to use her own name, etc. If you love as you say you do, then you would chose to come here with respect *for this woman, who she is, and her experience. And* honor *such.*

Ramona Vickers says, "As far as people who know you not believing that 'Will' could be verbally abusive, you are dead wrong. He will be the first person to say he is an asshole. He has not changed since you met him. He is the same person and you know how to push his buttons, you always have."

I am personally very concerned about this statement. Are you implying that Kellie is to blame for all of her spouse's actions because he was an ass when she met him? Do you mean that she should put up and shut up or that because she desires happiness and love, she must tolerate acts of intimidation and coercion? Most of us who have experienced these situations are well aware of the devastating effects upon the psyche.

I see a sincere demonstration on Kellie's part to try to achieve these goals with the man who had come into her life, at the sacrifice of her being who she is. How does either one of the two people personally involved in this dynamic heal by doing so? What is it that you have learned in therapy? This statement is not helpful to either one of these people.

I also read that you believe Kellie knows how to push her spouse's buttons, and that may well be true. But in healing, the one who owns those pushed buttons needs to learn how to respond appropriately. This is the road to healing and emotional maturity for those intimately involved in the situation. One concept that we all must grasp is the fact that no one else is responsible, nor can make us feel or act the way we do. Our behaviors (our reactions) are our own choices.

With that said, we are human and certainly not perfect, and yes, each of us will fail now and then. If one goes through life continuing the same negative behaviors, giving excuses and validating their behavior by blaming others, they do nothing to heal or improve any situation. It remains stagnant. Would it not be the desire of all of us for healing to occur, and for those we love to grow in love? In this life, we are tested and placed in situations in life sometimes so profound that we must acknowledge that someone sent us a wake-up call. We cannot claim ignorance or be held blameless. We must be accountable and acknowledge what is before us, within us, and work on our own growth.

Also, if Will indeed admits he is an ass, does he not then admit that he has issues to work on? Or is his ego so inflated that he can only blame others and feels it unnecessary to work on himself? If so, what is there that anyone else but he himself can do to heal?

I live with a person similar to Will. In my working on my own issues, I realize he also has issues to work on. It is not my job to point them out or attempt to teach him better. He is an adult. There is nothing I can do except to provide support, but he has to want my support and he must want to change for himself.

Ramona Vickers says, "If you want your marriage go back to the therapist and listen to what they are truly saying, do not walk away because it is not what you want to hear. It's the hardest thing you will ever do!"

If one really reads Kellie's blogs, it is quite clear that she has made quite an extensive effort to work things out between her and her husband. She has attended therapy, she has searched for knowledge and she has tried to communicate with her spouse. She has learned, she has admitted that there are things in her life she needs to work on, and has gotten busy with it. She has made positive progress. She admits there is more for her to learn.

A marriage involves two people, therefore it takes two people to work on the marriage, otherwise it is destined to fail. I have yet to see any therapists who think otherwise. In therapy and counselors in general, there are those who specialize and are good at certain issues. There are those who are generally inexperienced in certain areas. Some will admit this; some do not see and are in denial, or for whatever reason attempt to do the best they can. This attitude can cause more harm than any good. Mental health professionals recommend that we seek other counsel when treatment with one professional appears ineffectual. This will involve a bit of intuition from those experiencing the situation. We all need to acknowledge, respect and listen to our intuition.

How could you or I know what took place? We can offer only our opinion based on what Kellie shares with us. I hope that if you love both of these people, you will also discuss your concerns with Will; express your concern that he too must work on his issues. Also, work on your issues so that when you speak, it is with love, compassion, hope and empathy for the one you are speaking too. Blame has no place in love.

Ramona Vickers says, "Someone who loves you!"

Demonstrate the love you claim, by respecting the experience of both individuals, avoiding blaming statements, providing genuine support, setting a loving positive example, allowing both to heal in the way that is best for them, and giving them the space to work on this without negative interference.

You are responsible for your words and actions. It is my goal to point out the hurtfulness of your written words. I felt it necessary for me to address what I felt and perceived in your words, the negative way they made me feel, and my concern as to how they may feel hurtful to Kellie Jo. I am not sure what your true intentions were, but I sense it was not a positive intent.

I appreciate Kellie's blog. I find it very helpful in my own experience, and she often writes the emotions I forget or block out in my own journey. Her writing helps to validate my own emotions and experience, and it is most helpful to experience another's journey, not out of enjoyment of their misery, but to help one clarify the dynamics going on in their own life. Living with a person who is weak-minded and thereby abusive is a difficult experience that those of us who have lived it know all too well. If you have indeed lived this experience, then perhaps there would be far more compassionate and understanding in your writing.

I deeply respect Kellie's strength, courage and determination. She is one who keeps on trying and does not give up. She is an all giving, all loving, compassionate, and forgiving person. I am one who is thankful she is who she is. How do I know this about her? She shares that here, in her written word.

Kellie is responsible for her own healing; her husband is responsible for his. They are responsible to each other for the injustice they have inflicted upon each other, and for forgiving those of one another. They both must exert effort if they want to heal. If only Kellie exerts herself, only Kellie will heal.

Don't Worry
January 25, 2010
3 days of freedom

Understandably, I am not going to share the details of what is transpiring right now. There are things that are not safe to say to anyone besides the parties involved. Tomorrow, after a much-needed sleep, I will report on how I'm feeling and as much as possible, what I am doing.

Right now, I am acting on my emergency plan. It kicked into effect when I called the cops the other night, and it continues as I write. For those of you who worry for me, I want you to know that for now, I am okay. Each minute is different. During the horrible ones, I hold on, knowing that the next minutes will not be so terrible. The hardest part is honoring the anxiety I have without letting it overcome me.

I am very worried that he will break the no-contact orders. Of course, everyone here I know because of Will. They all say that they do not think he will do anything; it is okay to relax. How would they know?

If they knew my husband so well, then why didn't they see this abuse coming (again)? They tell me *not to worry* because they do not want their perception of him upset further. They will be happier when they see *him* smile, hear *him* say the right thing, so they can *believe the worst of me* instead of change their perceptions of *him*.

How dare they tell me not to worry! I am the only person in the world whom my husband will throw around like a rag doll and call a whore, a traitor, and a million other nasty things. Did he ever call *you* those names? Did he ever put his hands on *you* in an attempt to control and scare you? I doubt it. You do not know him like I do, so please stop suggesting that I should pretend to know him like *you* do.

Don't tell me not to worry.

Comments from Readers

QuietOne says - *I am so sad for you. Your tenacity and bravery are amazing. How are the kids holding up? Do you have someone there for you now? Do you have support?*

I am thinking of you always. I am praying, wishing, hoping, demanding that God do *something!*

I am here.

> **Erin says** - *Believe me, I* am *worried. The thought of how angry he undoubtedly became over the past few days has me sitting on pins and needles. He has* always *pulled the wool over everybody else's eyes. They have* no *clue what he is really like when nobody else is around. They only know the side of him that will do anything for them, say the nicest things to them, joke with them, and be seen as such a nice southern guy. They don't have a clue that he is bamboozling them right into the thought pattern that he wants them to believe.*
>
> *They don't realize that he is playing them. They do not realize that he is making sure they fall in line. They don't realize* at all *what he is like behind closed doors.*
>
> *To all of you out there that tell Kellie not to worry, you have no idea* what it is like to live with him. I have seen first-hand

what he does and how he treats his family. He has not showed this to anybody else outside of their immediate family but me that I am aware of, and I can only guess why he allowed me to see it.

It really irritates me that not only does my sister have to go through the pain, physical hurt, and anxiety she is going through right now - but on top of that she has to deal with people who think they know him so well telling her that all will be okay. I am here to tell you that you do not have a clue. *Please open your eyes before something* else *happens. I beg of you. My sister's life may depend on it.*

Thank You
January 26, 2010
4 days of freedom

I am grateful, very grateful, for all of you. Some of you have called more than once today to find that my line is busy. You left voice mails and sent emails too.

I am also very tired, and it is very late. For anyone I didn't call back today, please know that I will check in tomorrow - or so I plan. It so happens that most of the calls I received and did not answer came at a time when I was talking to another friend. I am feeling blessed. Once upon a time, no one could be calling me now because no one could have known. I am relieved that I reached out to all of you.

For those out there living in abuse, it is time for you to reach out too. It is time to begin remembering that people love you, really love you. If you can't think of any, then find a domestic violence group, book club, a gym, an online message board if you must; somewhere where you can be *you* and start to remember *you* are important. *You* matter. Trust me, the people you need will come to you, and you will build your support system.

You know in your heart of hearts that *one day* you will be in my shoes - anxious, hyper-aware and unable to sleep properly or even remember to eat - because your abuser finally did whatever thing you can no longer ignore. If you reach out now, people will do for you the same as they did for me over the past four days.

They will call you, message you, text you, email you and poke you. Some will stop by, and you will have to say, "I'm too tired" or "The kids are here," and they will understand. They will help you. They will invite you into their homes, unconditionally, whenever you feel the least bit insecure, scared or anxious.

They will tell you how proud they are of you, how strong you are, and how brave. You may not believe those things to be true when you hear them, but after hearing them enough, you will come to believe that you are worthwhile, that you are brave and that you did the right thing even though it was the hardest thing you ever did.

They will remind you that time is your friend, keep you sane when you think that you should have done 101 things today when you only did three. Even though your world has seemingly ended, the days are of the same length and the superhero strength it took to do the thing you did does not slow time, does not give you more time to complete the steps needed to get you from hell to peace.

They will also feel a little helpless because they *want* so badly to do *something* ... and you will keep them in your thoughts because sometime soon, you may need something that only that person can give. Like my old friend told me, *you will have to let people help you*, and that is one of the most difficult things to do.

To all of you who have extended your hand to me, no matter how you did it, I feel your support and love. I sense that even some who did not contact me directly are sending me prayers and warm thoughts. There is no word to describe how grateful I am to all of you.

This is far from over, but I know I am far from alone, and that, my friends, is the greatest gift I've *ever* accepted. Thank you.

Events of the Day
January 27, 2010
5 days of freedom

It sucks not being able to tell you everything. I wish I could live this part of my experience online, but for various reasons, I cannot. I can tell you that although I find myself crying at times, I also find myself laughing at times. Although my oldest son is livid with me, peace lives in the house and it was not here before. Perhaps the peace in the house is the peace I feel within, too.

Although I hate the events that brought me to today, I wish they had not happened, in some very real ways, they had to happen. I had to see that Will meant it when he said, "I am not going to change." He has thoroughly convinced me. He will not change.

So if he will not change, will not examine his mind and heart to extricate his own demons but chooses to continue demonizing me in their place, then he will continue to live inside the hellish environment we both experienced. He might be telling himself that *I* created this world alone and that the events between us are the result of the things I did; or, he might be coming to terms with the reality of our situation. *I cannot know what he is thinking*, and I remind myself of that 20 times a day.

I also cannot know, nor do I want to know, what he is doing, what he is saying about me, or what he could be plotting. The longer I think of the darkest side of him, the more frightened I become. I know that living in fear results in not living, so I refuse to let fear control my thoughts and actions. I am as prepared as I can be, and that will be enough.

I am also aware of the duality of his personality. I know that there will be a time when he comes to me softly. I don't know what he may request of me at that time - perhaps it will be to tell me goodbye - but it will happen, and I know that even then, I cannot let my guard down. His darker side is too real, and his softer side too infrequent, for that delicate moment to carry further than the time I am face to face with him, hearing him say those things (whatever they will be).

I already miss some of the kind times we had together. Our first kisses, our first laughs, the births of our children. Even so, those things are memories and will always be memories – things like them will never happen again. It has been so very long since we've had *any* kind times together, so wishing for them so I would have one last good memory with the man I loved through it all is pointless. What we have is what we have, and it will be enough.

Besides, even though apart, we still get to watch our sons grow and fall in love. We still get to be grandparents, and there will be joy in the upcoming days, even though we now live separate lives.

The way I see it, in a future not too far away, I will see more of the goodness of Will in the rest of my days than I will see the darker bits of him. There won't be the opportunity to see the bad because if the darkness pops out of him, I will leave wherever he is and go to my own peaceful home and be thankful that, although alone, I am safe, content and prosperous.

Comments from Readers

Lori says - *As sad as it is that this breaking point happened, find beauty in the fact that you have enough perspective now to know that you will be happy, you will be successful and you will know a better and more content life once this chapter is put to rest. You have grown more than you even know, and your new growth will fuel your success in the next phase of your life. I wish you nothing but the best and I am so proud of you for taking action when it had to be one of the hardest things you have ever done to this point in your life. Bravo.*

> **QuietOne says -** *It is good to hear the hope in your words. Well done! I am at a real loss for words that will have any value or meaning to you now. The box that Will put you in was too small to contain you. You once wrote something about being afraid of your own power - I hope you are not afraid any longer. Whether you like it or not, your own powerful nature will prevail.*

Cara says - *This is terribly inspiring. Thank you for sharing your journey.*

> **Erin says -** *You are so spectacular, Kellie. I love you, I am proud of you, and I have nothing but admiration for the strength you have (in good times and bad).*

Slippery
January 28, 2010
6 days of freedom

I've been considering the best ways to proceed with this blog, and I've decided to continue writing it pretty much the same way I've always done it - honestly, openly, and with the focus being on what I'm doing and how I'm feeling as I deal with the abuse in my life. This blog is about my world and me as I sense it. It exposes, often in hindsight, the dire truths of my situation. It is a record only because I cannot and do not know what is to come, or to become of me. I write what I feel. It is the truth according to me. It is not the truth according to Will or the truth according to my boys, but the truth according to me.

I trust that everyone readily understands that there are always at least three versions of truth when there is truth to tell - your version, their version, and the indifferent record of events imprinted upon the universe that may never reveal itself. Sometimes all three versions line up perfectly. Usually, the three versions of truth do not align, and we people dive into the business of *sorting things out* which usually results in a fourth version of events which is not the truth either.

The law engages in *sorting things out* and, although the process works (because we the people empower it to do so), there is much omitted from the final report. The understated language of the law, although forceful, is often not as clear or forceful as I wish it would be. The law is not my voice, but I must adhere strictly to it because to ignore it would cause the court to *sort things out* in a more biased way.

Legal issues, such as separation and divorce, require discretion. Today in court, nothing happened that surprised me, and that was a good thing for my side of the truth. The ex-parte order stands with one revision: my attorney requested visitation for the boys with their father because I asked her to request it. My attorney also requested and the judge granted a line on the amended protection order that reads, "Parties are not to discuss this case or make any remarks about the other parent while in front of or around the minor children."

I consider this blog to be *in front of or around* my children. They know I have a blog. I don't think they are interested enough to visit it, but fact is that they could, and there is no way to stop them from viewing it. So, here we are back at the first paragraph, how to proceed with this blog. I will not write about the specifics of this case, and I will not bad-mouth the boys' father. I believe that I can share how I'm doing, what I'm thinking, feeling, and (to an extent) experiencing without violating any court order.

I can share, as it pertains to our separation, any event that I would share with my boys. For example, when I saw them today, I told them that they get to visit their dad, and neither dad nor I can say anything bad about the other in front of or around them. Those are facts they must know, and probably both facts relieve their worry to some extent. It may be challenging at times to refrain from adding specifics to my posts, but I am willing and able to write with the constraints.

Comments from Readers

RandomlyK says - *I'm so glad to hear that you will keep writing. I also respect that you are going to need to be very careful in what you choose to write here for a while.*

> **QuietOne says -** *I am so glad the ex-parte order is continued. That must be a load off your mind. As for your blog - just the facts ma'am. Fair enough.*
>
> *I would feel confused by "no bad-mouthing" as the facts clearly speak for themselves. I don't think I have ever read an entry where you bad-mouthed Will. You don't call names and you don't pass judgment on his behavior. You say you do not like it, you say his behavior is damaging to you. I hope the order does not attempt to make you squash the facts in an attempt to protect Will from his own behavior.*

Emergency Money
January 29, 2010
1 week of freedom

Will revoked my access to our money by closing all our joint accounts at the bank. I don't know if or when I can pay the bills. I am not concerned that this situation will persist. In fact, I know that it cannot continue under law, and Will is not going to risk more legal trouble than he faces.

I would like to take the opportunity to address *money* as it relates to emergency plans. If you leave your abuser and take marital funds with you, you will owe back half to the marital kitty when you go to settle financially. However, if you take money with you, then you have not broken any law. The money is yours as well as his. Keep your receipts, document why you spent the money and spend prudently to stay on the safe side.

Likewise, all debt incurred during the separation is also the responsibility of both parties. You do not relieve yourself of joint credit card debt during the divorce - like all other monetary issues, debt is a marital concern and you deal with joint debt in court or in your separation agreement. You are as financially responsible as your spouse for all assets and debts incurred during your marriage and during the separation period. To that end, remove yourself from any joint accounts to protect yourself.

So, as you make your emergency plan, go into it fully aware of your responsibilities. You are *not stealing* if you take marital funds with you when you leave, but you will be required to settle later.

Speaking of things you can count on, count on your would-be controller to do everything in their power to leave you helpless and insecure. The more miserable you are, the more likely you are to return to the environment you left - and your abuser knows it.

If you believe he wants you to stay gone, at least admit to yourself that *he does not want you happy.*

Your happiness is possibly the biggest threat to your abuser. When you feel happy, then you feel strong. When you feel strong, you may well realize that you don't want the life you created with him. I've known this for a while, and it feels odd to have my innate knowing become such an accurate predictor of future events.

> There's no threat of a weak and broken woman walking out on him. No threat of a woman unable to provide for herself walking away. As long as I doubt every single skill I possess that creates beauty and value in this world, I am impotent against his brutal verbal, emotional and mental attacks. ~from *Turning Inward*, 2009

I'm happy. Watch out.

Laughing
January 30, 2010
1 week and 1 day of freedom

As Marc and Eddie sat on the couch with their computers, they called me in and began a *conversation* between Stewie (from the sitcom *Family Guy*) and Ashton Kutcher using a soundboard with recordings of things the two have said. My boys' imagined conversation between Stewie and Ashton turned out to be the funniest damn thing I have heard in forever.

Part of the conversation went something like Stewie telling Ashton not to mock him, at which point Ashton teased Stewie about his job at the drive-through window. Stewie got madder and Ashton kept ordering food.

Ah well, this story may not be funny to anyone outside of my living room anyway. But really ... Ashton Kutcher and Stewie? They're funnier together than you might think.

Another possibility for these soundboards is prank calls ... but I wouldn't know anything about that childish nonsense.

It feels so good to laugh aloud without worrying about Will's icy stares. He hates it when I am *silly* or *childish*, but I love that about me. I have *that* part of me back.

Red to Blue
January 31, 2010
1 week and 2 days of freedom

My emotions are whirling. I feel victimized and angry about temporary injustices. Then I'm sad. Then I'm impatient. Then my stomach is sour. I suppose my stomach being sour isn't an emotion, but I seem to feel it like one.

It is tough to talk with people who question my actions instead of questioning their assumptions. My explanations don't match their assumptions, and they think I am lying. I am finished explaining myself to anyone but my attorney, but I doubt I'll have to explain much to her. Funny thing about *healthy people* like my attorney is that they recognize abuse for what it is, and understand most actions resulting from abuse show defensive posturing, not offensive manipulation.

If I could have one thing for myself tonight, I would not give a *damn* what anyone else said about or to me. I would realize that my inner knowing and strength is *all* I need, and that seeking to convince anyone of my position wastes my time and precious emotional energy. The ones I most desire to convince are the ones that I could never convince; it is time to let them go. It is time to fortify my environment with people who believe me; I need the strength saved by *not* explaining myself to people who don't want to see my truth.

My motives for convincing these same people are questionable, at best. What would I gain from convincing them their friend/kid/brother/soldier was less than what they assume him to be? Vindication. I'm not after vindication. I'm after peace. It is time to stop trying to garner validation and understanding from people who will never give it.

I wish I'd had a little more time to prepare myself, to get myself to a healthier place. But then, alongside that thought comes the realization that me being healthier, reacting in healthier ways toward the abuse, is exactly what threatened him the most.

Comments from Readers

QuietOne says - *I disagree that you are not in the healthy place you want to be. Women (and men) go entire lives and never stop seeking validation from others. Their need of approval cripples them, and they never even see the pitfall.*

I have been through some of what you have experienced and I used to try to talk to my mother about it. It frustrated me that she would never say "Oh my poor girl! It's awful that you are going through this. Your husband is rotten for treating you this way." I wanted to hear those words so much!

But one day I confronted her and asked her, why, if you love me, don't you give me your passion? Actually, I said, "Have you no passion for your children?" She confessed to me then that her mother was so controlling and demanding that she never wanted to visit her mother upon me. She said she withheld her opinions and comments because she wanted me to validate myself.

It took me many weeks to understand what she was asking of me. But I finally understood that she wanted me to see my opinions and judgments as the most important thing. She did not want me to rely on her for validation and approval. Her methods were harsh but I finally understood that she was trying to give me the gift of breaking the abuse cycle. As much as I hated her methods, she was trying to give me a wonderful gift.

I hope you can see the resistance around you in that light. It's hard and harsh, but it is a gift. Gawd - that sounded like a lot of tripe. But I did find it to be true. I have appreciated my mother more ever since.

Am I Happy He Is Gone?
February 1, 2010
1 week and 3 days of freedom

I had a long day. I haven't experienced any emotional upheavals, and the doubts and fears I carry seem to be at bay. I'm feeling great. But I noticed something weird. There is a lot of time to fill when there is no anxiety. At least, no anxiety that is dependent on Will's actions. Here is a list of some of the things I did not feel anxious about today:

- Did I remember to pack his lunch last night? Did he go to work without it? I hope he had socks that were acceptable to wear - he must have because I didn't hear any drawers slamming this morning.

- Is the house presentable? Will the other things I've done today excuse the dirt on the floor and the unwashed dishes?

- Should I keep under wraps what I did today, or should I remind him that I went to the Woman's Club meeting? Is what I purchased at the store needed or wasteful and do I tell him about it or let it appear like magic from the toiletry closet?

- Did I sit on my ass too long after I got home? Could I clean and wash clothes and pick up after the kids and clean the litter boxes and care for the household-running minutia? Will he look around the house tonight with that disgusted look on his face? Is he going to say something to me before or after he starts drinking?

- Is he going to come home already smelling like alcohol?

- The report cards are due. I need to see them before him so I can guess how he will react and prepare for it.

- Is he going to mutter about having chicken for dinner again after we take our separate rooms? I'd like to watch Medium tonight, but I don't want to sit in there with him - he thinks my shows are stupid. Maybe I can write without him getting mad that I am writing. It depends.

- He didn't ask me how I was or give me a hug when he got home. Does that mean something?

- He is dumping ice in his glass. I wish he weren't having another drink.

- He is in there talking to the air as if it were me. He doesn't want a response; he just wants me to listen. Should I acknowledge him or pretend not to hear?

- Now he talks to our son about me without saying he is

talking about me. Women always do this or always do that ... He is being so hateful. Do I say something? How much has he drunk already? I almost wish he were drunk so I could more easily pretend his words are unintentional.

- He is quiet. What time is it? Let me go see if he fell asleep on the couch.

- Should I wake him up to go to bed? Will he be madder that I woke him up or that he woke up on the couch tomorrow morning? Will he try to continue the conversation with the air if I wake him up?

- Is it okay to lie next to him or should I keep my distance. Maybe I can put my feet on him ... that way I can pretend we feel close.

You tell me. Am I happy he is gone?

Comments from Readers

Javanejoon says - *You must feel a huge sense of relief now that you have some peace in your life. You made a brave move and good on you girl. Stay strong and keep safe.*

> ***KeepSmiling says*** - *Yes, I think you're happy. One time my ex came home and first thing he did was take his finger rub it over the dada. He held it up to me showing me the dust, and then he ran his finger across the top of the door. He made a point of holding his dusty finger up to me again, and I wanted to scream, "Are you fucking crazy? If it's so important get a cloth and do it yourself!" What an imbecile. I am so rid of that loser.*

Erin says - *Ummmmmmm... I say that you are...happy! Woo hoo! When is the last time you felt such peace? I am so, so, so, so, so glad for you, Kellie!*

Kim says - *Hi Kellie, Oh my days! I am so happy for you, but I doubt you are the happy bunny of all your up and coming tomorrows. As you said, you must sort out with what you you want to fill your mind. It's like being lost, and up until now, you met with a violence of one sort or another, or all sorts together, every time you turned a corner.*

Now, this next corner you're turning, you are met with space and time, and most importantly (and somewhat scarily) yourself. These, unless you know exactly *who you are can be frightening and (key word coming up) unfamiliar. We tend to fall back into familiar territory, if it presents itself.*

So watch out. Be present in every moment. Enjoy and practice the stillness of a moment. Just be. For you, I think, this will take some doing. Your life has existed on a knife-edge, so you will have to accept that some hard work is ahead. But enjoy it, because every day will get easier and easier.

Are you happy he is gone? You may feel relief, but you may also feel grief too. That would be perfectly natural, I think.

Thinking of you loads and sending love across the pond.

Kellie Jo says - Kim, you're right about the bunny bit. Yes, I am sad about many things (my marriage is over for goodness sakes!). I am happy that he's not in my presence now. Underneath the conflicting emotions is something unfamiliar ... it's the budding of joy, the emergence of freedom that I took back after giving it away to him. Joy is replacing the fear I carry in my heart, slowly perhaps, but it is there and I will allow it to grow.

DonnaLee says - *Oh man, Kellie, the anxiety that I felt reading that. Unfortunately, you cannot change the other person who creates that atmosphere until they see what they do and change. You may feel sad at times at the loss of a relationship that was full of dreams, but a relationship that eats away at your very soul is not what anyone really wants. You sound like you are happy about what is not going on around you right now and don't you dare feel guilty for feeling happy. I bet your house feels so calm.*

Tiffany says - *Oh, I love the budding of joy and the emergence of freedom. I am excited to see what goodness is coming your way brave girl! I think that even when sadness or grief settles in here and there, you have to remember that the grief is for what you* wish *your marriage had been. Not for what it was. And I think that since you got two beautiful boys out of it, there is no reason to regret what was. At the same time, there is every reason to celebrate what will be. Only the best for you as you move forward!*

Potty Talk
February 2, 2010
1 week and 4 days of freedom

I had a little conversation with God when I was on the commode today. God didn't mind and was glad to hear from me. I asked God to take my worries and promised to be on the lookout for signs to guide me.

The guy side of God invited me to put my worries on his shoulders - He would bear them for me. The girl side of God said she would go before me to clear my path, to light the way, and to remove the burdens from her counterpart's shoulders until they were no more. They work well together.

God is All.[1]

Now I have to let them do their thing, and that could be the hardest part of all.

Emergency Plan = Emotional Pain
February 3, 2010
1 week and 5 days of freedom

It's one thing to know you need an emergency plan to escape domestic abuse, and another thing entirely to create it. My first emergency plan was to drive a half mile down the road and sit on the farm road with my lights off. That was it. I didn't have extra keys; I did not pack an overnight bag. I took nothing but me and (I hoped) my purse. The plan was not realistic.

I worried about how Will would react when I executed the plan. I couldn't tell him about it ahead of time because telling him gave him the chance to either increase the abuse or convince me that I was not *in danger of abuse* despite my feelings on the matter. On top of feeling guilty about keeping a secret from Will, I felt confused and upset that I had to leave my home for even an instant. However, the assault in 2008 opened my eyes somewhat. Will *could* put his hands on me. He *would*. He did so a few times before 2008, and I could safely assume he would do it again.

I spent the next weeks pissed off that if he misbehaved, then I was the one who had to leave the house. *Why couldn't he leave when he felt his temper rising? Why couldn't he take responsibility for the intimidating airs he put on around our home? Why couldn't he admit that he was at least part of the problem?*

Stewing in anger, I realized something else. What Will had been doing was not right *and* he was doing everything and saying anything he could to avoid accepting one bit of responsibility. *I would always be the one to have to leave. Always.*

With that realization, I fleshed out my plan a little more. I knew that I needed enough cash to cover a hotel room and probably at least one meal. So I opened a bank account in my name alone. It felt terrible to build layers of secrets. I rationalized away the secrecy by deciding that if I had not used the emergency money by our 25th wedding anniversary, then we would take a vacation. The vacation would be to celebrate how far we'd come as a couple and how happy we were together. In the aftermath of our marriage, I see that it was a great idea to have money *for me*. At the time, I truly wanted that couple's vacation because I wanted my marriage to last. The fantasy of us being close some day continued, but my emergency plan was a little stronger.

Soon after, I worked up the nerve to ask my friend if my boys and I could run to her home in an emergency. She agreed, and I felt better for talking to her, but bad because I we would be a burden to her family. In my heart of hearts, I know she would have us stay as long as we needed to stay, but still, I felt like a yet-to-be discovered leech on someone's leg.

In so many ways, creating the emergency plan *felt* like planning to *leave*. It was hard to follow through by making keys, telling neighbors, getting a post office box, securing documents, creating my own log in information at the bank, signing a contract for a phone that accessed the Internet...it felt sneaky. I don't like sneaky. I prefer an open approach, honesty, integrity. This did not feel like integrity to me.

I had yet to put a change of clothes or toiletries in my car the night I left forever. I packed them while the cops were here. I forgot to take important documents. I didn't remember to secure my files on the external drive. I was not ready because I had hoped it would never come to that - I wasn't ready because I wanted to *stay*.

The night I left, I planned to return home the next day. However, I remembered that he told me to take myself off the bank accounts as I walked out the door. So, at about four in the morning, I used my phone to check the bank. Emails from the bank reported that he had changed the username, password, pin number and phone password ... all of it. He had tried to lock me out of the accounts. Fortunately, he did not know about my personal login information (one of my secrets). I used my credentials to transfer funds from our savings account to my personal account. Just like that, in those 3 minutes, I realized that I was not going home.

Later, I received more emails from the bank showing that around 7 AM, he called and withdrew all the remaining money out of all of our accounts, even the boys' accounts. I imagine he felt as if I stole the money from him; I know he was extremely mad about it. What had he expected me to do? He said in his voicemails that he hoped I would go. Yet when I left, he seemed to want to make it impossible for me to stay gone. How could I leave with no money? Perhaps he wanted me to go groveling back to him after learning that his *real world* required sleeping in my cold car without money for a burger. I'm too wise to ask him to explain his reasoning because his reasons only lead to more abuse.

The emergency plan I created wasn't perfect, and it wasn't nearly *enough* - I wish I'd had a pre-packed bag, I wish I'd ... it doesn't matter. My two saving graces were my high-tech phone and personal bank login information. If I had to do it over again, I would have pressed through the emotional pain of creating an emergency plan, a *thorough* emergency plan, before I had the need for it.

Comments from Readers

Kunjii says - *Wow, it sounds like you were forced into leaving, but thankfully, you were somewhat prepared to go. Are you in the family home or did you move out? Where does he stay? Actions make you stronger. You're probably realizing this already. Take it day by day and best of luck to you.*

> ***RandomlyK says*** - *Kellie, you are so right. I think that is the hardest part of what those of us who are living in abuse go through. The safety plan has been my biggest obstacle because of my preconceived notions, expectations and emotions. Ladies, any of you in this situation, even if it hasn't escalated to the point you need a safety plan, make one, be realistic and follow through. Remember to keep your plan strictly* need to know *(and your abuser does* not *need to know). It's difficult to keep secrets, but protection of your children and yourself requires it.*

What Would You Do With Omnipotence?
February 4, 2010
1 week and 6 days of freedom

I feel anxious tonight. I woke up anxious this morning. I could be anxious about this weekend in general. The boys are spending Saturday night with their father. I am anxious about things I cannot control and never could control - although I thought I had the power to control them.

You see, once upon a time, I believed Will when he said that I made him angry. I made him yell. I made him go into asshole mode. I made him want to hit me. I made him cut me down. I made him use physical force to subdue me. I must have thought I was damn powerful, being able to spin that grown man around in such a tizzy that he lost control of himself. He justified his behavior by blaming me for it.

I could make him mean, hateful, vengeful even...but I couldn't make him love me, I couldn't make him respect me or be nice to me. What is the point of being *omnipotent* when your *powers* only work against you?

In the beginning, I tried to make him love me for me, and when that didn't work I thought he would love me as his baby's mother. When that didn't work, I morphed into the house frau he said he could respect. Along the way, I tried to be his mother, his Maw Maw, his aunt; I even tried to be more like random women he pointed out to me. I tried to make him love me, and I could not do it.

So why did I buy into the idea that I could make him angry?

Believing I could make him feel *something* was better than acknowledging he would *never feel love* for me. I thought there was something broken inside *me*, something that I could fix. I forced myself into pits of depression thinking that there, at the bottom of the pit I would find the thing that made me so unlovable. Once I found it, I thought I could pluck it out and dispose of it, then rise to the surface of myself to find that he was able to love me. I do not wonder why I spent so long looking for something that was broken. I wanted a happy marriage, a loving husband and a close family. I wanted to be a part of his life, to share my gifts and myself with him. I once believed that we complemented one another and were unstoppable. I wanted the dream so badly that I stuck around for almost 18 years trying to create it.

Until recently, I believed I could have the dream. The dismantling of the illusion is the most painful part for me. Taking our children to their father for visitation is an outward and visible wrecking ball hell bent on destroying our marriage, my dream, and that's why I feel anxious.

Comments from Readers

Martha says - *Kellie, my thoughts and prayers are with you.*

> **Ramona Vickers says** - *Kellie I'm not giving you permission to do anything. You don't need it. I'm sorry you took it that way. I am not as eloquent with words as you are, obviously. I believe that you feel the way you do, and I'm not trying to lessen that in any way. I don't doubt that his behavior makes you feel that he hates you, all I wanted to remind you was, it wasn't always that way.*
>
> *He married you and wanted to spend the rest of his life with you, at one time. You were the best thing that happened to him, at one time. He did love you. You did love him. I watched the two of you in love, and it wasn't fake. I believe you no longer love him, and I believe he no longer loves you. The situation has deteriorated to him lashing out at you in anger, and you responding to him here. Both of you will have to grieve the loss of the relationship in your own way. I also know that situations are never as simple as they seem in black and white. What a perfect world it would be if they were, but we don't live there.*
>
> *As sick and saddened that it makes me, after news of the things that have been happening since your last blog, you have both crossed lines that can be uncrossed. You know what I am talking about. As I stated before, you are intelligent, so think about the future in your next moves. By screwing him, you screw yourself.*

Kellie Jo says - *You are uninformed.*

> **Ramona Vickers says -** *No, Kellie, I'm not uninformed, perhaps under-informed. What I am very informed about is that "Will" loved you very much. I remember, in the beginning, when he went up against his entire family to defend you. I am well aware of the ties that bind that family together. I listened, on many occasions, to "Will" talk nothing but praise of you. As different as you two are, he did appreciate so much about you. Your artistic ability, creativity and beauty.*
>
> *As you know, it does not sound like there is anything left for you there. Get your divorce, and move on. I hope that sometime in the future, you will be able to see that he did care. I do know when you are in a situation, it is hard to step back see that situation for what it is, and was. There is no reason to be anxious, "Will" loves and would never hurt his children. As I'm sure your attorney told you, it is best for the boys to continue a relationship with their father. Whether right or wrong, his anger is with you not them.*

Kellie Jo says - *You are uninformed about what goes on in Will's home. He has hurt his children; we have hurt our children. He will cross any line to win, and Will behaves as if every conversation has a winner and loser. He turns our boys into losers daily.*

Will usually said nice things about me to other people. He says that I'm smart, that I'm creative, that I'm pretty, that I'm a good mother, that he wouldn't be where he is without me.

At home, he turns those phrases into how stupid I am, how my interests and creativity are worthless in the real world.

My beauty evidently leads him to call me a whore. According to Will, I've never been a good mother: I twist the boys thinking, I make them lesser men. And let's not forget that he got where he is despite of me - my whining and complaining and spending all of his money makes it too hard for him to control himself.

Those pretty things he tells everyone else about me is a front. He tells me to show him, not tell him; what he shows me is that he hates the core of who I am.

You may think I'm lying, exaggerating, and that is fine. I don't need you to approve of my truth. Perhaps, sometime in the future, you will be able to see this situation more fully. I'm not counting on it, and it doesn't matter to me if you do see it fully. I do not think you are contacting me to hear my side or to be objective. It seems as if you're attempting to project his side of the story onto me. That's why I said you should stick with Will.

My attorney doesn't tell me anything I don't already know. The boys are almost grown; they want their dad. I will not ever deny them their father. I hope that Will continues to modify his behavior around the boys. Since coming home in December, he has given them much needed time and attention.

Thank you for giving me permission to move on. I suggest you do the same.

A Necessary Evil
February 6, 2010
2 weeks and 1 day of freedom

I saw Will today. He looks good. Softer. I caught him glance at me sidelong and I wondered what he was thinking. Will gave Marc a bag to put in the trunk of my car. It is going to stay there, unopened. Marc relayed that his dad didn't have room for whatever is in the bag, and I feel sad that Will is living in a travel trailer. Things will get better for both of us. Right now, there is a lot of waiting. I keep telling myself to be patient, but I wish I could snap my fingers and make what will be the future become the present.

I thought about how difficult switching parents must be for the boys. I wondered if they sensed the finality, and I wondered if they were okay with it, right now, at that moment they removed their bags from my car and transferred them to his truck. I thought of my parents' divorce. My sister and I didn't have to see our parents together after they separated because I was old enough to drive us back and forth. I remembered standing in the hall of the courthouse, thinking someone was going to ask me to testify on behalf of one or the other, and I thought about how angry with them I felt for having to *think* about choosing. I don't want my boys to have to choose.

There are aspects of Will and my relationship that I wish the boys never witnessed and never felt - like our fighting, my crying and the tense family time playing Uno. Why couldn't we ever have fun? Why was it always so damn *hard*?

When things get too much to bear, I force myself to envision the future in as much as it pertains to Will. We will learn to parent apart while remaining consistently together in the discipline and care of our children. We will attend the boys' graduations from high school and college. We will eat dinner at our boys' homes together (if they'll have us). We'll attend the births of our grand babies and wait together in one room to see the red little darling pass through on the way to the nursery. We will spoil those grandkids and go to their birthday parties, kindergarten graduations, see their first new cars. We'll do all that stuff together, kind of.

Right now, that future is far away. Right now, there is a lot of waiting. I keep telling myself to be patient, but I wish I could snap my fingers and make what will be the future become the present. But if I did that, then I would miss all of *this* ...and *this*, painful as it is, is a necessary evil.

Comments from Readers

Ramona Vickers says - *Nowhere in what I wrote assigns blame to you or him, and I am trying to be extremely careful not to do so. I remind you that I care about you both.*

Your escape plan put you in a somewhat comfortable situation as far as money is concerned. But that will change if the military dishonorably discharges "Will." I understand that there is no person or institution you can talk with that can remove the charges. But what are you going to do when "Will" has no income? If he has no income, he can't pay child support, which he will pay otherwise until the boys get out of college if they choose to go. The armed forces will see to it that.

Because he is in the military, you guys are legally residents of Texas where there is no alimony, only community property. If what you have already taken from the accounts is less than half you'll be okay for now. But how long will that last?

Texas also has one of the most conservative child custody systems in place. In other words, unless you are a prostitute, turning tricks for a fix, which I know you're not, the mother gets primary custody of the children.

The current charges don't have to have anything to do with the divorce, unless you plan to make them such. Actually, the ball is in your court. I'm pretty sure "Will" feels betrayed by you taking the money. I am not saying you were wrong to do so; I'm trying to make suggestions that will bring about the best resolution of the situation for everyone involved.

> **Kellie Jo says -** *I invite you to read more of the blog. There is no lack of thinking or considering on my part. I've done nothing but ponder our circumstances for over a year, including what I see as best for my boys. What is best is for them, Will and me to get the help we all need.*
>
> *Perhaps Will has not heard what I've told his father and his friend about these charges when they pressured me because he cannot stand not having control over them. The charges are a heavy weight for him to bear; he will have to bear them until the State of North Carolina dismisses them. Or doesn't. I don't want his career ended; I don't want him dishonorably discharged. To limit his income in any way is financial suicide for myself (at least for a while).*
>
> *Yes, the consequences of being found guilty of an assault on a woman charge could be devastating, but he chose to attack me. I wonder why people think it is my fault that he is in the position he is in. I told him what I would do the next time he put his hands on me* during therapy; *he chose to physically attack me anyway. He must not have believed me. He must have thought that I would be too afraid to lose what we've worked for to risk involving the law.*

What he couldn't comprehend was that what we've worked for isn't worth being intimidated and man-handled. It isn't worth allowing him treat me like a bag of shit that he plans to light on fire for someone else to stomp. I promise you, I've laid it out carefully and clearly, in private and at counseling, what he could expect if he put his hands on me one more time. And in counseling, in front of the therapist, he said he understood.

Court will test his patience. I will appear at every court date knowing that the judge will continue this case until our attorneys reach an agreement as to how they will attempt to handle them. No matter what our attorney's intentions or my intentions are, it's up to the judge what happens in the end. There is no office I can go to, no judge I can approach, to drop these charges. Refusing to attend court in this matter could work out poorly for the boys and me in the future.

Keeping money from me, sending veiled messages through friends and family, insinuating adultery and, in general, attempting to keep me under his thumb is not *going to result in a speedy end to the serious charges laid in front of him. The ball is in his court. I'm sure his divorce attorney will contact mine soon.*

Ramona Vickers says - *The waiting sucks. The boys will be fine.*

When I say that if you screw him, you screw yourself, I hope you see the full consequences of what's going to happen at your next court date (not for the divorce). Not the immediate, but the long term, and how it will affect you and your children, not just "Will."

This One, I'll Address above Board
February 7, 2010
2 weeks and 2 days of freedom

This post is in reference to Ramona Vickers's continuing *support* in the comments sections of this blog. I will continue to answer her for as long as she chooses to submit comments, but my patience is wearing thin. Despite Ramona's claim to love both Will and me, she continues to believe that what Will tells her is fact. I don't blame her. He's very good at convincing people.

Thanks to everyone who helped rebuke Ramona's insistence on *caring* about me. Anyway, this post is for Ramona.

Ramona, you are assuming a lot. Or maybe you're repeating what Will has told you, there's no way for me to know. However, I am tired of bantering with you.

What do you know about how comfortable I am financially? I took what amounts to less than two months of his net pay. I took the money out *only* after receiving emails from the bank, time stamped, showing that he had attempted to lock me out of all of our accounts. He changed all the personal information on the accounts, thinking I had no way to access the money. Fortunately, he forgot to change the email notification address in his haste to deny me a way to sustain myself.

When I found out what he had done, I took the lump sum from the emergency account because it was obvious he wasn't going to share. I had no way of knowing when I would receive any more money, only that I would, eventually, and a good portion of the money I had went toward attorney fees.

You are also assuming that I have no means of financial support besides my husband, no way to provide for children and myself. Besides my own ability to earn an income sufficient to cover our needs, the Army gives Transitional Compensation to women divorcing their soldier due to domestic abuse. It isn't much, but it is enough to fill in the gaps, and it lasts for three years. That assumes him found guilty of the charges; there is no guarantee of that, and I've already told you how I feel about the charges.

The military sees to his paying child support only so long as he is in the military. After he retires or is discharged, the Army has no further interest in what he does financially (except for Survivor Benefit Plans and *if* I receive a portion of his pension benefits). If he retires, that will be in about 5 years; if he's discharged, the Army's disinterest begins immediately.

Currently, Will plans to give each boy two years of his GI Bill. Because Will earned the GI Bill by the time he left the Army the first time in 1996, the GI Bill is his to keep regardless of the outcome of this stint in the military. And, even with Will's contribution of his GI Bill to the boys, there will be a need for financial aid. Depending on Will's and my income in the coming years, the boys may or may not qualify for federal aid.

As it stands right now, with us married and him providing the only income, we do not qualify for Pell Grant money - he makes too much. I know because I applied last year. Separated, the situation may change.

Yes, it is true that his attorney could refuse to hear this case in North Carolina. I don't care. There are benefits and drawbacks to either state; I'm sure Will's attorney will fill him in on all of that.

I find it odd that you mention a prostitute turning tricks in your assessment. Is this something you know about directly? Or is this a dig at someone else?

And finally, you are wrong about the current charges having

nothing to do with the divorce. They are domestic violence charges; they have everything to do with the divorce.

Will has felt betrayed by many things. I am not surprised that he discounts what he has done in his assessment of my perceived betrayal of him.

I am done explaining things to you. Besides, what I say doesn't hold water with you. You evidently know more about my situation than I do and have spent more time considering my best options for me. If you see fit to call me or email me personally, please do so. For this weekend at least, I am done with this conversation.

Comments from Readers

Ramona Vickers says - *Prostitution was the worst situation I could imagine. Perhaps you would prefer this example: The state of Texas will give kids back to a raging alcoholic mother, who tries to commit suicide. That was meant to be catty.*

Sorry you see this as banter, I'm trying to get an understanding of the situation instead of listening to rumors and second-hand information.

Thank you for giving me some insight in to the situation. Certain things make a lot more since now.

> **RandomlyK says** - *Where's the duct tape?*

Adding To It
February 7, 2010
2 weeks and 2 days of freedom

Some people don't see how they're abusive. Will has said several times that he's an asshole, but he doesn't see it as being abusive.

Acting like an asshole is something one might do on a bad day or once in a blue moon. And when someone is an asshole and *not* an abuser, they usually apologize for it quickly, embarrassed by what they've done. For example, the asshole who cuts me off in traffic then flashes me the bird when I honk the horn is easy to forgive. The asshole had a bad moment; no skin off my nose! Maybe, if we both ended up in the supermarket later eyeing the same head of cabbage, that guy would apologize. At least, that's how these nerve-wracking scenes play out in my head. Gives me peace.

But someone who acknowledges that they're an ass, is proud of being an ass and seems to thrive on doing ugly things to other people in order to get his way...well, that person is abusive.

There are abusers that grew up in a home where abuse was normal. A home in which everyone felt isolated and struck out at the perceived weaker ones in order to relieve the stress on themselves. No one ever told them they were wrong; in fact, the example given by the caregivers showed them they were right. These people, once out in the world, recognize some clues proving that their behavior is not exactly *normal*.

Some of them may take notice, wonder why they always feel put upon, mistreated, distrustful and pessimistic 99% of the time. They may wonder why other people seem to look at them sadly or become upset in their presence. There is a chance that these abusers will seek to discover what others find off-putting about them. They may discover that their own attitudes and beliefs are holding them back from enjoying life, love and happiness. These people may seek change.

But some of these unhappy people stick with what they know because it is what their grandparents did. What their parents did. It's how they were raised and what they've done all their lives. Gosh darn it they love their family. To admit that their upbringing negatively affected them perhaps disrespects their forebears. Perhaps, as children, one criticism of their parent caused such an outrage that the child who made it was shamed and felt afraid. Now, as adults, the subtle memories of multiple shames and frightening moments prohibits them from even considering that something that grandparent did was, in any way, *wrong*.

"So if Grandma was right, then I'm right! If the world thinks I'm an asshole, then I am. It works for me. It's who I am." Those people will not seek change. They become abusers in part because they won't admit there's anything wrong with their behavior.

I've been an asshole before, but I'm not making it my life's work.

Comments from Readers

Ramona Vickers says - No need to respond. *I find it interesting that you chose to write about abusive families today. It makes me wonder if that is how you see "Will's" family. At this point, all I'd like to say to everyone who reads these journals, there are always three sides to every story. The perception of each of the parties involved, and what the others on the outside see and perceive. I believe Kellie Jo actually said that. No jab intended, I just liked the comment. I so didn't want to believe that "Will's" family was telling me was the truth. Unfortunately, I see for myself.*

As stated by another person in a previous blog, blogs are for supporting one another. I support Kellie Jo leaving her husband, but I can't support the way she is doing it. I sincerely believe she is, and has been, using this blog to better her position in her divorce.

> **Kellie Jo says -** How would you suggest I leave him, Ramona? Should I let him come home (as if he would seeing that I've done the unforgivable thing and reported him to the law)? Would it be okay with you if I stayed with him and waited to see how long it would take him to hurt me again? How many times does he have to lay his hands on me before it is okay that I leave in this manner?
>
> Maybe I should have left last month when he was promising he would change, that he would work with me, that he wanted us to last. I am sure you wouldn't have judged that so harshly, right? (Poor Will - he was trying so hard and the bitch left him anyway!) Perhaps I should put my tail between my legs like a good woman and slink away without standing up for myself, the boys or what is just or fair. How would you dictate I do this, Ramona?
>
> As you and I both know, domestic violence is always a case of he said she said because the abuse happens at home, in the privacy of home and the secrecy of isolation. Proving abuse is difficult at best.
>
> However, writing a blog is easy. Anyone could do it. I could have started this blog and wrote nothing but lies in it for a year. Is it evidence for my use in court? No. I don't think a blog the alleged victim writes is reliable evidence in court. There has to be proof beyond a reasonable doubt that Will

did what I said he did. The proof must be solid, and a blog written by me, the victim, is not solid proof of Will's actions.

There's no input from Will on this blog. He could claim the blog is fiction I wrote to jump-start a writing career. He could say Ramona Vickers is not his sister, friend or acquaintance. Those statements are as provable as the truth (not at all). The blog would be inadmissible. It doesn't matter to a judge what I write here. The judge wants proof.

What goes on behind closed doors always stays there. Blog or not, any domestic violence charge is only that - a charge.

Will and I remain heavily invested in this case. I for one would like to think it is the most important case going. But for the judge, it is one of fifty she will hear this week. We aren't important to them. The judge looks at us through the lens of the law; we're no more important than are the others sitting in the courtroom. I am no different from any other woman alleging domestic violence, and I'll bet not all of the people who allege it tell the truth. I'll also bet the judge knows it. So the judge not only looks at Will, she has to look at me.

In a domestic violence case, the victim is as much on trial as the abuser. Because the domestic violence charge aligns directly with our divorce, they are at this point inseparable. My blog falls into the category of shady evidence. The only legitimacy this blog receives is the input of Will's family members. And even you are an alleged participant in this blog as I could be paying you to pretend to be a family member so I could use this opportunity to defend against all you say. I give more information than I normally would in response to your statements.

I like the idea of three sides to every story, too. However, I wrote it a little differently than you described. I said,

> ...there are always at least three versions of truth when there is a truth to be told – your version, their version, and the indifferent record of events imprinted upon the universe which will probably never be revealed. Sometimes all three versions line up perfectly. Usually, the three versions of truth do not align, and we people dive into the business of "sorting things out" which usually results in another version of events which is not the truth either.

Ramona, what you perceive falls into the sorting things out category.

Comments from Readers

IBelieveYou says - I am in a similar situation. This post spoke to me - my husband's entire family is conditioned, from several generations back, to attack and turn on each other, and to relieve stress by attacking the weak. His father, mother and sister have all done it to me, repeatedly. I know when I leave him, they will attack me and discredit me.

I think it is highly likely a sister of an emotional and verbal abuser would behave like Ramona Vickers. I know nothing of her or you specifically, but after living with someone who sounds similar to your husband, I would assume their families are also similar.

I am sorry your difficult process of sorting this out and getting on with your life is made more difficult by whoever this commenter is, and by members of Will's family. I hope that, when his family reacts like this, it helps to convince you that distance from this is a good thing.

Apology at the End
February 8, 2010
2 weeks and 3 days of freedom

I question my darkness. I know that I have tried to hurt Will before. I know he likes a clean house, so I let the housekeeping fall to hell. I know he likes me to serve him food, so I stopped. One time recently, I even tried to make him mad - on purpose!

There have been times where I wished I were more like how I perceive Will to be. I have wished I could somehow learn what he was doing so I could do it back to him.

I always feel horrible about it.

Wait. Let me clarify that. There was a time when I didn't know I was doing it. I didn't feel horrible about it then because I was acting out in the only way that came naturally to me. Since I've learned about co-dependence, I've been able to see how my passive-aggressiveness was a form of manipulation. It certainly didn't work well, but it was my attempt to gain control. If Will came by his aggression naturally, then I certainly came by my passive-aggression naturally. I knew passive-aggression as an acceptable means to handle my anger. I grew up with it, accepted it and never questioned it because it was what the people who I loved modeled to me.

Sound familiar?

There are reasons people like Will and I get together. We complement one another perfectly. We're two opposite ends of the same spectrum, both as harmful as the other is emotionally or mentally. Will's bad luck of the draw is that aggressive people get physical. When Will and I first got together, we both had the same traits as we do now. But our deficiencies weren't as pronounced; they were easier to ignore and forgive. But neither one of us wanted to take responsibility for our own feelings. We wanted the other to *make* us feel better. Over time, our anger at one another for not making us feel better led to button pushing. Every time I pushed his button, he inched further toward aggression. Every time he pushed my button, I inched further toward passive-aggression.

Now, the distance between us is insurmountable. There has been so much pain, too much pain.

I am working my way toward the center of the spectrum. Sometimes it seems like a slow crawl, and other days I seem to teleport with ease. This weekend has seen my slow crawl. The exchange with Ramona brought out feelings that I thought were confined to Will's behavior, but they aren't. I am *healthier* when it comes to Will because he is the obvious perpetrator, but I realize that my co-dependent passive-aggressive behavior is not limited to Will. A part of me wants to bring Ramona over to my side because to do so would hurt Will. Her appearance on Facebook and on this blog took me by surprise, and the language she used sent me spiraling backward into my darkness. She is right in saying the last post is how I see her family. *Growing Up Co-Dependent* focuses on mine. Neither family is healthy.

One family has an outward appearance of aggression, and one has an inward expression of aggression. But the language I used in the posts is different. I am much more forgiving of my family than I am of Will's. His family acts hostile toward me. I do not feel comfortable around them, and I learned to distrust them.

I passive-aggressively lashed out at you, Ramona, with that post, and I am ashamed of myself. I thought about taking it down, trying to make it seem like it never happened, but I won't. This blog is a record of my journey, and to ignore my mistakes or pretend I don't make them at this point would be more shameful than making the mistake. I do apologize, Ramona, for adding fuel to this fire and I promise you, I will overcome the nasty habit that is mine and mine alone.

Comments from Readers

Ramona Vickers says - *Your last post is based you believing that I am part of Will's family. I am not. I grew up in a more passive-aggressive world and learned that behavior, which I also displayed in my responses to your blog. I am sorry for that. Bad habits are hard to break.*

You don't know my family.

> **QuietOne says** - *You did not lash out - you defended yourself.*

Ramona Vickers says - *I agree with QuietOne. You owe me no apology. I wish I could tell you who I am. Unfortunately, I agreed not to get involved. Now I see that would have been the best thing to do. I can say this; I understand a family like Will's. When you married him, he said you would be a part of that family. But, in reality, they did not allow you inside the family circle. Sometimes you stand outside the circle, like a kid at a candy store, face pressed against the glass, wishing you were a part, and other times, thanking your lucky stars you aren't. But never truly feeling a part of it.*

> **Kellie Jo says** - *Sorry Ramona. I did think you were one of Will's sisters. In one of your comments, you referred to Texas giving custody to an alcoholic mother bent on suicide. I wrongly assumed that you were the alcoholic mother because I don't understand why someone else would bring the alcoholic mother we obviously both know into this blog.*

I figured you were the alcoholic mother and used yourself in that example of Texas justice. The mother you referred to has made great strides in establishing mental health.

So no, I have no idea who you are, Ramona nor who your family could be. Our exchange has been beneficial to me; it helped me to see my shortcomings more clearly. I don't know how long it will take to establish new habits, only that I will.

Conflicting Thoughts
February 9, 2010
2 weeks and 4 days of freedom

I spent the last few days obsessing and sad. I feel no clarity at all. I am angry that part of me wants to pretend this [physical violence/separation] never happened. Part of me wants him home. Part of me wants to be sorry and sad and compliant.

I know part of him wants to come home. (I am guessing though I say I know.) If he does want to come home, the romantic version of his return goes like this:

He is sorry. He languishes in that tiny trailer where there is nothing to do but think. He wants help because in his heart of hearts he knows I am doing what I need to do to feel safe. He knows he is more than a bad husband - he is a frightening one. He is apologetic and shamed. He wants to make it right.

But I imagine his thinking is more along the lines of "I will win. I will make her lose it all." This is his house, his family, his wife, his boys, his property, his money, *his his his* and he hates that I took it from him. If he returned home, he would eventually feel empowered enough to let me know that he came back for the money that was his. The boys who are his. Not for me, not for love, not for change.

He would go about dismantling me the best he could financially, mentally and emotionally. We both would know that the next time he put his hands on me they would be fists. The beating wouldn't stop until I was either dead or too damaged to recover.

Anger. Denial. I'm in denial, shifting back to anger, then denial again. How else would I explain the romantic notions that I cry over, the fiction I long to live? I heard a man in Staples the other day answer his phone, "Hello my love, my life, my wife." I felt torn between wishing my husband would talk to me that way and thinking that the man was hiding his abusive nature behind sweet words.

I don't know if I will ever trust a man again. As soon as I love him, will he show his true colors?

Tired and Weak
February 10, 2010
2 weeks and 5 days of freedom

I'm tired and weak. Today's been a rotten crying day. I'm going to blame it on my period. But if I weren't on the rag, I'd still feel low today. I've been going through paperwork. Dividing it up, mine, his, mine, his.... I never ever wanted to do this. I didn't.

Comments from Readers

PrincessLuceval says - *Oh, I'm so sorry. I feel your pain in your writing. Baby steps. Tiny steps forward. Stop and rest a lot.*

> **Kunjii says** - *Yep, you're gonna have horribly awful days; and you might start to regret what you did, but you never know - this might be the wakeup call that you both needed*

> to change your lives and re-commit to each other. If you love each other, it could happen. If not, go in peace. Each of you deserves happiness. Spending six months or a year apart may make you appreciate each other, or it may open your eyes to all the possibilities of happiness out there for you to explore. Take it one day at a time.

NewDirection says - *I learned that being forced to divorce your abusive husband is the final act of violence. He left you through his abuse and behaviors, but you are forced to make the choice and to do the emotional and logistical work that goes along with it. You get to bare the guilt, shame, sadness, ambivalence and all there other fun emotions that come with being forced out of a marriage due to abuse. When I'm not in a self-pitying mood, I try to act like divorcing my abusive soon-to-be-ex is empowering, and then hope that I'll believe the show. It sucks.*

> **Kellie Jo says** - Divorce, I hope, is the final act. It does seem violent. You sound angry today; I suppose that anger goes along with the rest of it. I don't always feel empowered, but I keep moving forward. Looking to the horizon. What's on your horizon? What do you want for yourself?

Half Life
February 13, 2010
3 weeks and 1 day of freedom

Yesterday I visited the Women's Center that acts as this area's Small Business Association. The Center offers two programs that fit me. One caters to displaced homemakers and the other helps people wanting to start their own businesses. Under the displaced homemaker's program, The Women's Center will pay so I can attend some classes offered at one of the colleges here in town.

I feel torn between wanting a job that makes money and one that is light on cash but heavy on connections to people. For example, the center would pay for my certification in many different types of health care jobs (aging baby boomers are making the career field lucrative). However, I don't want to work in health care. I barely have patience when my own children are ill. Why would I want to inflict myself on aging ill people?

Come to think of it, I'm not torn. I don't care about the money. Not right now. I'm willing to work hard and make a name for myself, but I do hope the money comes at some point! I want to be a writer. I'm willing to forgo the starving artist mentality if something comes my way that fits me well. Maybe the money will come easier than I fear; I won't know until I put myself out there.

Under the business program, the center will help me write a business plan and introduce me to people in the community in the writing field, at the paper, at area magazines, etc. I look at a business plan as verification that the service I have to offer is a viable commodity. Is there a market for my writing? What topics pay? Where? How much can I earn freelance? What's the best way to publish my writing? Would it be better to get a day job (related to writing) right now and write my little arse off about whatever I wanted in my down time?

Will doesn't pay attention to the labor forecasts because he knows that there will always be a market for him - he is skilled at both soldiering and mechanics. He's proud of his blue-collar mentality, and frankly, so am I. I'm a big fan of a good day's work.

Will and I differ in that I see pursuits such as writing and art as valuable. Creating a work of art (whether it's a story, a website, a painting) is challenging and rewarding. It's not exactly blue-collar, callous-creating work, but that is okay. We each have our different skill sets, and I'm tired of putting my skills at a level lower than his. Yes, *he* is the one who places my skills at a lower level than his, but I am the one who went along with it. I don't much feel like going along any more.

How the heck did Will get into this post? I didn't mean to drag him into it. I suppose that Will and his ideas will be in my head and heart for quite some time. They've been here for almost half my life already.

Some of his thoughts I will miss.

Army of Snot
February 13, 2010
3 weeks and 1 day of freedom

I doubt whether I will be able to make it now that I'm free. I know my thoughts are normal - I think almost anyone in my position would hold similar ones. Shoot, probably most people have these thoughts at times. None of us have any guarantee that what we do will result in financial or any other type of security. Maybe we're all winging it.

These thoughts are new to me though. Always before, I had a husband who took care of me financially. I had faith that if I did my part, then we would be fine. Now I have to do everything I used to do *and* do his part so I can earn money for the boys and me. I don't know if Will thinks about it that way. Does he think that now he has to do my part too? But then, that's not my business.

Wondering what he thinks keeps me stagnant at a time where I want to be a rolling stone. You know, gathering no moss.

So when I start to doubt my viability as a writer, when I start to wonder if I should take the promise of big money tomorrow in exchange for a career that doesn't involve creativity, then I have to remind myself to stop diminishing my thoughts and denying what I know I want for the sake of imagined security.

My security up to this point has been a sham anyway. What do I know of security? I've deluded myself into thinking that I was safe at home when I wasn't safe at all.

I noticed something else. Ugh. I feel secure when I am sad. Shit. Now I'm crying ... but it's not sadness. What is this? I feel familiar emotions. I feel crushed, hopeless and alone. My sinuses are friggin' stuffed up as if the snot hung out behind my eyeballs hoping for a good cry. I don't know the words for this.

After writing the section above, I needed a break. I refilled my coffee and noticed that there is almost four inches of snow on the ground! Real snow! I called the boys to look at it, and they took off into it. I watched them, and then thought, "Why not?" I ran to put on my shoes and coat but stealthily snuck up on Marc with a snowball! We ran around the yard, Marc, Eddie and me, throwing snowballs. A snowball hit me in the eye so I declared myself *winner* 'cause I got hurt. The boys said I was the *loser* 'cause I got hurt. Boy, the rules have sure changed since I played with my dad in the snow.

We ran and threw and laughed. Marc took a high position and creamed me, so I took it out on Eddie hiding on the other side of the boat. Eddie was too sweet to get me back. Now, back in the house, snowy pants exchanged for pajamas, I think that the best way to describe those familiar thoughts and the feelings that go along with them is not to describe them at all. Those are old thoughts about old things. The best way to stop tormenting myself with old thoughts is to create new ones. Soon, the new thoughts of laughter and my boys and snowball fights in the crisp night will replace the old ones that required an army of snot to fuel them.

Part II: … and the living begins

"Life isn't about finding yourself. Life is about creating yourself."

~ George Bernard Shaw

Transition Title
February 13, 2010
3 weeks and 1 day of freedom

One of the best parts about blogging is making up titles. Sometimes I know the title before I know what to write, and sometimes I must finish a post before the title reveals itself. But it is tough to come up with titles this week.

I don't know what I'm doing; I don't know what I'm feeling. And when I consider what I'm thinking, I feel afraid. There is no good title for that kind of confusion. There is no good title for this time in my life.

I'm not married but I'm not single. I don't want to be married, but I don't want to date. (Puh-leeze! Will I ever be ready to date?)

I don't have a home of my own, but I'm living in one.

I don't have any money of my own, and the thought of having my own cash worries me. Having my own money means that I'm alone.

I am alone, but I'm still Mama. I am alone, but I'm still sister, daughter, friend and even wife. How can I be so many people but feel lost? How can I be Mama when I don't know what the hell I'm doing?

I'm afraid but trying to be brave. Courageous but wishing I'd been less so for a little longer.

Smart but feeling like an idiot.

Sad and not wanting to honor it. Happy but fearful of letting happiness go, not trusting that it will return.

What the hell is *this*?

Too Soon
February 14, 2010
3 weeks and 2 days of freedom

As usual, I'm reading books. Tonight's subject is divorce. The thrust of this book on divorce is deciding what kind of divorce I want, then considering how I want to get there. Do attorneys hash it out? Do we have to go to court and air our dirty laundry? Or would mediation work for us?

But then there's the big question: Am I on the path to divorce? Is there *no* alternative? Am I going to get divorced in the same hasty manner I married? Did I throw out the brakes on this vehicle on a downhill road? If we lived in Texas, we could get a quickie divorce (so long as we were happy with the separation agreement). In North Carolina, we must live separately for one year. I am beginning to see the wisdom in the forced wait.

I find myself wishing Will and I could talk. We both want separation from each other. We both want the other to change. We both want to renegotiate a *lot* of crap. And there I go speaking for him again when there is no way to know what he is thinking. I cannot, by choice and by law, talk to him now. I need time.

But my attorney wants my financial documentation yesterday. She wants to know exactly what I want when all I know is that I don't want him around me now. Isn't there some way to slow down? Will wants me not to show up in court for his next appearance. If I don't show up, then chances are the court will drop the charges. Good for him, makes me look like a liar. I'm no liar; I'll be in court.

What he says doesn't align with what my attorney says. He says I can't trust a civilian attorney; but I must trust a civilian attorney because I have *no access* to a military one.

I trust that everyone knows military courts are completely different from civilian ones. Even Will, an active duty soldier, cannot hire a military attorney to represent him in civil court. The Judge Advocate General (JAG) is not a free attorney service for the military. JAG only governs what happens to a soldier under military law (discharge from the military, dock pay, reduce rank and that sort of thing).

Because the military now pays attention to domestic violence and abuse, *if* civil court convicts Will of domestic abuse, the Army will dishonorably discharge him. That's what Will says JAG says. I haven't been able to get to JAG yet - they have a class two times a week and my other appointments have taken priority. So here I am, being pressured by Will to "not show up" in court and to get financial documents so "we can proceed," and all I want to do is to sit with this for a bit.

There may be a smart way to handle this separation and divorce that doesn't involve ridiculous amounts of pressure or money. I'm no attorney, but given a little time, I can get a handle on *what I want* and then find out *what he wants* and then see how close to agreeing we are. I'm thinking a mediator is necessary. Will wants the cheapest way out, but I have a lot at stake. If I don't have someone who can protect my interests, then Will loses nothing and keeps everything *we* worked for and created in the past 18 years.

I think he doesn't care about that. I suspect he wants to rush things so I don't have a chance to think. Or maybe he wants to rush things because it hurts. But *all* of those ideas are simply me projecting my own thoughts onto Will, and that isn't going to help me one bit.

Instead of blogging, I am going to write out what I want. I'm going to give that to my attorney (for record keeping) and have her send it to Will. Then maybe he'll tell me what *he* wants. After that, I can be pleased, hurt or angry, but I would be able to move ahead without feeling unheard and rushed.

Semantics
February 14, 2010
3 weeks and 2 days of freedom

Victim or Survivor? There has to be a different word for what I have experienced and what is to come. I don't feel like repeating the word *victim* to myself or portraying myself as such. I am a *survivor* of abuse; however, the word survivor brings to my mind those who have been shot, bloodied or on the brink of suicide due to the abuse inflicted upon them. I don't want to run around calling myself a survivor when I haven't survived any major types of physical harm. I won't taking away from the fear and pain physical abuse has caused in me - those feelings are for a reason, real and valid. But I've never looked like Rhianna in her post-violence photos; I've never been hospitalized due to physical abuse.

I'm looking for a word that describes what I've experienced. A short, small, easily understood label. I also have to be careful of what I say to myself about my experience with abuse. I don't want to blame or label *him* in order to describe myself. Will and I have different understanding about our experience together, and that's all there is to it. I cannot force him to admit to nor accept responsibility for any of it; I cannot somehow force him to stop blaming me for it. I can't even convince him that his behaviors are abusive, let alone that his behaviors have affected me in a negative way. So how do I describe me (within the confines of abuse)?

- Sufferer (no, I definitely don't want to live my life as a sufferer of anything; I prefer to recognize and correct instead of suffer)
- Contributor (I did contribute to the abusive cycle because it takes an abuser and a victim of the abuse to make the cycle spin. I don't like contributor because it implies I approved of it in some way.)
- Participant (somewhat close, but implies the word *willing* to go along with it and doesn't quite describe the confusion mental and emotional abuse inflicts)
- Victim (yes, I am a victim of abusive behavior, but like the label *sufferer* I prefer to not live my life under the victim umbrella)
- Survivor (have I survived it? are there degrees of victimhood that hold greater claim to this word?)
- Wife of an Abuser (labels *him*)
- Casualty (closer...implies that I am still living although I've previously been in the thick of it)
- Recovering Victim (yuck. plain yuck.)
- Misused (not right because it implies that I can be somehow used or did agree to someone using me)
- Living with Abuse (begs the question *Why?* and that requires an answer that the questioner wouldn't understand anyway)

I cannot think of a word or phrase that succinctly labels my experience. Yet maybe the lack of vocabulary for the *abusive situation* speaks more than one word could. Abuse itself is insidious, tricky, sneaky and quiet. It makes sense that Abuse would not *want* a label pinned to it.

Abuse creates victims for a while, and then either disposes of that victim (killing body or spirit) or the victim becomes something other than Victim. Abuse uses someone else to inflict its pain; the longer the abuser stays in the dark about Abuse, the longer Abuse lives. Likewise, the longer the victim doesn't recognize Abuse, the easier it is for Abuse to infiltrate the victim's behaviors as well.

Abuse seeks to win, live and thrive in two people, not one. When Abuse is able to accomplish that feat, it is more likely that Abuse's two victims will stay silent about the torment they inflict upon one another. There is probably no one word to describe the abusive relationship and that is probably why I've written about Abuse for over a year.

I also have to be careful of what I say to myself about my experience with abuse. I don't want to blame or label *him* in order to describe myself.

Comments from Readers

QuietOne says - *"Abuse's two victims will stay silent about the torment they inflict upon one another." So right you are.*

The best I ever came up with was "I have experienced abuse." It is inadequate. There are not many people I will discuss the situation with, and even others who have experienced abuse seldom understand that the both parties inflict and receive abuse. I also hate victim and survivor because both leave a person sounding helpless and inactive, and it is not that way. I don't blame myself but I recognize that I have been an active participant in my own abuse.

> **PrincessLuceval says –** *I heard the phrase, "You are a target, not a victim." Target isn't always correct, but quite often feels so.*

Change is Stability
February 19, 2010
4 weeks of freedom

Today I drove to the swamp and sat in the car wondering what my next move would be. There are so many possibilities. The possibilities could be paralyzing, but I decided to choose one and go with it. If it doesn't work, then I will choose another possibility.

So after I thought about what I wanted to do I thought, "What is the one thing I don't know that it would help me to know right now?" I sat there for a while, not knowing, and thinking that All wouldn't answer this question. I mean, I didn't know what I didn't know, so how was I going to get an answer?

I got quiet, waiting for the voices. But the swamp was silent. Smooth. Still. It was a still-life painting, un-romanticized and brown. There were no voices.

I thought about how different this swamp looked the first time I ran to it. On that day, the water was almost overflowing the banks. There were swirls and eddies, fish jumping and forest noises. The swamp flowed that day, life exploded. But today, there was nothing but quiet. I thought about how much the swamp had changed and how it may be different the next time that I visited. Mossy green and stagnant? Then I realized that it did not matter how the swamp would be different next time - it would be what I needed it to be. It would change. It would change into what I needed it to be.

And so will I.

In the Way
February 22, 2010
1 month of freedom

The weekend is over, and the boys are home. I started putting together my first book this weekend. I have a publisher and an idea, and I'm hoping for the best.

I didn't start to feel anxious until about two hours before picking up our boys. I don't feel void and I don't feel overly paranoid or extremely sad. I don't feel happy or entirely empowered, either. I feel ... strange.

Marc got mad at me on the phone about an hour before it was time to pick him up. He yelled and used a word I don't like, told me my reasons for telling him he couldn't go to his friend's house were "bullshit." He said it was unfair that he had to choose between seeing friends on the weekend and seeing his father, and I agreed with that. I told him I would talk to Will about weekday visitations.

When I spoke to Will about it, I didn't get a definite answer. Will implied that by visiting the boys in the middle of the week that I was not keeping their best interests at heart, choosing to disrupt their routine over keeping it stable. I said that these were extraordinary circumstances and that if Marc or Eddie wanted to see him during the week, then we would make the concessions to see that it happened.

He also said that the magistrate gave me everything I asked for (I didn't correct him by saying I didn't ask for all of what she *gave*) and now I'd have to deal with it. I don't know what he was arguing about exactly. He and I are in charge of visitations and we can communicate about the boys (no-contact order amended on January 28).

Because our boys want to see Will during the week in addition to weekends so that they have less guilt over visiting friends on weekends, then we as parents should make it happen. I left the ball in his court. I asked him to think about it, and if he decided it was something he could do then he could email my attorney and we would start figuring out how to go about it. (Due to the no contact order, he cannot contact me directly although we can discuss the children and see one another at a public place for visitations.)

I cannot comprehend much of what Will does and says. I understand that no matter what my opinion of Will or his behaviors, our boys see him as Dad and love him unconditionally. Marc and Eddie both would like to see him during the week if it is possible. Will said that he would like to see the boys, but feels I'm not using good judgment in requesting a midweek visit. I wonder if, because I asked for a midweek visitation, Will would rather not give me my way than agree to see his boys.

My other suspicion is that Will is drinking during the week and doesn't want to interrupt his own routine. I don't think his reluctance to visit midweek has anything to do with him not loving our children, but I don't see how his explanation for not agreeing to see them midweek makes sense. [Sigh.]

Maybe he is trying to build a case against me and it has nothing to do with my other suspicions at all. I don't know why he's arguing. I feel like there has to be something more to it, but after I publish this post, I'm going to let go of it entirely. I left him in charge of deciding, and now all I can do is wait without trying to figure him out. I have to let it go.

It is 15 minutes later. I'm still letting it go.

Fixing It
February 23, 2010
1 month, 1 day of freedom

My therapist helped me understand more about my frigging compulsion to *make things right* (co-dependency) during our session yesterday. It feels wonderful to know that I am on the path out of co-dependency, but sometimes my path doubles back and forms a loop that I must travel a second time. That's okay. I'm learning. A day or two ago, I wrote a post that described how I hoped that by talking to Will and setting up a midweek visitation, our son's would be able to visit their friends (during dad's time) on the weekends and feel less guilt about doing so. Honestly, looking back, I hoped to smooth some of Will's ruffled feathers by showing my willingness to work toward equitable visitations.

So, what was I trying to do? I was trying to make my sons and Will feel better. It didn't matter that I don't *want* to have midweek visitation because of my jacked-up weeknight schedule (from now until the end of this semester). It was more important to me to make two people (Marc and Will specifically) feel better after the actions I took a month ago. (And why am I feeling guilty for leaving the man who put his hands on me?)

In effect, when I spoke to Will about Marc's wishes, I opened myself up to Will's habitual attacks. I truly thought that Will would say, "That sounds good - how about Wednesdays?" or something similar. I didn't expect a 20-minute argument against an extra hour or two with the boys. And why didn't I expect an argument? Because I was doing a good thing, a self-sacrificing thing that may (or may not) benefit our boys, and I expected Will to see that and maybe not be so mad at me. And then, I wrapped myself up in knots wondering why Will behaved as *he* did, and assigned motives to Will (motives I cannot know), and berated him for his decision. In short, I created a situation in which I had no business and then amplified the negative result it in my own mind to punish myself.

My therapist presented an alternative solution, one that makes sense and would have cut out all the drama. She said that Marc's feelings of guilt were *his* to deal with. It sounded harsh to me at first ... didn't I *cause* Marc's bad feelings? Wasn't I responsible for this whole mess? Shouldn't I do everything I can to *fix it* for Marc? Well, no, no, and no.

Marc's bad feelings are a result of a conflict between spending time with his dad and spending time with his friends. Do you see my name in that statement? No. I'm not involved in Marc's bad feelings. When he told me he felt like he had to choose, I could have said, "Well, maybe a weeknight visitation with your dad would help. Talk to him and let me know what you decide and I'll work with you."

I am not responsible for this whole mess. Will and I separated because of his act of violence.

I cannot fix anything for Marc. When I decided to insert myself into the conflict, I took away Marc's power to solve his problem on his own. I so wanted to eliminate Marc's bad feelings! I don't want my child to feel bad, ever. But if Marc is to grow into a fine man, he's going to have to learn to deal with his unpleasant feelings on his own. I mean, will I be there when he has a conflict with his co-worker? His boss? His girlfriend? Nope. He's got to learn to deal.

So, my assignment for this week is detachment. Specifically when it comes to allowing the ones I love to own *their* problems. I'm here for them if they need suggestions or if I can do something that will help them sleep easier at night so long as I am a component of their own solution and not attempting to fix it for them.

Comments from Readers

Erin says - *Hmmm. Sounds like a good time to listen to your hypnosis mp3!* [2]

> **EagleWolfeSpirit says** - *Kellie & Erin! I've been meaning to tell you, I have listened once to the hypnosis and although not 100% sure, I have felt so much better, so much stronger, and insight and outlook is clearer! A few days ago, I had my 7-year-old listen to it as well, for as long as her father is around, she needs all the ammo she can find to repel his antagonistic/abusive comments and ways! Thanks ladies!*
>
> *Kellie, I cannot begin to tell you how much you sharing your situation and thoughts are helping me to see the light on so many things!*
>
> *There is good and bad in all things, and what you do for me is a small portion of the good that will come from this bad thing! Some of what you realized yesterday, I have realized in the past, i.e.: we each own our own troubles and the resolution of such. What stuck out for me in this post was:*
>
> *#1. The way you describe co-dependency gave me a greater understanding of it. I see how it applies to me in certain situations. I never (before today) was quite able to grasp the definition of co-dependency. And as a footnote, I have read tons of material!*
>
> *#2. In describing your desire to want to help your child, I think it is a commendable and rightful place for a parent to be. For example, our children are in our care for us to protect and guide into adulthood. As in your specific situation, your*

children being older, I can understand where it is more appropriate to support them making their own decisions and acting upon them, 100%. However, with a younger child, I can also see where the situation would be different. There are many variables (as to the whys) to take into consideration with this particular situation, and it is only understandable one would take those steps, and make that fumble.

Something a dear friend has said to me is "You're not raising kids, you're raising an adult."

#3. I like the way you addressed the guilt aspect of this scenario, the fact that it does happen. We most certainly should not feel guilty for leaving such a negative situation. You are certainly making progress, and I am grateful for that blessing!

In my situation, during a conversation I initiated (which later turned into an argument attempt that I refused to engage in), I explained that I can no longer engage in this relationship intimately, until it is realized by both *of us that there is a problem, and help is sought. I can see where I have been involved in the dance of abuse, and as much as I hate to admit it, an enabler for him to continue the bad behaviors. I'm sure this situation will follow where most go, and I'm fine with that. Angry and resentful at times, but I'm working through that every day!*

Rules
February 24, 2010
1 month, 2 days of freedom

It is important to understand that the rules we follow later in abusive relationships are not the ones we accepted at the beginning of the relationship. In the beginning, I spent loads of time and energy rebelling against his abuse and assuming I could explain the asshole out of him. However, over time, I made concessions. I adjusted my behaviors both consciously and subconsciously thinking that Will was a *partner* in the relationship as well. He was never my *partner* and did not want to be.

After years passed, I found myself quite unhappy. On inspection, I found that I had agreed to *certain rules* out of my desire to keep him happy (or at least, not angry). It happened slowly, subtly, and completely.

Comments from Readers

KeepSmiling says - *I would break every rule in life's imaginary rulebook if I knew I was right. Some rules are supposed to be broken. Without the breaking of rules, we would still be living in the dark ages (no votes for women and our voices silenced).*

Rules can be imaginary shackles placed on us by others for control. Why set yourself more rules? Life is too short. Be kind, don't intentionally hurt others, do the best you can do, and don't listen to people who say the only right way is their way. Freedom.

Liar Liar
February 25, 2010
1 month, 3 days of freedom

This morning, I sat down with my hot sweet coffee and my daily planner. I have a lot going on. I scheduled therapy sessions, domestic violence group meetings, a meeting to hear the results from the military investigation, a court date on Monday, a class next week called *Career Makeover* in which I hope to practice networking skills, and of course, taking Marc to that stupid school that runs from mid-afternoon until way past dinner every day. Of course, that isn't all there is to do...it's a sample of what's happening next week.

This separation is overwhelming. There are many things to do *now*, and that leaves little time to do what is also important and must be in place before the end of this year. Namely, I must financially support my boys and myself *despite* the demands on my time.

So, anyway, I was sitting there with my hot sweet coffee and daily planner, and decided to write in my journal pretty much what I just wrote above. You know, *get it out* so I could move on to what I must do today, trying to take one day at a time and all that happy horseshit. But when I started to write, all that came out was:

LIAR!

You damn liar. You promised that you would love me, take care of me, for the rest of my life. You said that if I stayed at home to raise our children, you could go out into the world and provide for us. You told me that if I waited to make a career for myself then you would support my dreams as soon as you retired - we were down to five short years! You said to wait, to trust you, to be a good wife and my turn was coming.

LIAR!

You said that you knew we had problems and you were willing to work on them. You said that when you got home things would be different. You said that it would be hard, but you were willing to put in the work. You said you loved me and keeping our family together was what you wanted too. When I told you back in July of '09 that I had decided to stay, to trust that what you said was true, you had relief in your voice. You said you were so glad to hear those words, that you were happy for the first time in months.

LIAR!

You said that you wouldn't be where you are in the military today without me, and now you're doing your best to get rid of me, one rank from the top. You fucking suck, you abusive, sneaky, foul-mouthed, manipulative, lousy husband. You fucking lied to me about all of it.

LIAR!

And then you have the nerve to call me a traitor.

LIAR!

I am angry from my bowels up. I don't know how long this will last. I don't know how long until I am a good enough person to let it go. I don't know when I will be free of you, of thoughts of you, of love for you.

Back in July, I decided to keep loving you. You had given me every reason not to love you, some reasons you gave more than once. I was willing to look past it, to look deeper into you for the man I married. I was willing to live with rough around the edges - you're a self-proclaimed asshole and chauvinist, you stereotype people, you drink, you party, you work before you love me ... I decided I could live with all of it. I was willing to look beyond who you are, who you are proud to be, in hope that *one day* you would treat me well, love me like you promised.

LIAR!

I only wanted you to be nice to me. Treat our children and me with respect and civility. You can be who you are and still learn to be nice. You could have even looked at it as if you were playing a game with me, fooling me, manipulating me to believe good things about you - that may have been fun for you. But you wouldn't try. You wouldn't listen. You wouldn't tell the truth.

You LIAR.

Wasted Time
February 27, 2010
1 month, 5 days of freedom

Today Will requested to come by at 3 PM to pick up some of his things. The time wasn't good for me, so I suggested a different time in the morning. I didn't hear from him, and he didn't show, but that's not what's bugging me. It bothers me that I waited in the way I did. I didn't do any writing or anything that I would consider productive because I was waiting for his interruption. Anticipating it. Instead of going on about my routine, I put it all aside so I would be emotionally ready for his arrival. What *did* I do? I played a video game on the computer. Bored out of my skull, and waiting.

By noon, the deadline I gave came and passed. I felt angry with myself for wasting the morning. I thought about how I spent this morning, anxiously anticipating his arrival. I felt nervous, borderline panicky; the match-three game numbed my mind and made it tolerable. Then I considered how many other times I played that stupid game and under what circumstances.

- I played that game in the hour before I expected him home from work.
- I played it while he was working outside expecting me to be at his disposal to prepare and serve his food.

- I played it when he stalked around the house, pulling up couch cushions and bitching about the dirty socks and candy wrappers he found there (but didn't throw away).

I played that game *lots* not because it is fun or engaging, but because it allowed me to jump up from it at a moment's notice and *tend to him*. That is what I was doing this morning – putting aside important activities in anticipation of his arrival and whatever emotions would accompany him. You know, I made a video about this called *Effects of Verbal Abuse*. In the video I said, "I've been trained to receive permission to be myself, and then to have it taken away from me in an instant."

I would now add that he trained me to *anticipate* having that permission taken away. I did it today and last night, too. Last night, I cleaned up the house some while telling myself "If he notices, I don't care" (and not believing it). Holy cow, the house wasn't even a *mess*! This morning, I agonized for long seconds over whether I should make the bed or not. He's been telling people I cheated on him; part of me wanted the bed to look like two people had slept in it and part of me wanted to make the bed but didn't because then he'd suspect someone else slept in it because I *never* make the bed?! I decided to leave the bed looking as it did when I rolled out of it.

I brushed my teeth and put on some make-up because I didn't want to look like I was a mess. I'm not a mess, not as much of a mess as I sometimes think I should be, and I worried about finding the right balance between *okay* and *overwhelmed*. What do you think of this? Mascara so he'd know I hadn't been crying, but no blush because I didn't want to look too healthy. That's what I went with. Ugh! Craziness.

Then I sat down at the computer to work on my book, and then shut it down because he would be here right as I got going with it and I didn't want him to interrupt the process. So I let my anxiety over his upcoming arrival preempt the process entirely. And then he didn't even show.

Despite the past 24 hours of self-induced craziness, I am ready to do something else I said in that video:

> ...[when] I hit that invisible wall where everything falls to pieces, I feel like I can't handle anything, that I can't do anything, then I'm just gonna tell myself, 'We're changing the training. My ideas are important. What's going on in my head is important.' And even if what I'm doing has gotten a little harder or hasn't turned out exactly as I'd planned, that doesn't mean that it's never going to be [the way I planned]! It just means that it is time to learn something new. It's time to figure out another way to get around an obstacle, and from this point forward, I will recognize when I am falling into the pattern of denying who I am.

So, here's the good news. I recognized the pattern. Next time I see it, I will press on and do what I want to do instead of anticipating disaster. I am resisting the urge to calculate how much time I've spent in the past 18 years *not* doing something I wanted to do because I was anxious about something that he *might* do.

20 Minutes
March 1, 2010
1 month, 1 week of freedom

Twenty minutes until I have to leave the house. I could waste it playing Solitaire, or I could spend it writing. Writing every chance I get is proving to be an easy new habit. The other night, Marc's school put on a presentation. I wrote down observations and snippets of prose (not good prose, but prose!) while listening to the lectures of area business people. I carry a notebook in my purse, and now I use it to jot down words other than reminders and family business. Easy. This morning, with 20 minutes before I must leave the house to attend a *Career Make Over* class, I could have done any number of things that need doing.

- Fold the basket of laundry.
- Wipe the kitten footprints from the floor.
- Clear off the end tables.
- All things I would have done in the past to avoid problems later in the day.

However, I chose to write and feel good about it. I don't know who is going to do the household stuff. There is no one here to tell me I am a horrid wife because the house isn't up to his expectations. No one to tell me what my job entails or complain if I let them down because there are crumbs on the table.

I'm free to write. Much like Will has been free to soldier. He is required to go to work every day, and look how far it has taken him! He is one rank from the top, and he got there because he soldiered day in and day out, religiously. He didn't have anyone telling him to stop soldiering and clean the car. He didn't have anyone breathing down his neck to fix the leaky faucets or clean up the dirt he tracked into the house. I left him to mind his own time and be a soldier. Any other demands of his time he chose to attend to when there was an opening in his schedule - not before and not after. He decided when to do something other than soldier.

I will learn from him when it comes to writing. I will write even when I don't want to write. I will go to work even if I'm sitting here at home, and I will not worry about other menial chores that will be there later. When I can, I'll tend to the laundry, the car, the faucets, the dishes... Until there is an opening in my schedule, I'm not going to worry about the things that can wait. I'm excited!

I Love Who I Am Becoming
March 1, 2010
1 month, 1 week of freedom

Recently I found as website called *Six Word Memoirs* that asks you to define yourself in six words. My latest memoir reads, "I love who I am becoming." My other one reads "Thought love meant pain. Was wrong." When Marc returns to a normal school day schedule, my memoir may be "Got Kids on Bus Now Write!"

The truest memoir is the one I came up with today. I love *becoming*. When I was a little girl, I loved becoming a tree-climber. When I was a teenager, I loved becoming an artist. When I was in my twenties, I loved becoming a mother. Around 30, I loved becoming a woman. Now, at 38, I don't know for sure what I am becoming, but I know I am enjoying the process. I am enjoying becoming with all its hazards, failures, unexpected joys and successes. I love that I may not see what I have become for another 5 years when I'm already working on becoming something else.

All in all, I love my life with all of the successes and failures, blind spots and divine interventions. I really love the successes and divine interventions, but the failures and blind spots are learning experiences and without them, I wouldn't have become who I am right now, at this moment.

I am right now this moment.

Top 8 Signs It's Time to Leave Your Marriage
March 1, 2010
1 month, 1 week of freedom

Today, looking through past journal entries, I found conversations between Big Me (my true voice, the one connected directly to All), and Little Me (my everyday self). Without boring you with the internal workings of my mind, I would like to share what Big Me said about my marriage.

Little Me wrote: I wonder how long I will be able to go on with abuse at the forefront of my mind. At some point, it will truly exhaust me. How will I know if it is time to cut out of my marriage? How will I know if I need to continue healing on my own, when me trying to force Will to stop his part in this if fruitless? How will I know if it is time to leave? Hey, Big Me, I'm talking to you. Signs that it's time to leave the marriage? Hello?

> Big Me said: You don't want me to answer that question.

Little Me wrote: No, I suppose I don't want it, but I need you to answer me. Don't make me dance around like Squirrel Nutkin here. Please, tell me. When is it time to let go of this marriage?

> Big Me said:
>
> When you can no longer hear Pauline [my guardian angel] or me.
>
> When you do not write, draw or express your truth in any new way.
>
> When you see darkness in the middle of the day.
>
> When no one wants to listen to you anymore because you encourage them to do things you cannot or will not do.

> When you cannot bear the sound of his footsteps, it is time to hear those footsteps no more.
>
> When you feel as if everyone would be better off without your crazy ass self.
>
> When you feel dead, your eyes are puffy and you have headaches from all the cry-snot you generate.
>
> When you feel all hope is lost.
>
> Those are signs that it is time to leave your marriage.

His footsteps don't bother me as much as they used to bother me. I still don't want to hear them in my house, but it is all right when I hear them as we meet to talk about the boys. He is not *here*, and I'm satisfied with that for now.

However, I experienced most all of the other signs in the past. I considered being untruthful with you, the readers of my blog. I've considered encouraging you to do something that I am not certain I can do. If you're interested, you will have to read the next post. It may be a long one.

I Want to Lie to You
March 1, 2010
1 month, 1 week of freedom

I visited my attorney for the first time on January 26 - two days before our first court date. On that day, she asked if there was any chance of reconciliation. I told her that he would have to do many things he swore he would *never* do if we were going to reconcile. I told her that reconciliation was out of the question as far as I could see. On February 13, I wrote:

> Instead of blogging, I am going to write out what I want. I'm going to give that to my attorney (for record keeping) and have her send it to Will. Then

> maybe he'll tell me what *he wants* and I can be pleased, hurt or angry, but I would be able to move ahead without feeling unheard and rushed.

I wrote it out, everything I wanted. What it would take to maybe repair our relationship and maybe save our marriage.

I never sent it to my attorney, but last weekend, I gave a copy to Will. I told him that I was holding it back because I didn't think he'd agree to it. I did not tell him that if he didn't agree to it that I would be hurt because I'll know that he didn't think I was worth the effort. If he does not agree to the terms, then it means we are finished. Completely.

Yet I want to know. I want to move forward in this life knowing I did absolutely everything I could to prevent our divorce. To prevent my children's hearts from ripping in two. To prevent my heart from ripping the rest of the way. To prevent destruction. To give him a chance to face his demons as I face mine, individually, but together.

In the document I gave him, I tell him what I want. I tell him he can add to what I wrote, but not take away from it; if I cannot agree to his additions, we divorce. I wanted to lie to you for a while longer, waiting to see if he would agree or not. If he did agree, then I would tell you all about it. But if he never agreed, then I would keep the shameful secret to myself.

I do feel ashamed. Once I left, I knew I had done something that my family and some of you had prayed I would do. I feel ashamed because by giving him this chance, by giving us this chance, you may see me as a loser. You may see me as someone who retreats instead of someone who fights. You may see me as a true abuse victim, willing to subjugate my wishes to his. You may lose confidence in me; you may think I am a fraud. I feel ashamed because I thought once I left, I would be gone forever, and here I am giving him another chance to break my heart. Even if he agrees to the terms, there is no guarantee he will honor them later. He has a tendency to forget things that are important to me.

I do not promise that if he agrees to the terms that all will be immediately well. I want this year apart. At the end of this year, even if we've both done everything I've asked, I may not want to stay married. He may not want to stay married. Maybe we'll go ahead with the divorce. Maybe I will think we're reconciling but he hits me with divorce papers. I know I am leaving myself wide open. That's what I do - expose my soul.

Maybe it is better if you read the agreement. The only difference between what I gave to him and what I'm providing to you is his name. I changed his true name to "Will" because that's how you know him.

I want:
- You and me to have a relationship in which we feel valued by one another.
- A loving, mutually respectful and financially successful marriage that lasts our lifetimes.

Right now, I do not feel these things are possible.

However, there are some changes that could be made that may help me feel more secure in our relationship and more hopeful for our marriage. If I see evidence of these changes explained below, then perhaps what I want would become possible.

I wrote the list knowing that I am not an innocent person. You are definitely not "all bad" and I am further from "all good." I know full well that neither of us are or will be perfect, but I expect both of us will have to work harder if our marriage has a shot at lasting.

Will, you may add to this list, but not take away. I feel strongly that what I've contributed is of highest importance to me. If you cannot agree to this list, or I cannot agree to your additions to it, then we will proceed with the separation and divorce.

If at any time you reconsider and would like to reconcile, I will be open to your suggestions. However, the following list is important to me and it isn't going to go away.

Like you said, love isn't the question ... the question is whether we can live together or not.

I. Behaviors That Must Stop Immediately

- **No physical violence.** No pushing, grabbing, shaking, choking, hitting, etc.
- **No physical intimidation.** No hitting tables, cabinetry, walls, etc. with fists or objects; locked doors stay locked and if one of us says we need space the other one gives it by leaving the area and refraining from muttering or attempting to continue the conversation indirectly. No bodily encroachment into personal space during any argument or tense discussion.
- **No threatening behavior** and if one person says they're feeling threatened or afraid, the actions that person takes to remove themselves from the situation will be respected.
- **No verbal assaults or verbal abuse**. No name-calling directly or indirectly where it can be overheard by the intended target or other people. No covert verbal abuse implying one person is less valuable than the other due to differing opinions and beliefs. No labeling of one another as unappreciative, uncaring, unfit, irresponsible, dishonest, etc. No word games, no rephrasing of another's words to

change their meaning, no more technicalities or meaning-splitting (i.e. "You didn't say not to do that on the list!"). No attempts to control through tone or word. No abuse disguised as a joke.

- **No emotional abuse.** No hinting to each other or to the children that one person is somehow deficient as a parent or a person because of differing beliefs. No implying that one person's feelings are less important or somehow wrong due to deficiencies in character or mental health. No withdrawing emotionally to punish one another (although it is understandable that abstinence from sexual activity or physical proximity is at times an appropriate response). No attacking one another's character or values.
- **No mental abuse.** No extended conversations designed to wear down the other person's defenses. No lying about how one feels or thinks in order to gain compliance on any issue. No insinuating that one person is more valuable than another due to income, technical skills, experience, etc. No condescension or righteous anger due to one's desire to visit a mental health practitioner. No denying events or statements with the hope of making the other person doubt his/her perceptions. No blaming the other for the actions we take, feelings we feel, or words we speak.
- **No abusive anger.** No yelling or swearing – if we're angry enough to yell and swear then we stop communicating until tempers aren't so high. No getting in one another's face, no walking up fast and then stopping inches away from one another, no flailing of arms or stares meant to intimidate, no tools/knives/instruments held while angry, etc.

- **No alcohol abuse.** No driving under the influence of alcohol alone or with family members. No avoidance of relationship or any other issues by remaining under the influence of alcohol for extended periods. No attempts to have important and/or sensitive conversations while drinking.

II. Behaviors to Begin or Continue
- Couples Counseling
- Individual Counseling
- Relationship Abuse Education (therapy, courses or classes, reading material, etc. but must be on more than one occasion and with regularity)

III. Outward Signs Changes are Taking Place
(some things I'm looking for)

- We verbally acknowledge the abuse in our marriage and family to one another and our boys. We say we are willing to change and start planning, individually, how to create the changes needed.
- We attend regular counseling sessions as a couple. We attend to our own self-help issues with qualified professionals via therapy or some other form of guided support.
- We willingly take responsibility for our individual contributions to the cycle of abuse in our relationship and family.
- We share what we feel we must change about ourselves and dedicate ourselves to improving communication in our marriage without abusing one another in any way.

- When we disagree, we respectfully disagree and then work together for a compromise without browbeating one another to accept our opinion as right and theirs wrong
- We accept that there are many changes make and that it will be hard work and will probably take some time.
- We are patient with one another, but we hold ourselves accountable for our own change without pointing out any possible deficiencies in our partner's change process.
- We respect for one another's need to feel safe and secure in our home; we don't have to agree with one another's feelings in order to respect them.
- We take time out as a couple even when there are other pressing responsibilities because there will always be other pressing responsibilities.
- We take time out as a family and work together to create a tension-free environment for our children.
- We do not harbor anger and then explode in a fearsome rage; anger deserves attention, but it is not always deserving of our constant attention. We no longer feed our anger by guessing or assuming what our partner is thinking. Instead, we ask them what they are thinking.
- We share our changing needs and desires with one another. We support one another's dreams and goals even if we do not want to pursue them or see value in pursuing them ourselves.

IV. My Suggested Timeline

(negotiable, but I think a year apart is about right)
Will, please consider this timeline of reconciliation if you choose to work with me to save our marriage. I think it will help us to not rush and carefully evaluate whether we truly

want to reconcile or not without involving the children (to the extent that they can remain uninvolved).

- **Months 1-3:** We continue to work on our separation agreement. If we decide not to reconcile, we will need the agreement. I need some time alone without talking to you except in a "business" manner; I feel we should limit our contact as much as possible during this time. I am comfortable with email without attorney involvement.
- **Months 3-5:** We return to couples counseling. We talk about whatever we need to about what's happened between us up to this point. We arrive to and leave from sessions separately for the first half; perhaps start talking on the phone more often during the second half.
- **Months 6-9:** We continue counseling. We begin to "date" or see each other alone for dinner during the week. We see "how it feels" and decide if we enjoy being around with one another and can discuss where we think our relationship is heading.
- **Months 10-12:** We continue counseling. We begin taking steps to consider seriously our future as a couple. Do we merge or separate? If we reconcile, are we going back to joint accounts or not? Do we think more separate time is required before we choose to reconcile or divorce? ...etc.

Comments from Readers

NewDirection says - *There is nothing wrong with wanting to prevent divorce. Your list is excellent. I would add that drawing the line at abuse is good, but you want a happy marriage, not only an abuse-free one. Him actively cherishing, loving, respecting and honoring you is not too much to demand and is necessary for stopping abuse. You need to replace the hurt with love for you to heal.*

My soon-to-be-ex refused my list. He wouldn't read one book I suggested and walked out of therapy. He wants to reconcile but wants to ignore the fact that he has abused me for years. He wants us to try to be nice and let the past go!

It hurts to know that he will not do the work. I must file for divorce and change my daughter's life forever, or I know that I will return to the ugly life I finally got the strength to leave. Please also consider that he should get therapy before you do couples' work. He needs to show remorse and a desire for restitution or he will use couples' counseling as a weapon against you. Therapists do not recommend couples' counseling for abusive relationships. No one is perfect, but the abuse is his issue, not yours as a couple. Sending you comfort and love on your journey.

> **EagleWolfeSpirit says** - *Absolutely excellent! You are a planner, and please, do not ever feel that anyone would ever consider you a fraud! You are 100% genuine and honest! By doing this, this post and these reconciliation terms, you are doing the right thing for you and your family. You are implementing assertive intervention, something anyone with an ounce of love and caring would do. I for one am proud of you, who you are, just you. You are a beautiful, loving woman and those who have you in their lives are truly blessed. Thanks again and always for sharing; it helps those who read more than you may ever know!*

Of Guardians and Demons
March 2, 2010
1 month, 8 days of freedom

I confess. Several others live inside of me. I talk to them, and mostly, they talk back. In the beginning of this exchange, I'm speaking to Big Me, the part of me directly connected to All with no go-betweens. Next, I hear from a couple of little demons that Pauline (my guardian angel) pointed my awareness to earlier. Then, I talk to Pauline.

This conversation came out during the NanoWrimo Challenge in November 2009, a few months before I left Will:

Little Me: I know many things now that I didn't know ten months ago. *You* of course. I wasn't willing to question too much ten months ago, and now, when I do question, I try to do the questioning in a productive manner. Instead of asking loaded questions, I will ask questions that leave room for me to believe what someone says. For example, if I know you broke the plate, I won't ask if you broke the plate.

I'm physically tired. Is there a way to put this typing on autopilot? Could I turn over the keyboard to you? [I mean to turn the keyboard over to Big Me, but instead...]

> Demon 1: *[...almost as if I caught them mid-conversation]* ...you can to ddhea; but kdaesdkn don't know when we were planning to come over... Oh my. How did she just now recognize us? How did she only now figure out we were here?
>
> Demon 2: Pauline told her. Pauline has told her before, but she wouldn't listen. Didn't like the idea of demons running around in her. But that is what I am. How about you?

Demon 1: Yep. Demon. Demon, demon, demon. I love to hear my name. Why didn't Pauline say our names?

Demon 2: Because labeling us gives us more power. It is better to live with the demon you know than the demon you don't. That is true only because once these humans name us, they can fix us. More aptly, they're willing to believe that they are dysfunctional (which is what we want them to believe, no?) and once we're named, then they can launch an attack against us.

Once we know one human can identify us, we know others can too. We frequently try to get other humans to see our influence over the ones we've got, so they can feel proud that that particular demon is not in them. What they fail to realize is that Pride is the first demon. Pride always opens the door for the rest of us, call us what you will. If Kellie would let loose her pride, then most likely you and I would fall out the trapdoor with it. With Pride.

Demon 1: Look at her. She knows she is prideful. She is mistaken in thinking that all pride is sin. Some pride is not a sin. However, she's listening, so I'm not going to talk about that.

Demon 2: She's not listening for our names. I know she wants to know. What did I say to make her not want to know our names? Rumpelstiltskin! Rumpelstiltskin! Rumpelstiltskin is my name!

Demon 1: Dork. You cannot tell her your name. She doesn't want to hear it, so you're not allowed to say it. Geesh. We've told her too much.

[I hear scampering of four little feet and see a shock of red fur dart away. Weird.]

Me: Pauline? Why did you let it slip that there were two other demons in here?

> Pauline: Because I wanted you to know that you are a mystical creature, Kellie. There are vast universes yet unexplored. Those other demons have a possibility of simply going away. They may never ever come to bother you. As they said, if you can kick pride to the curb, then there's a good chance they will go with him.

Me: Pride goeth before a fall. I'm picturing pride falling out of me followed by two red furry demons. Why are those guys kind of like comic relief? Why are they not serious?

> Pauline: Because not every demon in you is serious. In fact, not every demon in you is as important or serious as you give it credit for being. You are concerned that you are an abuser. You worry that you are a manipulator and a hurter. Whether you are or are not is not your worry. Now that you know that you do not want to propagate certain behaviors, you can rid yourself of any characteristic of an abuser. I know you will discover that you developed the characteristics in question through practice, not due to a deep-seated evil nature. There is nothing wrong with you.
>
> You are at present merely the characteristics you absorbed before realizing you had control over what you absorbed and expressed. Now that you know, you do not have to fear being an abuser. Now you are one who is overcoming the characteristics of an abuser. With that as a focus, you cannot fail.

Me: Pride has come up twice tonight. Am I really so prideful?

> Pauline: Well, if you think you know what everyone else is intending without asking them, then you are prideful. Think of it. Do you know what another person intends with his or her words or actions? No. Can you always trust what they say when you question them? No. So in reality, you will never know the whys of someone's behavior. You will only see the effects.
>
> You must decide for yourself if the effects are ones with which you want to associate. You cannot change those people, and even knowing the whys of what they do (if they're honest) does not change the effect of the action on you. So, do you accept what they did as good for you or not? If not, distance yourself.

Me: [silently wondering about love, how it fits]

> Pauline: Love. Love is a misunderstood term. Pride uses the facade of love to promote its standing in your soul. It is not love to forbid your children to mess up, embarrass you, dishonor you or hurt your impression of yourself. Doing so merely teaches them to fear you, not to respect you. Forbidding them their humanness forbids them to be themselves, to learn, and that is a prideful act. If you take on the embarrassment that you think another person should feel, then you assume that you CAN take on responsibility for that person. Since you cannot control other people, you cannot rightfully take responsibility from or for them. Doing so is prideful.
>
> You assume that you can usurp the shame or accomplishment onto yourself. You cannot. Love is not prideful. Love lets other people be who they are and allows you to be who you are.

Will can never tell you who you are. He can yell from the rooftops that you are a whore or that you are a chaste woman. It doesn't matter what he yells because he cannot tell anyone who you are.

You want someone else to write your author's biography [for NanoWrimo profile]. You want someone to tell you who you are. The biography is a daunting task for you because you are unsure of who you are. Take off the label *survivor of abuse* and what do you have? You have no clue, do you? Well, I am not going to tell you, and I am not telling you because I love you. What you are, who you are, is an ever-evolving definition. Feel free to shed the old and embrace the new, even if the you being shed is but 10 days old. Who cares? Even though you will be mom for the rest of your life, that doesn't mean that you cannot be more and less and other and in addition to ... you decide who you are every given second. Every single minute. Every single day.

Seek and Ye Shall Find
March 3, 2010
1 month, 11 days of freedom

Will and I were unhappily married and I blamed him for every one of our missteps and evils. Although I thought I was trying to make him happy, I was trying to make him happy *so he could make me happy*. When I failed, I wanted to run far and fast.

I tried running away into motherhood. I tried running away into shame. I tried running deeply into loathing and hate and sickness. I have run, but I haven't left. There must be a reason for it.

There must be a reason greater than my experience to explain why I haven't run from here. Why must there be a reason? Why must I seek a reason explaining why I stayed? I want to say I stayed for love; but by my own admission, I don't know what love means. So if not for love, then why? Maybe I'm tired of running.

On the other hand, maybe when I ran into the arms of my husband, I did it for a reason other than escape. Is it possible that he offers something that I need to be me? Does and has he challenged me to finally find the All within myself? Is that why I am with Will?

I know that being with him, in part, has caused me to find Big Me. Being with Will forced me to look and listen inside myself, peeling back layer after layer. Most of the peeling hurt badly. Most of what I peeled back tore me apart, exposed old wounds. It fucking hurt.

I turned inward, away from him, away from what he said and how he treated me. I sought refuge in my scarred and burned flesh, painful but so familiar that I didn't want it ripped off. But in my frenzy to run, I ripped it away and discovered the All deep inside. Now that I'm getting a glimpse of the All, I want to pluck it out of me like an unskinned grape and present it to him. I want to show him what I have found so he may believe that the All is within him, too.

My old habits tell me that I am supposed to use the All in me to save him. Yet that is not what All is telling me to do. All tells me to stay quiet about what I've found. I am not supposed to define it for Will because he, out of habit, will try to shame me into putting All away again.

You see, Will has bad habits, too. He cannot bear to think that All is in me because he thinks he should have All only to himself. If my sin is pride, then Will's is probably selfishness. I don't think selfishness is on the Seven Deadly list, but it's enough of a sin to cause problems. I digress, selfishness is on the Seven Deadly Sins list; it is called *greed*. I could be wrong about Will's sin. I have no business in his mess right now anyway. This is about my mess. My pride.

In today's psychology, there is a less deadly word for pride. It is codependence. Ask a hundred people what codependence means, and you will get 100 answers. Codependence is practically indefinable because it is a catchall phrase for people who do things they shouldn't at the expense of themselves but happen to have an alcoholic or other dysfunctional person in their periphery. Codependence is a problem in itself; the co-dependent has their own set of problems, presumably exaggerated because of the people involved. My definition of codependence is the belief that I can fix everyone around me and that they, by doing certain things I decide, can fix me. Sounds like pride to me.

Pauline clued me in to two little demons running amuck within me, waiting for their day in the sun. I haven't asked her why she did it, yet, and I will. First, I want to take a stab at guessing.

As science now shows, we find what we're looking for. We thought an atom was as small as it got; then we discovered protons, neutrons and electrons living inside the atom, then smaller bits making up those bits. Light measures in waves and in particles, depending on what we are looking for it to be. No matter what we look for, we're going to find something; the act of expecting to find something else always results in finding something, if I keep on looking for the bad shit floating around in myself, I am going to find it. Imagine for a second that I found every little demon wandering the halls of my mind. I named it and exorcised it. When I exorcised the last demon, when I became flawless, what would I feel? Probably, you guessed it, Pride.

Pauline tells me that it sometimes doesn't matter what demons run around in my head. Punishing myself by trying to exorcise tiny laughable demons is a waste of time. It's not that I'm bad and there's nothing that can be done about it, the key is that I'm bad *and I'm good* and there's nothing to be done about it.

I'm going to seesaw back and forth at times, and that is okay. The challenge is to keep looking for the good until I find pride, then back off and fix the bad until I find pride again. I play this game over the course of seconds, days, weeks, months and years. It is a constant, and it is to be an experience. Period. Not a good one, not a bad one, but always a grand one. It is the mystery, the life, the quest of a human. I will push the limits and feel the push back, continuously. This is what we're here to do. Stretch and contract, stretch and contract, but above all, remain flexible.

I became inflexible. The years I wasted are years that I refused to stretch or contract. It took me longer than some and not as long as others to realize that I must keep moving. Standing still denies the All the opportunity to live through me. Being stubborn in my belief that I am any one thing (co-dependent, abusive, victimized) causes All to stop experiencing life through me. Life ends.

All is inside of me. All is constantly moving, growing and being new things. Consider God, Christian format, for a moment. Old Testament God was full of fury and vengeance. He turned women to salt and burned cities, flooded the earth and murdered men who spoke contrary to Him. New Testament God was full of love and gentle guidance. He sent and sacrificed His son so the rest of us could take a lesson on what it meant to love outside of possession and desire. You could say the Christian Bible is a snapshot of God, or perhaps a three-minute YouTube video of God expanding and contracting. He definitely is not staying still.

God also fractured himself in the Bible. He created angels to worship Him, and humans to look like Him. Then He allowed a piece of his creation to go rogue. Lucifer (turned Satan) is the best of God who found Pride in Himself and exorcised that piece of Himself to the Earth.

Why didn't He send Lucifer and his buddies straight to the promised Hell? Because God knew that killing Lucifer wouldn't solve the problem.

You see, God is *All*. He is darkness and light. He lives. He experiences. And He put Himself in each one of us so he can experience what we create as well. God knows that to stand still means that He will die. Yet He gives a portion of Himself to each of us, as a loan, so when we return to Him, our bodies decaying in the earth, we can watch our selves reunite with All, and we will know, beyond the shadow of an earthly doubt, that what we experienced was worthwhile.

Murder Suicide
March 3, 2010
1 month, 11 days of freedom

Abusers kill their wives and then themselves because once she is finally dead and motionless on the floor he realizes that the life spark was hers and hers alone. In killing her, he sought to absorb her; now that all is gone from her, he realizes he will never ever and had never ever been able to use her life spark for his own. Overwhelmed with true grief because he feels unable to live without leeching from her, he turns the weapon upon himself.

He truly loved her life force. His mistake was thinking he could ever take it from her and use it as fuel for himself.

Scary.

Running Away
March 6, 2010
1 month, 12 days of freedom

Marc, Eddie and I went to the movies tonight. Marc met two of his friends there. Marc left with them without telling me; he went to get a refill on popcorn and didn't come back. Texted me that he had a change of clothes and a place to stay and that he would be okay. I called Will who lamented the *drama queen bullshit* that prohibited him from ... from what?

So Marc is gone (again), Will is referring to his limited legal position as my fault, and there is nothing new with either of them.

I'm not worried about Marc. He has no money, no job, and soon he'll have no phone. His friends will eventually tire of housing and feeding him, and he'll come home (eventually) to find school uniforms and two changes of clothes in his closet. He'll always have a home here. Yet I'm tired of providing luxuries for a child who doesn't appreciate them and compassion for a man who forgets who he's talking to when he's pissed or worried.

Letting Go
March 8, 2010
1 month, 14 days of freedom

Marc left the house with his dad yesterday. They're going to live together for a while; maybe it will be permanent. A piece of me feels like I decided what behaviors I would and would not tolerate *too late*. A big piece of me wonders, "What if I had realized my marriage was abusive three years ago? 10 years? 17 years ago? How would my life be different now?" The question fuels my guilt. I feel guilty for not doing something sooner. On the other hand, when I look over the past years, I know I was doing the best I knew to do at the time. Whether I was compromising, negotiating, caving, pretending, yelling, fighting or crying, I was doing the best thing I knew to do.

I've been in communication with an angel (an *angel*!) for about 15 of these years. I've had the best guidance possible. If an angel wouldn't tell me what to do, then I can surmise that no one could have told me what to do. I wasn't ready to hear it, wasn't ready to do *this* that I've been doing for the past year and a half. Now that I am ready and now that I know, to do differently could only result in feelings of failure and anxiety.

When I'm 60, I don't want to look back over this period wishing I had pretended I didn't know about boundaries, co-dependence, abuse, manipulation and control. I do not want to pretend I am wrong for doing what is right for me, or wrong for doing what I believe is right for my children. Every action has a consequence. Positive action, such as standing up to my teen, can have hurtful consequences in the short-term.

But what about next year? Where will Marc and I be next year? Well, it won't be a world in which my words and beliefs don't matter. It won't be a world in which I allow my boys to run all over me and I anguish about giving in to teenage hormones and emotional manipulation. Better? Worse? Only time will tell. Right now, I'm doing the best I can with the knowledge I have. That will have to be enough.

Comments from Readers

Kellie Jo says *- It is now March 3, 2011. I ran across this post and noticed it is dated almost a year to the day Marc came back to live with me. It seemed he was missing from my life much longer than a year. I like the last sentence in this post that says, "But right now, I'm doing the best I can with the* knowledge I have. That will have to be enough." It was enough. Life is good.

Wrong
March 10, 2010
1 month, 16 days of freedom

Will says that I don't admit my faults, and that I am verbally and physically abusive. The idea that I'm the abuser is one I've struggle with more than once (*Trick or Treat*[3] and *Participant in My Own Abuse*[4]). The problem with listing all my faults at this point is that I am only now realizing how my actions contributed to the abuse in my marriage. I do not intend for the following list as an accounting for every single time I was wrong in my marriage, nor give an example of every single *way* in which I was wrong. I am trying very hard to face up to my actions, and I am working hard not to make the same mistakes I made in the past.

I am changing. I did the best I could with what I knew at the time, and now that I know a better way, I'll do it differently. Some of the links on this list lead to pages that tell of ways in which Will was wrong; in those cases, you must read between the lines to see my fault. The point is that I have faults, and I know it. Anyway, here we go:

Recently Will reminded me that I threw keys at him in 1992. I did throw the keys and fortunately I missed because if I'd hit the target he may have gotten a bump on the back of his head. And I don't mean that lightly; if you've ever caught a set of keys that you wished you'd let fall, you know the pain. I was wrong for throwing the keys whether they hit him or not.

I was wrong for throwing the dishtowels, too. Not because they hurt anyone but because I was in the midst of a childish fit and allowed my anger to spill out into physical action.

I was also wrong for slamming doors in anger.

I was wrong for slapping him last year. It doesn't matter why he said it or even what he said. I was wrong for slapping his face.

I was wrong for calling him a bastard and an asshole, and labeling him in other ways. It's not my place to tell him who he is or to expect him to accept it.

I was wrong for saying things to hurt him. I wonder why I don't feel as badly about slapping his face as I do about intentionally hurting him emotionally. If physical abuse is punishable by law, then why do I not feel worse about putting my hands on him than anything else?

I was wrong for telling him that I hated him.

I was wrong for nagging and for not being able to forget anything bad that happened between us.

I was wrong for partying when I should have been a better mom and wife.

I was wrong for being angry and bitter.

I was wrong for being arrogant.

I was wrong for yelling at people who were trying to help.

I was wrong for communicating in passive-aggressive ways.

I was wrong for many other things, too.

I made the list to illustrate the point that I am not trying to glorify myself in relation to Will. I am sorry for all the bad things I did, all the times I knew I was wrong soon after committing the offense and all the times when I look back and see where I was wrong but didn't know it at the time. I am very sorry for the ways I contributed to this nightmare, and the ways in which I hurt Will.

I know this blog also hurts Will; I feel conflicted over whether to continue writing it or to erase it from the web. I also know this blog helps many other people. You tell me so. This blog is validation for others experiencing abuse, and a peek into the abusive cycle for people who are not a part of one. For the latter group, *they* would more easily recognize my faults than I can.

I know writing this blog, chronicling my experience, saved my sanity and soul through the past year and a half. Without it, I would be more likely to gloss over and try to ignore the events and pain I've experienced. I may not have had the strength to leave the night I left if I did not have a record of my truth to review. I'm torn. If you were to ask Will, erasing this blog and all memory of it is the right thing to do. I'm not so certain - it would certainly be right to him, but would deleting it be right?

I went to the courthouse today and registered two business names, *Kellie Jo Holly* and *Verbal Abuse Journals*. I figure between the two, I can completely eradicate my surname from any Internet searches including the WHOIS directory in relation to this site. It will take some time, but any online hint of who I am will disappear.

I am also going to go back and comb over the site looking for pictures and removing them or making the people in them unrecognizable. I thought I had done them all already, but while looking through to complete my list, I found a couple that need to disappear. I'll be doing that promptly. Doing those things is, I know, an unacceptable compromise for Will. But deleting everything is an unacceptable compromise for me.

Admitting wrongdoing does not suck. If I sat in denial of my own wrongs, then that would suck the life out of me, eventually sculpting me into a bitter, lonely, mean-spirited blamer. I didn't try to bring change to my marriage to become THAT.

Please don't respond to this blog saying, "But Kellie, you were justified" or "You were in a horrible situation!" or any such platitude. I did what I did. I want to be ashamed so I can remember never to do those things again; I want to be ashamed so I can begin to put this horrible situation behind me, and so I can move on in strength and in harmony with my true nature.

Comments from Readers

Erin says - I understand what you are doing. However, please don't let this worm too far in your mind. You asked that we not comment things like "But Kellie, you were justified" or "You were in the middle of a horrible situation!" You said that for a reason. You know they are true; but you are also trying to figure out exactly where you stand in the whole situation. Please don't deny yourself the courtesy of realizing you ultimately re-acted, even if you were the one to start this particular offense.

About your blog. I swear. Don't let Will (or anybody else) convince you to take it down. That blows me away. You are speaking the truth on here. You are using it to work your way through a horrible life situation. You deserve this; and so does anybody else who reads it in order to have realizations in their own lives. If it embarrasses him then perhaps he shouldn't have acted in the ways he did. By Will telling you that it is an embarrassment I see another form of manipulation. If he were working through this problem, he would realize that he has to own up to his actions. He is not doing that. He wants them gone.

If you don't want to continue on, I will. I will write about being the sister of a woman who endures this abuse and manipulation. Your story must be told. It will be much, much better coming from you. You are on a life path here, Kellie. Keep it up, and don't feel the least bit guilty. After all, you are presenting the truth. (Good job on registering those business names by the way!)

In the spirit of the first half of your post, I am biting my tongue, or tying my fingers, when I say the following: nobody's perfect. I love you. You are a wonderful person; and you are doing the right thing.

> **QuietOne says -** *Kellie - you are right that the abuser will use the victim's acknowledgment of responsibility or being at fault against them. I have experienced that repeatedly.*
>
> *I urge you not to take down this blog.*
>
> *You discuss and demonstrate the varied and twisted paths of an abusive relationship so well. There is much for other abuse victims to learn here.*
>
> *I am sorry Will feels threatened by this site, but you cannot allow his feelings on the matter to sway you.*
>
> *I seem to recall the need to always fix and please as a contributing factor to the abuse in your marriage. I believe if you allow Will to persuade you to take down the blog, it will be for those reasons.*
>
> *You are not intentionally out to hurt him. Your blog is not directly tied to him. If he is hurt by your blog, he should stop reading it.*

KeepSmiling says - *You and Will are both very strong characters, have strong differences of opinions and could both be seen as stubborn and wanting to be right. You two are like chalk and cheese, so when you bring this together in* *a marriage then you create problems of control within the dynamics of the marriage. Kaboom!*

When two people are head strong, one of them has to lay down the sword and admit to some of the wrongs they contributed to the buildup of problems within the marriage. You admitted you made mistakes, now maybe Will can admit some of his.

Also, nobody in the world is perfect; we all make mistakes because we experience human emotions and sometimes say things we don't mean in the heat of the moment. It is sometimes a defense mechanism, or born from frustration to get a reaction, so don't over analyze things said in arguments.

> **Kellie Jo says** - *One of the problems in an abusive relationship is that when the victim admits fault, the abuser uses that intimate information against her (or him, whichever). For example, when I told my husband I felt depressed and then sought professional help in 1996, he used my depression as a point of entry for attacks. Recently, when I told him I was learning about co-dependency and trying to change, he started telling me all of my problems existed because there was something wrong with me and that he is right on all counts because I admitted to being wrong on some. My apologies are accepted and used as ammunition later; he does not apologize to me.*
>
> *You see, it is easy for me to admit my fault when I see it. It is easy for me to apologize when I know I am wrong. There is no* new *laying down of the sword in this post. I've done this type of thing consistently throughout my marriage and the other facets of my life, too. There is no way that this post*

will somehow cause Will to magically change and stop attacking me. He will use this post as he has taken advantage all of my other apologies; maybe he will pause briefly to grab a bigger sword because I'm weakened (in his eyes) and he can take the opportunity to arm himself more fully.

KeepSmiling, are you involved in an abusive relationship or do you know someone who is?

RandomlyK says - *I have to agree with Erin on all that she said. May I also add that in reflecting in my own situation, being it is what it is, that I am finding in being immersed in such a life that this insidious disease leaks into all aspects of life. I find that many of my wrong-doings are due to reacting to the life I have been living, reacting to the reactions of those around me, and hence, my children are beginning to do the same. I can admit to many of the same wrongs you have, and possibly thousands more.*

No, we in these situations are not innocent, but it is important to note that we do wrong and to figure out why. For me, I was not always this person I am now. I know what because I have spoken with several people who knew me way before I got sucked into this life. They have reminded me that these wrongs are not me; *I am still me deep down inside. I'm sure you are finding the same. And the blog: keep it Kellie Jo. This has become bigger than you and Will. It is a living breathing thing that inspires, validates and is truly helping hundreds of women if not more.*

Fix and Please
March 15, 2010
1 month, 21 days of freedom

QuietOne said that she remembers me saying my desire to *fix and please* is a factor in the abuse. She is right. If I took down this site, it would be to please Will; the more I think on it, the more I realize that removing my blog is another way to *erase me*.

If this blog were to vanish, then (as Erin says) our transgressions would *go away*. It would be as if the abuse (and co-dependency) never existed.

I will take a different course of action. The blog stays, but I will do everything in my power to remove any trace of my true name from it. In time, the only way someone could figure out who I am is to go to the courthouse in the county in which I live and dig through the volumes of documents to find me. I doubt that anyone's curiosity would extend to such extremes. I paid to privacy protect this site in the WHOIS directory upon its inception. If you go to WHOIS online and look up this domain name, you find *nothing* about me.

Will said that when he typed his name into google, all kinds of "crap" turned up about abuse. I typed in his name and there is nothing about abuse there. In fact, there is precious little mentioned about him except an offer to find him in the white pages. Under my real name, I get hits on my volunteer work and contributions to Wikipedia concerning that work ... nothing about abuse. Kellie Jo Holly is the only name that turns up hits on abuse. As it turns out, his complaint is a lie.

I think it says a lot about my thinking that I took his word on this and tormented myself for a week about it when I could have done the google search in the beginning and put my mind at ease immediately. I want to do a better job verifying facts when it comes to our relationship. I've been with him for so long that I don't fact check him anymore. Why would one fact check their lover? Maybe I will change my view on fact checking everyone. From now on, if I cannot verify your feelings on google, I'm not paying attention to them. Just kidding.

Feelings cannot be fact checked, but I can verify proclamations of fact! Ronald Reagan said, "Trust, but verify." That is a great idea.

Choose
March 18, 2010
1 month, 24 days of freedom

I decided to fight for custody through the legal system. Will has wanted to do a consent order in which he and I sit down together and hash out the details of our separation. Whereas this may be possible concerning our financial matters, I am not willing to do it for custody issues.

I am, at this point, unskilled at negotiation when it comes to my spouse. I give up something I want in hope of creating a mutually satisfying agreement. I see now that I've been wrong to do that. He says that he gives me an inch and I take a mile...in hindsight, I do not see how that comes even close to the truth. There was a time when I would second-guess myself on that point, causing me to give up even more of what I wanted or needed or thought was right. Now, when I imagine sitting down at a table with him to reach a fair settlement via a consent order, I smell bullshit. I sense that I would give up things that I don't legally have to give up - at least, not yet.

A few nights ago, Will and I were on the phone talking about our court date on March 17. My attorney initiated it as a custody hearing. Because Will and I planned to pursue a consent order, he did not want to go to court for custody issues, and I didn't see the point in it either. That was, I did not see the point in it until he told me what he wanted.

He wanted primary custody of both our boys and for them to live in our house together. He explained that he should be the one to manage their day-to-day lives and make the final decisions on issues regarding them. I said that I wanted joint custody. He said that was an interesting idea, one he hadn't heard of, and would be willing to negotiate it.

I smelled bullshit. He knows about primary custody but hasn't heard about joint custody. Is he serious?

At this point, I have two options: I could negotiate a consent order concerning custody with Will, or I could go through the legal system and let a judge decide. I know that I am not yet capable of negotiating a fair agreement with my spouse. In prior conversations, Will has indicated that I should explain to the boys that when the time comes, they are choosing a residence, not a parent. I initially thought that the boys would be choosing a lifestyle, not a parent. I see now that both Will and I are wrong. In the eyes of a child, any such choice boils down to choosing a parent, one over the other, for some reason.

In Will's version of a Consent Order, we force the children to eventually choose. I considered both Marc and Eddie's positions. Marc already chose. He wants to live with his father. Eddie told me that he does not want to choose a residence and that he doesn't want to choose at all.

I cannot do anything about Marc. Even if a judge assigns primary custody of Marc to me, no one can force Marc to live with me because of his age. When he ran away, the law in this state would not even bring him home if they found him! They would call and tell me where he was, and it would be my prerogative to retrieve him - if he agreed to come home. That law sucks, and I wish someone would do something about it; but that someone isn't me, so I have to live with it. Therefore, because Marc has already chosen, I have only Eddie to tend to in this decision. By going through the court, it will force both the boys to talk to a judge. The judge will then make a decision in their best interests. No one will force Eddie to choose because the judge will do the choosing for him.

I am fully aware that I may lose primary custody of both of my boys during this proceeding. I am distressed about it, I am worried about it; I am horrified at the thought of losing any of my legal rights as a parent. I know that my spouse (and probably Marc) will say everything possible to convince the judge that I am an unfit mother, a horrible mom, and that I am mentally ill and emotionally unstable. I am willing to take that risk in order to save the heart of my youngest son. Choosing would absolutely hurt Eddie, but talking to a judge, nervous as he is about that, will not force him to choose anyone or anything over the other.

Eddie asked if the judge would ask him whom he wanted to live with and I told him that I didn't know what the judge would ask. I told him that I have not been in his position, but I will do everything in my power to get him in touch with someone who can explain the procedure to him - maybe a kid who went through it or an adult who works in the system.

I also told Eddie that if a judge point-blank asked him that question, then he could answer, "I don't want to answer that question." In fact, he could say that in response to any question asked by anyone at any time (including me). If I can save Eddie from choosing then I will have done the best thing I can do.

Now all I must do is stay the course and prepare my own heart for the worst as I pray for the best.

Comments from Readers

Deby says - *Kellie, you are going through a lot, and you are definitely in my prayers. Do you have a lawyer? I hope so because it would be dangerous to believe anything that his lawyer is telling you - they do not have to tell the truth! It might be possible to have the judge appoint counsel for your son. During my custody issues, I became overwhelmed and was talked into giving up custody without understanding what that meant. A mistake that I pay for every day. Good luck to you.*

> **Kellie Jo says** - *Fortunately, I got lucky and opened the yellow pages to a wonderful attorney. I must admit that even with an attorney, I do not understand all the legal terminology. The worst part is that I don't know what I don't know, so I don't always know what questions to ask until it's close to being too late. Fortunately, my spidey-sense kicked in when Will said he didn't know what joint custody meant and I was able to communicate to my attorney in time to save myself from at least* one *mistake.*
>
> *I will find out about appointing counsel for my boys. I think they are hearing a lot of confusing words and attitudes and it would be nice to know that someone was advising them, setting them straight to what it all means for them in the end. Thank you for the suggestion.*

EagleWolfeSpirit says - *Kellie, I know the difficult situation you are in, and bless your sweet heart, you are thinking! How honorable of you to think of everyone involved in this situation, trying to work it all out in fairness and out of love* *to your family. I have been on both sides of the fence in my opinions of the court system; but in all fairness to them, I do think they try hard to do what is right for the children. At least that has been my experience in California.*

Will I Survive This?
March 18, 2010
1 month, 24 days of freedom

The pain and agony, heart-wrenching gut-churning sadness that I am experiencing is worse than any I have felt before. It is worse than when my grandfathers died, worse than when my dad died. It is worse than when I lost those babies in miscarriages, worse than when I suspected that Will cheated on me. It is worse than when we left Texas for the Army. It is worse than the nightmares I used to have about my children dying. It's worse. Every minute of every day feels like a do or die choice.

> Do I go to the Women's Center and sign up for classes? (Yes.)
>
> Do I wear sneakers or boots? (Sneakers.)
>
> Do I get into the car or run back into the house? (Car.)
>
> Do I listen to rock or AM radio? (Rock.)
>
> Do I keep driving or do I pull over and cry? (Keep driving.)
>
> Do I ask to see that one woman and then collapse into tears in her office? (No.)
>
> Do I pay $30 for this class or forget it altogether? (Pay.)
>
> Do I keep on deciding or stop thinking? (Decide.)
>
> Do I let the tears flow or hold them back? (No choice. they flow.)

I miss the times Will deployed because I could imagine that we were happy and pretend that everything would work out. I had peace, calm and security. Now I have no peace or security. It takes every ounce of energy to think, to decide, to move, to breathe. At night, I am exhausted but cannot fall asleep. I occupy my mind with thoughts of Eddie falling asleep in the next room, so close, still here, so strong, so trusting. I envision tomorrow being brighter, my breath coming automatically without having to remember to inhale.

Tonight, I will remember taking Eddie to shop for snacks and working in the front yard with him under the hazy sky. I'll wonder what is going on with Marc, wonder how he can text me with happy news but stare at me with blank eyes and a smirk. I will tell myself to be patient, that there will be brighter days, and force my thoughts back to Eddie, by now sleeping soundly in the other room. I will decide to hold back the tears that seemingly serve no purpose and instead visualize a happier time, away from now and this soul-less blackness that surrounds me.

In the morning, will I get out of bed or sleep and pretend this is not happening? (Get out of bed.)

Comments from Readers

KeepSmiling says – *I want to answer to the question you asked me on an earlier entry. I'm sorry I didn't answer before, but I just now saw it. You asked if I had been in an abusive relationship or knew of anyone who had. I've had numerous friends in abusive relationships that ended up with police involvement. Also, I was married to a verbally abusive man for 14 years who threatened to kill me. I also know a lot about alcoholism as a child of an alcoholic parent who was abusive. I hope this answers your questions.*

Kellie Jo says - *Thank you, KeepSmiling. I am grateful that you are here and contributing. I am sorry that you have experienced so much abuse over the years. What is your advice? How do you keep smiling - or rather, how do you smile on the inside? What keeps you sane, peaceful and happy?*

Jane says - *The sadness and pain will be worse than anything you have experienced before, for a while. For me, the first year was unrelenting sadness. Now in my second year of separation, it is getting better and better. I am amazed how increasingly positive I have become. I was negative during the marriage, and was in terrible emotional pain for the first year of separation. However, things do change for the better over time.*

One more thing - my own kids were older when I separated, but still were devastated. One sobbed and begged me to come back. The other was bitter and angry, and told me I had ruined their dad's life. I tried not to discuss their father's verbal abuse (did mention it once - hard not to mention it). Things changed, and now, 1 1/2 years later, I see my daughter demand respect from her new boyfriend (she never did this before) and my son compliments me on positive traits he says he never saw when I was with his father. They still have pain, but kids make up their own mind about these things, and they begin to understand after a while. As they grow, your children will figure out what was going on in your marriage. They may never tell you they understand, but their actions will show a change over time.

Also, think about this: I know I am unhappy when forced to make a change (new job, move to a new town, etc.). Kids are the same way. Part of their negative reaction is because they must make a change too, when you leave. This doesn't mean, however, that you should not separate. In fact, the boys may someday see your strength, and they may pick girlfriends who are able to make decisions for themselves, too.

> **Erin says -** I am so happy this time is over too. It was horrible to know what you were going through and not being able to hug you, to help you, to look in your eyes and tell you that it would all be okay.
>
> On the flip side, however, I am so proud of you, Kellie! You faced every day. You got up and did what you needed to do. You did the hard stuff. Over and over. Just as you went through this a few years ago - and things got a ton better - what you are going through now will pass as well. If you were to look at a graph of your life, you would see the average keep going higher and higher. Keep going because from here, I see how wonderful you are doing. I love you so much.

Kim says - I have two friends whose abusive partners isolate them; it is easy to give advice knowing the game they play. Abusers will always reel in the vulnerable and kindhearted. The game is to isolate, set you up to look bad, to play with your head.

I Was Happy
March 20, 2010
1 month, 26 days of freedom

Despite the heartache involved in separating from my husband, I am noticing something that is always present but I ignored. Any one day has in it beautiful moments. On Friday, I received a phone call from Marc. We talked about something important and things not so important, but we didn't talk about *this*. We didn't talk about how we were feeling or what we thought of the future. We laughed and I smiled. My phone told me I spoke to him for 32 minutes and 11 seconds, but for a little while, time was not important. It was as long as it needed to be. It didn't matter where he was or where I was; it did not matter what has happened in the past nor what may happen in the future. I was happy.

Later in the day, I picked up Eddie from school and drove to pick up his friends for an overnight. I have not had a bunch of kids in this house since the end of January due to weekends spent at dad's house. I heard them talk and laugh and checked on them without them knowing I was checking. I saw Eddie smiling and heard his now deep voice discussing things of interest to him. Things unrelated to *this*. I was happy.

I wonder why I didn't pay attention to those moments before. I could blame the intolerable situation between Will and myself for filling up so much of my thoughts and stealing my emotional energy. Our relationship was all-consuming, at least for me, and I didn't notice the happy times ... at all.

No, that isn't quite right. I noticed them, I experienced these small instances of happiness but then quickly let them fade as I chose to tend to the pain, confusion and sense of merely living through the day. Maybe now, because I know the pain is constantly ready to surface, I am more willing to let the good feelings wash over and through me. I hope that the waves of joy will serve to diminish the pain, over time. Joy became more important to me this week.

Perhaps the darkest moments I have experienced are setting me up for the capacity to be happy once again.

Fantasy
March 20, 2010
1 month, 26 days of freedom

Although I am busily updating a client's web site, I am also fantasizing about Will.

In my fantasy, he asks his friends to watch the boys for a couple of hours. He drives over here to the house and knocks on the door. I hesitantly open it, and say, "Hi. What is it?" to which he replies, "Can I come in? I want to talk."

I let him in, turn on the kitchen light, and we sit at the table. From his jeans pocket, he pulls out a folded up piece of paper and I recognize it as the *What I Want* document I gave to him a couple of weeks ago. He unfolds the paper and lays it out in front of us. Placing his hand on the paper, he says, "Okay."

"What?" I say.

"Okay, Kellie, I agree to what you want. I will do the counseling - we'll do the counseling. I've been more than an asshole, but I don't want to give in to my abusive tendencies anymore. I want to fix it. I am so sorry for hurting you, Kellie. I want my family back."

Of course, I start to cry. "Okay," I say. "I want to do the counseling and I want us both to stop hurting each other, too. I will do everything I can, everything I asked you to do I'll do too. I want my family back."

He stands up and I walk over to him awkwardly. I give him a hug, and then we pull away from one another.

"When will you be home?" I ask.

"Tomorrow's Sunday," he says, "it would be a good day."

"Okay," I say. I walk him to the door and he drives away. No kisses yet. Mostly unsaid words. My family will be back tomorrow.

That's the end of the fantasy. Maybe now that I wrote it out, I can concentrate on the site instead of impossibilities.

Justice vs. Right
March 24, 2010
2 months, 2 days of freedom

I signed a form today that says I want the state to dismiss the assault on a woman charge against Will. I walked into the attorney's office and told the receptionist that I was there to sign some kind of dismissal form for the domestic violence charge on my husband. A woman took me to her office, pulled out a form and asked me for my identification.

When it was time to sign the form, I started to cry. I moved my hand holding the pen behind my back and looked around for a tissue. I put my hand to the paper three more times before I managed to sign my name, and when I did sign, I did it quickly and without watching what I wrote.

I turned from the notary and she asked, "Mrs. Helget, are you sure?"

I wanted to grab the paper and rip it into shreds, but I told her "I am sure," and she notarized my signature on the piece of paper that will help dismiss the charge against Will.

He and his divorce attorney will go to court and say that I dropped the charge because I lied about what happened. His attorney asserted in court last week that "there was no abuse in Mr. Helget's home," and I'm sure she'll say that line again and he'll love it when she says it. Then she'll hold up the paper I signed today as proof.

Why did I sign the paper? Because what is *just* is not always *right*, and *what I want* cannot always be the best deciding factor between the two. I receive justice if the judge pronounces Will guilty of the charge, and Will ends up in an orange jumpsuit. It would be briefly satisfying to know that Will had to live in a situation where he was uncomfortable and unloved with the threat of violence (physical or mental) hanging over his head from day one.

I will flat out tell you - I feel vengeful. I want him to suffer as I've suffered. I want him to know what it feels like to live with an angry, irrational man who thinks he is right and will not apologize for anything. If I could choose his cellmate, I would choose one who is like Will but bigger and louder and who hits him on the first day and, after that, rarely does it again because the sidelong looks and muttered comments are enough to keep Will in line.

I've told Will more than once that I wish he hurt as I hurt. The difference now is that I know Will cannot hurt as I hurt. He does not have the ability to take it as I have. He told me more than once that if he felt like I said I do, then he would have left me a long time ago.

I wondered how he could understand my pain enough to know he wouldn't stand for it, but not enough to make him want to change his behavior. He seems to want me to be in pain, inflicted by him when he chooses. His controlling nature will continue to reveal itself as time goes on, in court and out.

Maybe Time will reveal Will's truth on my schedule, but most likely, I'll have a long wait. Therefore, I signed that paper in order to give Time what it needs to reveal Will for all he is. Vengeance is fiery hot, but short-lived. If I got what I wanted, there is no way to know how Will would exit the jail cell. Would he understand any better? I don't think so. I think he would emerge an angrier man, not a gentler one, and the lesson I sought to teach him would backfire on our children and me in Time.

When I consider the ways I've tried to *make him hurt*, I see that the only one who felt anything was I and those feelings were guilt and shame, not satisfaction. The guilt and shame caused me to become less of who I was because I absorbed the punishments he inflicted afterwards - I felt like I *deserved* punishment because I was a bad person, and it seemed fitting that the one I sought to hurt was the one who did the punishing.

It is not my job to do (or seek) what I consider just - it is my job to do what is right to the best of my ability. For one, a father imprisoned and dishonorably discharged from military service is not right for Marc or Eddie. They love their father as much as they love me - we are equal, almost one in their hearts. What happens to him reflects on me, and what happens to me reflects on him. Will and I cannot end the *oneness* our boys consider us to be – we are parents.

The choice to sign the paper was right for me. If I refused to sign it, then I would know that I gave in to the lesser part of me. I would have given in to the part that wants him to hurt. Now, the right thing to do, the hardest thing to do, is to let go of today and the fact that I signed a piece of paper that eradicated justice in favor of what I think is right. If there is any justice, it will come in Time.

Comments from Readers

***EagleWolfeSpirit* says -** *Very hard choice ... a very unselfish one, but that is who you are - unselfish. I agree with your decision, not because you were/are wrong in any way, but* because you are right. Do not feel defeated. You did what's right; you listened to your heart.

> **Lily says -** This is such a thoughtful post.
>
> I wanted to tell you briefly, of my ex-boyfriend's amazing, unselfish mother, and the unfortunate consequences of her loving kindness.
>
> My ex-boyfriend's mother is one of those rare women who can take anything and come back with love. Her ex-husband was a controlling, manipulative, aggressive man who ground her into the earth until she couldn't take it anymore. She decided to leave, but wanted to allow her children to have a relationship with their father, unbiased by her opinion. She hid from them the extent of his abusive ways because she wanted them to make their own opinions. The unfortunate result was that she gave up the ability to educate her children to learn from his cruel mistakes.
>
> His son, my ex-boyfriend, was incredibly crazy making abusive and controlling. It took me a long while to realize he was not the love of my life, but a predator controlling my world. I wish she had told him the truth, and I hope you will tell your children the truth about their dad. I hope they grow up loving the man but wary of his behavior and manipulation; then they will have the tools to escape the cycle.

Paradigm Shift
March 25, 2010
2 months, 3 days of freedom

Steven Covey's book titled *The Seven Habits of Highly Effective People* says a paradigm shift occurs when you suddenly see a situation in a different way. The introduction of new knowledge can cause a person to change their thoughts, feelings, actions, etc. I am having trouble shifting my paradigm.

Intellectually I know what abuse is and how it affects me. I know that abuse follows a textbook pattern. I know my ex-husband abused me. However, what I know too slowly filters into what I feel. I wish that when I discovered the abuse in my relationship that I could have completely detached from it. I wish that *knowing* solved the problems that come from *feeling*. It would have felt liberating if I had said to myself, "Kellie, that no good hunk of flesh abuses you. Do not love him anymore. Don't listen to him anymore. Do not try to help him anymore. Get out." Then automatically *felt* the same way.

However, that did not happen. My emotions cling to Will even though my thoughts are free. My heart holds back my paradigm shift.

Someone told me that when I found my thoughts and feelings focused on Will, that I could imagine Will attached to me by a taut rope, and then imagine a pair of scissors cutting the rope. Will falls away, leaving me the space I need to think on other things. It works (pretty well), but Will is attached to me by *multiple* ropes! It will take a while to locate and cut them all. I wish my paradigm shift were as simple as the examples in Covey's book.

One example is a man's annoyance with unruly children until he discovers their mother died in the hospital hours before. Another is when an egotistical battleship commander sees an oncoming ship in his path and radios "Change your course; I am a battleship" only to get the reply, "Change *your* course, I am a lighthouse."

When my paradigm shift finally happens, this is what I envision: I see a relationship with my ex-husband in which we can discuss our children. When he acts out in, I recognize it immediately and exit the situation. After leaving, I do not give what he said or did a thought other than, "He was right when he said he wouldn't change" and I snip the thread that binds me and continue with my day, my thoughts and my feelings unscathed.

Chocolate Bon Bons
March 26, 2010
2 months, 4 days of freedom

On December 18, 2009, I wrote a post called *You're a Housewife* in which I explained how Will told me who I was. I wrote,

> But to Will, I am a housewife. He said so. He also rejected any of the other labels I listed because none of them brings home any money.

I remember that conversation well. Will yelled that he was king of the castle. He acted infuriated when I said he must *earn* that title because it is not an *entitlement*. Then he labeled me as nothing more than a housewife and said I should be happy because "You have a roof over your head, food on your plate, a home to clean, a man who is willing to work, and children to care for."

I bring this up because today Will told me that he wanted me to go to work when the children started full school days. That would mean that he's been encouraging me to work for years and inferring that I refused to work, sucked an income off his sweat and sat around eating chocolate bon bons on his dime for years. Interesting. Hurtful, but I'll get over that.

He wants me to believe it because that is what he tells his attorney. That's okay. He wants out of alimony payments.

I listened to his drivel, but when he said, "I told you I don't like crawfishers. This isn't a threat, but -" and that is where I cut him off. You can pretty much bet that when someone says, "This isn't a threat," that the words that follow will be a threat.

We were standing in front of the same attorney's office in which I signed the paper requesting to dismiss the assault against a woman charge he faced. Mind you, I just did *him* a favor (that I didn't have to do and was difficult to complete), and here he was telling me that because of *another* sin I committed, I therefore forced him to ... *to what?*

I did not hear what he planned for me because I know two things:

- I do not ever again have to negotiate with him one on one. I can go through the court and mediation for every request and complaint if I must. I never have to face him on my own ever again.
- The threat is this: "Kellie, no matter what you do for me, it will never be enough. I will continue to tell you how wrong you are for making the decisions you make. I will continue attempting to punish you with whatever means are available to me. So long as you continue to be separate from me, so long as you choose to do things of which I do not approve, I will seek to hurt you."

And that is that.

Comments from Readers

QuietOne says - *Oh, I know these conversations so well!*

I quit my job to stay home with our son. I did it against my better judgment and at his request. I made more, but I quit my job because he assured me it was the right thing to do.

After 2 years of crushing verbal abuse, I decided to leave. Of course, his response was "No one will hire you! What skills do you have? You are nothing but a housewife." I walked out of the house and had a job that paid twice what my last job had paid in less than a week. I don't know why I went back; I do not know why I stayed.

I am sitting in my studio and coming to grips with one thing that will never ever change. I have not had sex in over ten years. Not with him or anyone else. He put a stop to sex by telling me I was humiliating myself, debasing myself with requests for sex. I work, I care for my son, I cook, I clean, I make friends and I create art. But I don't get sex.

I told him a few days ago, nearly a week ago, that I have realized I will never have sex with him again. He never responded.

Before I leave the house today, I will tell him that I intend to have sex again and I intend to fall in love - and I intend to do it all as a single woman. I tried divorcing him this fall; I did not stick to it. I told myself if we have sex we can make this work, but that excuse to stay is now gone.

Good luck to you Kellie. I love watching your mind unfold and your heart being so open. It helps me to be open with myself too.

Missing Time
March 30, 2010
2 months, 8 days of freedom

Recently Will accused of not seeking work. Somehow, I missed his words encouraging me to *go to work* and his subsequent *begging* me to find a job. Will's perception differs from mine when it concerns my activities during our marriage. To that end, I put together a timeline of my marriage to show when I worked, when I wanted to work, when I went to school, and when I didn't. It tells why I worked and why I closed up shop or quit working. It is quite the exhaustive list. However, I'm missing the years 2005 and 2006 on my time line.

I know I was working with my mother and sister on a joint venture, but I have no record of events like those that I do for the other years. I have not found my journals covering that period. Maybe I didn't journal at all during that time (doubtful, but maybe).

Therefore, despite the fact that I have marketing research to conduct and two resumes to write and some work on a friend's website to complete, I am going to ignore all of that for now. I want to find my record. I want to know I existed. I want to remember what I was doing or maybe figure out why I wasn't doing much. I hope that I will have some journal entries posted to the website by tonight.

Damaged But Not Broken
March 31, 2010
2 months, 9 days of freedom

I spent most of yesterday reading my old journal and putting new pages on the site. Turns out, I was depressed during the missing time I mentioned yesterday. During the missing time, we (my mother, sister and I) were attempting to turn our business into a personal coaching operation, but my heart was not in it. The entries show that my heart was into beating up on myself. Oh well. The conclusions I reached in those days fed my current realizations.

All of this, my blog, accusing Will of abuse, et cetera, began with me tearing myself apart. I guess when I finished (am I finished?), I knew our problems could not possibly be 100% my fault. I was damaged, but not broken.

Reading the journal entries made me feel sad for how lost I felt. I am better now.

How Did I Get Here?
April 1, 2010
2 months, 10 days of freedom

I was talking to my friend about how smart, confident women (as I was at 19 soon before meeting my husband) fall prey to men who end up abusing us, and then stick around for years of it. Are we asking for it? Are we seeking it? Is there something in our make-up that attracts this type of man? (Don't those questions sound similar to questions rape victims ask themselves? They are questions used to accuse ourselves of someone else's wrongdoing.)

Yesterday my friend and I hit upon one answer. Or rather, one question that is *relevant* to "How did I get here?" That question is "What was going on in my life when I met and fell in love with my abuser or decided to give the relationship another try?" I'll answer that one.

A soldier raped me less than a week before I met Will. The rapist drugged me at a bar. I woke up at least once after he was already inside of me, and I remember saying, "No, no, no ..." and then blacking out again. Next day, he came to visit me. He didn't mention the night before. I think he was checking to see if I remembered. After that, he started telling people what a good lay I had been. Sicko.

I didn't report it because the Army discharged my sister for failure to adapt to military life after reporting her own rape. I was new to my unit. I was happy to be a soldier. I feared military discharge or having to work with my rapist during an investigation. I thought it was best to ignore it.

Nevertheless, Sicko was running around blabbing about the sex. I was fresh meat as female soldiers always are upon arrival at a new duty station. When my soon-to-be husband tried to flirt with me at a coffee shop, I turned him down flat. Even so, something about him aroused me. Maybe I liked his deep voice, muscular build or overall manliness. Whatever the reason, I thought he was hot. But more than that, in hindsight, he was protection.

Will is manly. There is not a feminine tendency in his make-up. He is strong, forceful, confident, and everything else a woman in my position longed for. He was exactly what I needed, what I wanted. In fact, Will helped the rumors *go away* without even knowing it. His presence and his soon-to-be renown jealousy and possessiveness, kept all predators (er, men) at bay.

I looked at men as predators after the soldier raped me. Men sucked. However, I thought I had found the one good one in the herd. When Will's jealousy and possessiveness began to be problematic, I overlooked it. When he ordered me to throw away the box containing my letters, pictures, mementos and journals, I did. Well, I threw it away the second time he told me to do it. The first time, I *told* him I threw it out. The second time, he saw the box in my friend's room and confronted me so angrily that I did throw it out. I threw away the first piece of me because I thought doing so would keep Will from turning on me. I thought it would prevent him from becoming a predator of my mind and heart.

You see, I had to keep Will on my side. I wanted his protection from those other slimebag men (who, in hindsight I know were not all slimebags). I set Will up to be my all - my protector, my lover, my partner, my equal, my defense against all bad things in life. If I were to admit to myself that he was overstepping his role, that his request to destroy my box was irrational, then I would also have had to admit that he was *irrationally* protecting me.

Jealous rages are irrational protection mechanisms...but not for their victim. Jealous rages protect the rager - the one who cannot bear to lose someone whom he never owned in the first place. He thought he owned me because I let him think so. I wanted someone to protect me, know me and love me.

I can answer the question "How did I get here?" with one statement: I was not in my right mind when I chose Will. I was in survival and crisis mode. I was irrational and I based my decisions on fear. The solutions I devised came from *feeling*, not *thinking*. Will felt like the one. Will felt like my soul mate. My feelings for him were so strong that I overlooked a multitude of red flags.

I love Will to some degree still, but sense that love morphing into something different. Without Will, I could not be who I am today, and I like me today. I sucked him into my irrational world as much as he sucked me into his.

You would have to ask him what need I fulfilled for him 18 years ago. For me, his ability to protect me from the outside world was what I needed. I did not foresee his protection changing into abuse.

Comments from Readers

R.R. says - *"When he ordered me to throw away the box containing my letters, pictures, mementos and journals, I did."* Oh, my God ... mine made me do that too, early in our relationship. I threw my teen years down the garbage shoot.

Resisting Temptation
April 2, 2010
2 months, 11 days of freedom

I stopped myself from doing something manipulative today. I thought of sending Will an email after watching a YouTube interview[5] with Patricia Evans, author of *The Verbally Abusive Man: Can He Change.* Here is the message I almost sent:

> Will,
>
> I swear this is the last time I will bring this up on a personal note ever again. We are divorcing. I know you do not want to reconcile, and I am okay with that. I accept it. In many ways, I'm happy looking toward my future. It's been a painful adjustment not seeing you in it.
>
> There is a video on YouTube interviewing Patricia Evans, the author of *The Verbally Abusive Man: Can He Change?* She says that she's never ever seen a verbally abusive *woman* change, but men change all the time.
>
> I want the best for you. I've always seen your potential, tried to encourage you in that way. I regret the time we've spent hurting and hope you overcome all of it and lead a happy successful life full of love and respect.
>
> Our sons' mama,
>
> Kellie

Ahem. Let me shake off my embarrassment...

Only this morning, in an email to a Facebook friend, I wrote that we may *intend* our co-dependent manipulations to be for the good, but manipulation of any sort is wrong. Manipulation, even for a (hopefully) mutually beneficial outcome, is wrong. Integrity within myself must come first before I can exhibit it publicly.

The email I wrote is *true*. There is not one word in it that I don't mean, that I don't think (on some level). It is what I did *not* say that is the lie, the manipulation. Here is the email I would send to him if I were being completely honest with him and with myself:

Will,

I cannot promise that I will never bring up the abuse in our marriage ever again. I wish I could stop trying to make you understand, and that I could accept the fact that you do not want to see things from my perspective. Continually trying to force you to understand causes me great pain. I so wish that you would honor my opinion and investigate this subject for yourself. If you did, then I think you would want to change.

I begrudgingly accept the fact that you do not want to reconcile with *me*. It hurts to feel rejected. You probably feel that my actions rejected *you*, but I only wished to reject the actions you took that hurt me. I wanted to force that part of you to disappear so I wouldn't have to deal with it anymore.

I saw a YouTube interview this morning in which Patricia Evans speaks in positive terms about the ability of verbally abusive men to change when they realize their words and actions are abusive to the one person in the world they think they love more than anyone else does. I hope you will be receptive to her interview because she is not down on men and blaming them for abusing women. In fact, she says that she has not talked with a verbally abusive *woman* who changed her ways, but she has talked with many sincere men who do change.

I hope you hear that message and then think about the abusive phrases she mentions. I hope you hear your words to me. I hope you understand, and I hope you will *want* to change - if not to save our marriage, then for your sons. You still have time to set a better example for them of how to speak to the women they love.

You have the potential to be a great man in every way. This one area holds you back. If tended to, you could reap greater love, respect and admiration from not only your future lovers, but from your children too.

If you do change, if you do choose to stop the behaviors that helped to drive us apart, I am still willing to be your wife. I still want you to change and come home to *me*. But my emotions are changing and I do not know how long I will remain receptive to the kind of love that unites a husband and wife. I am looking forward to my future, but it still hurts to know you will be missing from it. These feelings will pass as I grow and because no one can hold this kind of pain forever. At some point, I have to let the pain, and you, go.

In some way, I hope that you knowing that I see a future without you sparks you to action. You tend to pursue the opposite of what I want. A part of me thinks that when you know I am considering a future without you, then you will start to reconsider a future with me.

I want the best for you. I have always seen your potential, tried to encourage you in that way. I regret the time we've spent hurting and hope you overcome all of it and lead a happy successful life full of love and respect.

Yours truly,

Kellie

I won't send the honest one either.

Why Did I Stay in My Abusive Marriage?
April 4, 2010
2 months, 13 days of freedom

Did you notice how questions that begin with *why* tend to be accusatory? As if the questioner demands to know why you would do something other than what is best (in the questioner's mind).

Even though the question accuses me of victimizing myself, I feel compelled to attempt an answer. I often accuse myself of making poor decisions, especially now with hindsight being 20/20 and all. I stayed, and my reasons for doing so are both rational and irrational. To answer *why did I stay?* I feel compelled to explain the irrational reasons first because they are the strongest.

Irrational Reasons:
- **I promised to love, honor and cherish him forever.** I consider this vow the most important and meaningful one I ever made; I assumed it was the same for him. What I did not take into consideration while holding steadfast to my promise, was that *he broke it* within weeks of making it. If a vow is the same as a contract (rationally) then my agreement with him became invalid the first time he called me a whore. Or, if that isn't enough, then the first time he put his hands on me. But I didn't let that promise go. Part of me still wants to honor it, even now.
- **My children deserve a whole family.** While that is true, our family was not whole. Our family fragmented a tiny bit every time I gave up a piece of myself to what I thought he wanted me to be. I was crumbling but imagining myself a foundation piece, a cornerstone. Over time, I eroded into the ground and could not be strong, which placed immeasurable pressure on the other members of my family.

- **I love him.** That is technically true in feeling but inadequately pure in practice. If I ably and completely loved him, I would have let him self-destruct (or surprise me to death by *not* self-destructing) instead of trying to constantly help or fix him, us and me. If I loved him truly, then I would have left him a long time ago so he could be who he wanted to be.
- **I am not as great as I thought I was.** That is not so. I was and am every bit as great as I was back in the day. Unfortunately, I came to doubt myself after years of listening to Will accuse me of being out of touch with reality. I believed him more than I believed me.
- **He is right about me.** I'm flighty, selfish, immature and living in a dream world. No. Not true. I am not explaining that one.

Rational Reasons:
- **Nope. I cannot think of one.** They are all irrational - in hindsight.

More Irrational Reasons
- **Being part of a team is safer and more stable than going it alone.** Not when the team can't work together and fights over every detail or when corporal punishment places one team member above the others.
- **It makes financial sense to stay.** In a way, this is true. Money pooled in one IRA is more powerful than the same amount of money divided into two. The one idea I overlooked is that money cannot buy happiness; I could never buy the kind of love I needed to thrive. Certainly, the money god is marking a big red X next to Will and my names in his book right now, but the happiness god is erasing previously made X's on my record.

- **I have nowhere else to go.** I never *truly* thought this. I always had somewhere else I could go because of the kind of family I have. Even if I had *no* family, there are government resources I could have tapped into and legal steps I could take. But, when I was desperate for a reason to stay, this was a solid stand-by reason, good for another bout of crying and convincing myself of the impossibility of my situation.
- **I am a horrible wife and deserve this punishment.** While I cannot say for sure I was a great wife, I now realize that no one, not even horrible wives who cheat, lie and steal, deserve abuse at the hands (or by the words) of their husbands. We all eventually get what we deserve - but it isn't up to one individual to determine what that is or how we receive it.
- **He has been to war and suffers post-traumatic stress disorder, so I need to give him some slack.** I'm not psychologist. How do I know what he suffers from? Quite possibly, my husband was unaffected by the war and his subsequent combat area deployments. For the record, everything has been much worse since returning from a deployment in 2008. BUT, two things: one, my husband abused me before seeing any war zone at all; and two, any mental/emotional issue he has is HIS...I cannot expect myself to tolerate abuse because I feel sorry for him or think I can help him along his road to recovery.
- **My husband is a good man and doesn't want to hurt me.** Maybe he doesn't want to hurt me. Maybe his actions are subconscious and maybe he doesn't remember what he did. Maybe my perception of him is false. Maybe I am unappreciative. Maybe I am too emotional. Maybe I

imagine our relationship to be worse than it is. Maybe I don't have it so bad. Maybe I am crazy. Maybe I am the one with the abusive personality. Maybe I'm sick and twisted. Maybe I'm the one who has it wrong.

Maybe that line of thinking is what led me down the path of self-destruction. Will told me repeatedly that I was irrational. Well, he was right about that. What he didn't know was that my irrationality kept us together, for better or worse, richer or poorer, in sickness and in health.

Comments from Readers

Tabitha says *- I hear you - and I understand all too well, having been there myself and having divorced one verbally abusive man to go straight into the arms of another because it felt comfortable and familiar. Did I know better? Yes. Did I do it anyway? Yes. What did it take me to learn? Waking up and thinking, "Is this what I want my children to be/have/know as good/right when they are older?" It still took years to break out of my own patterns to find a healthy me ... much less a healthy relationship.*

Looking for Work
April 5, 2010
2 months, 14 days of freedom

I am looking for a paying job, but I don't want a boss. I had a boss for 18 years, my ex-husband, and it has not turned out well. The more I tried to please my boss, the more he took advantage. The time I spent helping and pleasing him was wasted.

Well, not entirely. I do have two beautiful boys because of my marriage. And I did have plenty of time to learn new skills, although I taught myself and have no papers or degrees to show for my efforts. Not really. Not if what I want to show is job experience (for an employer) or an income. I fight the urge to run out and apply for a cashier position at Walmart. After all these years of enjoying his steady paycheck, I'm a bit frightened of having to create my own money. I am a little afraid of NOT having a boss. I do not know exactly how to boss myself.

I do know a job at Walmart would be devoid of passion. Some people love working at Walmart and other cashier type jobs, and I am grateful they do. In fact, I wish more people loved it because the lines at Walmart get super long and I highly value good cashiers! But I don't want to be one. After years of hiding my passion, or at the least crippling it, I want to use it. I want to live in it. I want to love my days, love my hours and love every minute. And make some money while I love it.

That is exactly what I want.

I have passion, I am gaining the expertise to use it and I have the skills I need to use it. What I feel I do not have is the *time* I need to decide exactly which path to follow first. I have many passions, many skills. As soon as I narrow it down to writing or web design, I feel constricted. Labelling my passion scares me. I want to be able to use it in *whatever* vehicle I *feel like* using at any given time. Crazy?

I read a book on this very subject called *Refuse to Choose* by Barbara Sher. She calls people like me *scanners* because we have loads of passion, possibly even loads of talents, but feel divided and unsure which path to choose. On top of that, we do not want to choose *one* path. We want the freedom to do it all.

Scanners like me also feel ostracized by a society that tells us to pick one thing and do it well. If we are not specialized or if we don't have a career with a name, then we're not doing something right. Other people call us flighty, indecisive and unmotivated due to a seeming lack of follow through. (If those people only knew what went on inside my head!) The trick is to embrace the passion, embrace the ability to do multiple things and to wear multiple hats. Then, we scanners can throw off societal blame for not living up to our potential, for not choosing one road. The book gives super ideas on how to go about creating a career for ourselves using our multiple passions or creating multiple careers (and multiple streams of income).

As I look for this elusive job, I will push away the panic of not having a steady paycheck. I do need some form of income, though. Perhaps my first stream of income will come from designing websites for small businesses. Simple, clean, efficient - so when a potential customer looks for the business online, there is an actual website and relevant information to see.

I'm writing one book and have a second one in line. I am also exploring affiliate marketing and website hosting. I would not mind writing articles for pay and I am willing to be a guest blogger for no pay.

I would also like to speak publicly about what people can do to escape abuse, and how the ones who love the victims can best help them. I plan to attend Toastmasters to work on that skill.

You see, I'm not short on ideas, but I am short on time. Maybe that is another idea that I have to extricate from my psyche. Maybe I have exactly the time I need.

Residue
April 6, 2010
2 months, 15 days of freedom

The residue from my abusive relationship clogs my brain neurons like smoke and nicotine residue clogs electronics. Enough smoke and the greasy nicotine will kill a computer, and enough abusive residue can kill my brain function. I *want* to clean the residue from my brain so I can start fresh.

My most limiting belief is that I am worthless. Despite evidence to the contrary, this idea underlies everything I do, every thought I think. I am worthless to my husband.

- I hinder him and hold him back.
- I don't know how to manage *his* money. I spend too much.
- I don't appreciate him. I was unwilling to love him how he wanted me to love him.
- I don't understand his culture.
- I don't understand men; I want him to be a woman.
- I am worthless to my family.
- I don't provide a monetary contribution.
- I warp my children's minds.
- I don't have any friends who can offer any positive benefit.
- I don't know how to support the people I love when they need me.
- I am too liberal in my beliefs.
- I give people too much benefit of the doubt.
- I trust strangers.
- I don't offer a skill that people could use.
- I am worthless to myself.
- I don't even have the common sense to know when I am wrong.

- I push and push and push to get what I want even though I know I am wrong for wanting it.
- I think about the wrong issues and sidetracked by unimportant details and ideas.
- I am too stubborn.

These are the ideas I bought into over the years. My abuser told these things to me. Those things he *believed* about me - or maybe he didn't. Maybe he said them only to bring me down, make me feel disheartened and easier to control.

When I have confronted him about the words he said to me, his response is, "I've always told you how talented you are." Really? That is what he has been trying to tell me? He is a lousy communicator.

What I want to do *now* is rid myself of *his* beliefs about me. I want to shine; but it is hard to shine when I feel suffocated in a cloud of doubt. Although I know the doubt I'm suffering is fictional - it *should not* be present - I also know that I feel it deeply. I feel like it could be true. I am trying to find my way clear of this sticky, murky residual abuse. I am doing it to myself at this point. He is not even here, and I still think these things.

Maybe the first step is to set this belief out in the open air - bring it into my conscious mind where it can no longer skulk and hide away. I will release it, and if it comes back like a boomerang then I'll release it again until I have thrown it so far away it can never come back. Maybe All will catch it and put it on the shelf with all the other self-limiting boomerangs people have thrown away so it cannot come back to me ever again.

Maybe He will give the worthlessness idea to a narcissist to balance them out a little.

Comments from Readers

Stefani says - Hi Kellie, I want you to know that the things you've said, both in your journal and videos, have helped me so much! I am 18 years old. I am stuck at home with a verbally and sometimes violently abusive father. I double guess myself so often. I've been depressed and have had thoughts of suicide since about the age of 14, but have only recently begun to understand why. I know I want to leave. I also know this may be a dangerous thing to do.

Then again, I know that even to speak is a dangerous thing to do when he's around! I'm so confused with what is right and what is wrong. I'm confused about who I should tell, how I should feel, and the right way to say it ... I want you to know how strong you are, and that you and I, my mother, all women and men out there in the same boat, can do whatever we set our minds to.

When I hear your thoughts, it feels as if I am having a conversation with you! I laugh and I cry, and I believe to relate to someone and know you are not alone is one very large step in the healing process. Thank you so much, keep it up, you are doing great.

> **Kellie Jo says -** Stefani, who to tell, how to feel, right way to say it ... I understand that well. You can anonymously call 800-799-7233 (National Domestic Violence Hotline) and talk to someone right now. Do you have a good friend? If you have a friend you can trust, can you trust her parents? (I'm asking because I don't know how well your dad has isolated you.)
>
> You are 18 ... Do you drive and have access to a car? If so, you could call the department of social services in your

town, ask them about their domestic violence program, and find out where there is a group meeting. You can do this anonymously, but before you give them any personal information, verify that you can remain anonymous if you choose. It sounds like you need help, but since you aren't certain how you want to deal with the abuse, be careful talking to the department of social services - they could initiate an investigation on your behalf and interrupt family life (something it sounds like you may not be ready to face). Because you're 18, department of social services may not initiate any investigation unless you have younger siblings.

How about speaking with a teacher or guidance counselor? A boss? A neighbor? Look online for resources in your state and city. Trust a stranger. You didn't say if your mom was living with you or not. I get a sense that she's suffering along with you. Have you spoken to her about your situation, feelings and fears? When I was still with my ex-husband, I tried to talk to him about my boys' feelings and fears. He wouldn't accept what I was saying He said I was twisting their minds, and used the information I gave him to further emotionally/mentally damage our boys. Your mom may be trying to help you too, behind the scenes, and having similar results. There's no way to know unless you ask her.

What is right and wrong? You are right - your father is wrong. If you confront him, he will do everything in his power to convince you that you are mistaken, that he is a noble man who is dealing with a bad situation the best way he can, that he may be abrasive but he is NOT abusive and you are too young to understand the difference. Or he may explode, using fear to make you shut-up. Even though you know you're right, you'll also know that saying anything results in scary anger, maybe physical violence.

You're right. You're in a dangerous situation - the danger lies in the unknown. Your father has accomplished his goal well. (Is it a subconscious goal or conscious goal? It doesn't matter to you if he knows what he does or not - the effects on you are the same.)

Your dad has probably instilled in you doubt about authority figures and counselors (school or otherwise), teachers and neighbors - anyone outside the family who may be able to help you. I am asking you to choose one person outside of your family to talk to about this bad crap going on at home. Choose one person and tell them. Maybe that person will not know what to do or how to help, but you will have opened the floodgates. Talking about it once will make it easier to talk about it again. Tell a second person, and a third. Align yourself with a network of people who know what is going on within your family. You will feel stronger; you will begin to see how strong you've been all along.

As much as you may want to rescue your mom or any siblings as you strengthen yourself, resist the urge FOR NOW. They will see what you are doing, how you are changing. There will be a day when they want to be like you, and when that day comes, you will be strong enough to lead them. But if you wait for someone else to rescue you, then your strength will continue to lie latent, you will continue to doubt it, you will continue to doubt yourself. Stefani, rescue yourself first.

You may not know how you feel, that is true. That happens when someone constantly forces us to gauge their emotional status before we're free to feel our own feelings. You have spent your life waiting to see how daddy felt so you would know what it was safe to feel. (What mood is dad in? What is going on with mom? Is it safe for me to laugh? Is it all right to cry?) You stuff your emotions away until it is safe to feel them. You've probably got so many emotions stuffed away inside that they're all bursting to get out and you don't know which to feel first. It is okay, Stefani, in time, you will sort out what you feel, you will feel it all and you will be safe to do so.

You know, the idea that you see strength in me and that you see what I'm doing as a source of support, speaks volumes about your own inner strength. If you didn't know what inner strength was, you wouldn't be able to recognize it in anyone else. You are a light, you are an agent of change and you are strong and very aware of the truth.

Lisa says - Kellie, worthless is not a word that describes you and you cannot let it define you. You are smart, intuitive, and if you really have any doubt that what you do is not worthwhile, re-read your reply to Stefani. You have a gift and I have no doubt that you will use it in the manner that you choose. You helped me tremendously; I stayed up all night reading the book you recommended and thinking about what you wrote to me. It made things so clear.

Designing web sites might get the bills paid in the short term, but your life's work is right there for you. You made me realize that I can accept the status quo and live in drudgery to keep a marriage going ... or I can identify today as the first day of my life and accept that I'm 40, I'm smart, and don't have any more time to waste with a guy who wants to control everything.

We married men, but also a culture that is male oriented, promotes the concept of the warrior, and requires that spouses sacrifice for the warrior to do his job. You and me, we think too much to do that. I love him, but I love me, too. And maybe we cannot reconcile that between us and maybe we are going to have to make a decision. I'm not sure I can give up me *and I know he cannot give up what he does and who he is, because that culture is so ingrained into him.*

Love yourself, Kellie. Many people out here love you back. We believe in you and we want you to be successful.

> **Erin says** - *I recently read something that fits this post to a T ... The only real power you have in your life is the power over your own thoughts.*
>
> *If you consciously choose positive, life rewarding thoughts, then that is what you will receive in return. You can do this. I believe in you 100%. Get your rubber band out and snap yourself every time one of these horrible thoughts (from your post) enters your mind. Take control of your thoughts and you will take control of yourself.*

18th Anniversary
April 11, 2010
2 months, 20 days of freedom

Yesterday was our 18th anniversary. I felt concerned about how I would handle it; knew I would feel something, but didn't know what I would feel. Turns out, he made it easy on me by being himself. I also reacted to him in a predictable manner. What he did, what he said, turned me inside out. It affected me all day. My thoughts about the incident were different, but my reaction to it was all too familiar.

So, yesterday he wanted to come out here to pick up a lawnmower and the boys. He got here around 9 AM (he later yelled that information at me), but he did not stop to knock on the door or let me know he was here. I didn't realize he was on the property until almost 9:15. His presence made me nervous mostly because it felt like he slithered into the yard to be sneaky. I made sure the boys had their stuff together and told them their father was in the back.

Both boys went out to greet their dad, but Eddie returned inside almost right away. Around 9:25 or so, Marc (who had been calm and seemed happy earlier) came charging into the house yelling at Eddie to get to the truck and yelling, "Mom, take a pen and go sign the taxes!" This kid was panicky...quite a change from before. Instinctively I knew something was wrong out there in the garage near my ex-husband.

Nevertheless, I had been asking him to get the taxes done since mid-February because he would not let me see his W-2 until last week, and then only on the promise that I would not file. I knew I had to get out there to see the forms. I did not take a pen though. I was NOT going to sign the taxes without having the opportunity to look them over. Last year, if he had them prepared I would have signed no questions asked. (That wouldn't have happened though - I usually did the taxes myself and he signed off on them.) But this year? No way in hell was I going to sign documents for the IRS without *knowing* what they said.

I entered the garage and there was Will, red-faced and apparently annoyed, using a tool on the old mower. His father stood over him, looking uncomfortable and maybe even worried. I don't know what his father was feeling, but that's what it looked like to me.

I asked, "What's up?"

He barked, "You have to sign one paper for the taxes so I can give them to [his friend the tax preparer] this afternoon."

I said, "I'm not going to sign anything until I look them over. I'll give them to you tomorrow when we meet back with the boys."

All hell broke loose. "Kellie, sign the goddamn taxes! It is the same number you figured up, all you have to do is sign! I have to turn them in today! There's only one paper you need to see, to sign –"

That is where I cut him off (kind of, he was still saying something) and said, "I've been asking for you to do the taxes since February, but you waited until now. I am going to look them over today and I will give them to you tomorrow if they look all right to me," and walked out.

As I was leaving to grab the documents from his truck, he yelled, "You didn't make any of the goddamn money anyway!" but instead of retaliating, I kept walking to the truck.

At this point, I'm wondering why he only wants me to see and sign one paper. I'm suspicious. It seems as if he is trying to bully me into doing things that will end up badly for me. I open the truck door, see the brown folder on the passenger seat, and step up and lean in to grab it.

Suddenly, he's right behind me yelling, "Get out of the fucking truck!"

I startled, but grabbed the folder and backed out of the truck. I half expected him to yank me away from the truck, but he didn't touch me. When I got to the ground, he grabbed the folder, opened it and took out the document giving permission to file electronically. He gave me the paper and told me to sign it.

"Stop the drama queen shit and sign the paper!" he barked.

I said, "I'm not signing anything before I look at what I'm signing!" and took the folder from his hands. I turned away, started walking up to the house. I was afraid he was going to come after me, so I watched for his reflection in the glass sliding door at the back of the house as I walked toward it. He didn't come after me.

I was safely in the house, but my heart was pounding like wildfire. I felt the fears and apprehension; I felt the pain and heartbreak. Nevertheless, I also felt so proud that I had *not* done as he said. I was proud of myself for not taking a pen outside with me. I was proud of myself for not engaging him when he tried to insult me. But I was shaking.

I went to the office and opened the folder, started looking through the documents. I realized I wasn't going to be able to consider them until I had calmed down, so I put everything back into the envelope. Right then, he banged on the side door to the office (from outside the house).

"What do you want?" I asked from the desk. I knew what he wanted, but I did not want him in the house and that was the first question to come to mind.

"Give me the goddamn taxes!" he yelled through the door.

"No, not until I look them over," I replied, more calmly than I felt.

"You and your goddamn drama! Gotta make something out of nothing!" He slammed the screen door hard, and then drove off like a mad man with my babies in the truck.

Shaking hands. Shaking heart. I didn't get to hug the boys goodbye or even wave at them because I was afraid to exit the house. I walked around, trying to shake it off. I grabbed up my phone and texted to Eddie, "R U okay? I didn't like how the truck drove off with my babies. I miss my hug! I love you."

Walking, pacing, shaking my arms.

Phone rings. Caller ID says my ex-husband's name. I don't pick up. *Who* is the drama queen?

Comments from Readers

Lisa says - *You have to love tax season, it brings out the best in some people. I hope that you celebrated your anniversary by acknowledging that you are in a better place and a better situation. It might feel lonely right now, but you are going to come out of this feeling good about yourself.*

I almost had to laugh at your account of yesterday's situation. That sounds like someone I knew, but with one twist ... after yelling at me, he would have tried to turn it around so that he was the one suffering because I caused all of the grief. And then he would have wanted to have sex so that he felt better about himself. It is so predictable now that I'm not in the situation anymore.

You made good and strong choices yesterday. Keep moving forward with us.

Not Over Yet
April 11, 2010
2 months, 20 days of freedom

He had left with the boys, but I felt like he was still outside, wanting me to do something I didn't want to do. I knew he wasn't there, but I felt him all around me; if he had intended to invoke fear in me, he succeeded. Eventually I watched the end of a recorded show. It didn't help, so I called my sister. That helped some.

I heard myself tell her that what he'd done was wrong. I wasn't wasting time thinking about *why* he did it or what he hoped to accomplish from it. I didn't care about those things. All I wanted to do was be free from the aftershock.

When I walked out to the garage to find out about the taxes, I knew I was walking into a minefield. I don't blame myself for not knowing how it would end. I needed to get the papers and he obviously wasn't going to bring them to me. He wanted me to walk into his minefield. But even before I walked into the battle zone, he had created it inside of his own *son*. The difference between Marc's demeanor before talking to his dad and after was like night and day. I was sad for Marc. I was sad that my boys were going to have to deal with their dad and his secret mines that could detonate at any second. I also instinctively knew that most of the mines had exploded already - at least for the boys.

Once Will left my presence, away from my influence, he would work hard to make it appear that I was the cause of his outburst, not the boys. He would make amends with them at my expense - or try to anyway. Maybe he succeeded; but maybe the boys saw and instinctively understood what happened at the house. Maybe. I suffer from something like Post Traumatic Shock from the current situation, which caused me to fear for my physical safety, and from prior times in which I *needed* to fear for my safety. My body was reacting in the same old way despite my mind's new awareness of what was going on.

But the day was still young.

After eating a little, I looked over the taxes. I found a problem and thought it was best that I ask the preparer a question or two. Plus, I was hoping there was a way to verify that the return I was looking at would be the one she submitted. The only signature needed was on the permission to file electronically form, and having signed that, he could technically submit any version of the 1040 he wanted as long as the main numbers matched. I was suspicious of my ex-husband's intentions, not *hers*. I don't know what he told her; I do not think she would jeopardize her career over him, but others have. (Like the female soldier who recently ... never mind ... I'll leave out the examples.)

I was concerned about him submitting other information that wouldn't change the numbers but could affect me later. At the time, I didn't even know if my questions were rational ones, but I knew I had questions that I could not trust Will to answer for me.

I texted Will for the preparer's number. He texted back and asked if there was a problem. I wrote that I didn't know, but I wanted her number so I could clarify some things. He stopped texting and called, said that (she and her husband) were *his* friends and I was only mad because I wasn't getting what I wanted. I did not ask him what he thought I wanted.

Instead, I said, "They're your friends, but these are *my* taxes, too and I have some questions."

He said, "They are doing *me* a favor - something you can't seem to understand. When someone does you a favor, you do as *they* ask and I'm supposed to meet her today because she doesn't want to work tomorrow!"

I said, "Well, you've had plenty of time to get the taxes to me. It's not my fault that you didn't do it sooner. What's her number so I can ask my questions?"

He wouldn't give me the number. In fact, he said he didn't have it. He had her husband's number. "Okay, give me his number and I'll ask him for hers," I offered.

"No! His wife is doing a *favor* for *me*, Kellie! You don't need their numbers," he said. I thought to myself that if he doesn't want me to have his friends numbers, then he probably shouldn't go to them for favors that involve both of us, but I kept it to myself.

Finally, I said, "I'll give the taxes to you tomorrow if [tax preparer who is his friend] calls me today."

30 seconds later, Will called me back and said, "He said that she says you can call her. Here's her number..."

I called her; she was the same person I knew from before the separation - no hate in her, as he seemed to want me to believe. No divisiveness in her answers, no hint of favoritism. She answered my questions. When I apologized for being unable to meet her requested schedule, she said not to worry that she planned to submit the form at work on Monday anyway, not today or tomorrow.

She told me that the refund would come in the form of a check this year made out to the two of us. He cannot put it in a non-joint account (at least not legally). She said she flat out told him that he had to split the return with me. She said that when Will had started complaining about the small return that she had told him he needed to be grateful to his kids and that his wife *hadn't* had a job this past year because if either of those things were reversed, then he'd most likely *owe* taxes.

What Will doesn't know about his friend and me is that our tax preparer and I share a limited connection. We are not friends in the normal everyday sense of the word, but we understand one another. The last time we spoke, we shared some of the commonalities between our situations, our marriages. We had similar misgivings, similar concerns and similar problems. She knows some of what went on between Will and me.

We did not speak of any of that during our phone call yesterday, but I know she remembers. I have the sense that she is going to be the same honest person when it comes to her work (she is a tax professional) as she is in her personal relationships, including the limited one we shared.

When we got off the phone, I looked over the numbers again and saw that she was right. Without the kids or if I had a paying job, our tax return would be tax owed. I signed the form, and I now feel confident about the information going to the IRS. If there is any future issue, I feel confident in my ability to correct it. Perhaps Will didn't want me to talk to her because he wants me to believe I am all alone in my assertion that he is abusive. Between you and me, I know I am not alone.

There is No Good God
April 13, 2010
2 months, 22 days of freedom

The judge gave Will custody of both of my boys today. The judge talked to the boys and read the affidavits from his family and mine. Then, he gave my boys up to Will.

I don't understand. I made my attorney explain it to me a hundred times. I didn't hear a word after the judge said, "Primary custody of the minor children goes to Will..." Didn't hear a word. My brain was not working.

This was a temporary custody hearing, but it's unlikely the judge will change his mind now. It doesn't matter that the boys witnessed Will verbally abuse me, physically abuse me, and probably intuitively know he mentally and emotionally abused me because he's done the same to them. It does not matter that we dealt with Will's alcoholism and anger as best we could. It does not matter that I am the primary caregiver. Nothing matters.

Nothing makes sense. Nothing is real.

I have all kinds of reasons for why the judge may have made this decision today. It boils down to "Your mother is a lunatic. Your father is sane. You're better off with the sane one." I lost my job as primary caregiver to my children. The fat lady sung today. It is over.

After court, I brought Eddie home so we could pack his things. I was heartbroken, but I did pretty well overall. Yes, I cried with Eddie. It is hard to be stoic when my child is crying. After we collected ourselves, we went about the business of packing his bags. I hated every second of it, but I got through it matter-of-factly. "Isn't this shirt too small? ... I don't think this one is good for school, so do you want to leave it here? ... How about these boxers? ..."

Around 4 PM, I called Will to tell him not to come to the house and that I would take Eddie to him. I had forgotten about my class tonight. No, I did not want to go to the class. I wanted to come home and cry and die and cry some more. I had the feeling All wouldn't take me to heaven because he has so much pain in store for me that I have to stay. I think she wants me to suffer.

I yelled at God. I told him that even *he* could not bear the pain of losing his son and so brought his son back to life to ease the guilt of allowing him to die. I asked why he would ask something of me that he wasn't willing to do himself.

No answer. I told you, God is not here.

I hope All's absence in my home means that she's doubly present with Eddie and Marc. I hope All curled up in bed beside Eddie tonight and is whispering, "It's going to be all right. Everything is going to be okay. Sleep, Eddie Boo, tomorrow is a new day."

Eddie texted, "I wanna go home..." with a crying emoticon beside it. Dammit, how can I respond to that? I want him to come home too. I cried and choked for air.

I wrote back anyway.

> Hang in there, Eddie Boo. It's going to be all right. I love you and your brother too. Nothing and no space on the earth will ever change that.
>
> All you have to do is live this minute and then the next
>
> Then the next.
>
> You can do this, Eddie
>
> love yourself
>
> be strong
>
> have faith
>
> I love you more than my own life
>
> I will do anything and everything in my power to erase your broken heart
>
> Know that you have two parents who beyond a shadow of a doubt are devoted to you
>
> And love you
>
> Everything will be okay
>
> I love you. Dad loves you.

I hope I am not lying to him. I hope everything will in fact be okay.

Comments from Readers

Mizzeponine says *- My God Kellie Jo, I'm sitting here, jaw dropped, grief stricken for you and your sons. I do know what you're going through. I was in your shoes 12 years ago* when the judge clearly should have given custody to me and did not. I still haven't gotten over it. The anger is with me, always. Kellie Jo, I am so sorry. I wish I knew something to say, some words of encouragement.

I am truly awe struck by this. I cannot imagine a situation where a man who was, just months ago, facing charges of domestic violence, could now end up with custody of two children. The justice system is not always just! I will lift you and your boys up in prayer. I wish you well. Stay the course, Kellie Jo ... stay the course!

> **PrincessLuceval says** - Oh my God. I'm dying, reading your post, crying for your pain, it's so palpable. This is another example that makes me hesitate to start anything, because of fear of that scenario for my babies and me. Hugs and prayers, Kellie.

QuietOne says - Oh God Kellie! My heart is breaking for you. I wish I could give some sensible answer but I have nothing that will help.

I can't even tell you I know what it feels like. I don't. One day at a time dear girl. One day at a time. Keep thoughts that your boys may end up hating you out of your head. Time has an amazing way of revealing truth, even if it takes a while. Keep your heart open for your boys. Big hugs to you!

> **Lisa says** - 1. Get a new attorney. Custody often comes down to how hard your attorney will fight for you and how skilled he or she is with custody fights.
>
> 2. Understand that your ex-husband will do what is necessary to get the boys to live with him, which may

include intimidating them. It is not about him having custody, it is about him winning.

I want to give you a bug hug and tell you everything is going to be okay, but I can't. I have to kick you in the ass and tell you that a warrior's wife is a whole lot stronger than the warrior himself. You have to fight with your mind. We're warrior women, Kellie, and we are stronger than we know or think. You can cry if you need to, but know when to stop and take action. Hoo-rah for the women!

NewDirection says - *I cried when I read your post. I will pray for you and your boys. I have seen suffering, for today it feels like death, but it is not the end. Don't give up, don't give in. Let your love for your boys fuel you, they need you more than ever. Stay strong, tomorrow is another day to fight the good fight. For a moment, we are forsaken, but then the feast.*

Mediation
April 15, 2010
2 months, 24 days of freedom

Will and I went to mediation yesterday. We did not sign a parenting agreement. We return to mediation on May 3, a date by which we plan to have a financial consent order in place. I told him I wouldn't sign *anything* until after the custody mediation. However, Will suggested I keep the boys with me last night, and Thursday through Saturday night, dropping them off with him on Sunday at 7 PM. Of course, I accepted. Will must want to drink to celebrate his victory this weekend. But he cannot drink if the boys are present. The judge's order for him to have no alcohol in his home stands.

I don't know why the judge did what he did that day. My

confusion is vast and unending, and I am not going to try to figure out the *why* at this point. Well, "Why?" *is* the biggest question on my mind, but since I cannot get into the judge's head, there is no way to know the answer. Will was flabbergasted to receive primary custody but not the house. *The house* was the furthest thing from my mind.

The Boys
April 16, 2010
2 months, 25 days of freedom

I am *ecstatic* to have my boys with me today. Will is primary parent right now, but he allowed me to bring the boys home with me last night and they will stay with me through Sunday. Will swears we'll do the same cycle over again until we get back into court on May 11, at least. Will says he is not happy with the judge's arrangement because he gets no weekends with the boys and is not back in this house. Seeing that I do not want to stay here, he will be back in the house soon. Even so, the judge let us know that the primary parent does not necessarily get the house, too.

Turns out that the fat lady hasn't sung yet. However, while she is warming up for her final number, I'll try to not worry about the courts and simply be grateful that my boys are with me as much as they are. It simply cannot stand this way. I have hope and I have fight left in me to see this thing through to the end. If Will turns out to be manipulating me with his statements about maybe dating me again after all this bullshit is over, I won't be surprised. I am not going to let his generous actions concerning visitations and soothing words concerning *our* future woo me away from what is right and just in my mind.

If he isn't willing to negotiate fairly with me, I will throw myself on the mercy of the court. I'm not giving in on the things I believe in. Namely, the boys need their mother in their lives, and I deserve at *least* half of the month's days/overnights with them. Shared custody at least. (By the way, joint legal custody remains in place. What changed was physical custody.)

I have not had the opportunity to speak with the judge. When my attorney requested affidavits attesting to my mothering, I did not write one in my own behalf. I thought it would be silly to write an affidavit for myself; I thought it look as if I was attempting to sway the judge. My attorney did not tell me to write one for myself, so I didn't. I preferred to have those who know me attest to my abilities. Will did write one for himself, but I didn't read it.

I started reading Will's father's affidavit, but when I got to a point in which his dad said something about me that, at the time it happened, never ever left his lips, I quit reading. I am not going to subject myself to any more lies about who I am as interpreted by people who love Will. [Sigh.] Unless my attorney requires me to read them.

I am happy the boys are with me right now although Will could take this delicate peace away immediately because he gets to make the call on extra visitations. So, my happiness is genuine, but so is my unease and distrust of the boys' father. I am able to be happy with them despite the undercurrents of doubt running through my heart. My only comfort is that Will told the boys the plan; if he breaks it, then he breaks their hearts.

If nothing else, this experience is teaching me to take NO ONE for granted. I became the primary caregiver of my babies the days of their births. It is what I do above all other callings. Now I face custody issues that I cannot understand and feel my precious time with them threatened. I will never ever look at *me time* or any activity that diverts my attention from those boys' faces ever again without knowing that the diversion robs me of precious time with my boys.

If I have to sit right beside them watching their programming, watching their game play, watching them watch the cats, or whatever it is they're doing...I will do so with interest. I will be more available than ever before. *Nothing* takes priority over being with my children during every possible moment that they are with me.

I took them for granted in many ways. The comfort of being their mother day in and day out allowed me to believe I would always be with them. I will NEVER take them for granted again.

Comments from Readers

Krista says - *I am so glad the custody arrangement is not final. Ridiculous. Either have a serious chat with your lawyer and rein him in or get a new one. What happened the other day should never have happened. You absolutely must write an affidavit. You now have the upper hand because you have access to what Will wrote and what everyone else wrote. You can rebut and defend yourself brilliantly. If you would like I will share with you my THREE declarations and my ex's responses to see the best way to word it, and so you can see how he is trying to manipulate the courts. Either email me or send me a message on Facebook.*

Do not give in to his sweet talk. A leopard can only paint his spots another color temporarily. What doesn't come off in the wash will always come out in the rinse. He will be as sweet as pie until you disagree with him on some little thing. My ex is still doing this. The best defense is to walk away. He will piss and moan but you need to keep moving forward. Not just for yourself, but for your sons.

Wishbone
April 18, 2010
2 months, 27 days of freedom

> Never grow a wishbone, daughter, where your backbone ought to be. - Clementine Paddleford

My wishbone is coming back. Or maybe it never left. Perhaps I am foolish for wishing what I wish. My wish is the same as the day I started this blog: I want the four of us to be a happy, healthy family. I do not want a divorce; I do not want to divide my family. Our precious boys deserve so much better than this. The problem is that I hate myself for wishing what I wish.

I have this idea that somehow, after almost three months, I should be more solid in my resolve to end it. I remember writing somewhere that the *hope* was killing me. Unfortunately, I still hope.

On another note, I have some ideas about what happened in court last week. I'm not going to share them here because, well, they're my ideas and I'm going to consider them alone.

I told Will that I'll work through a financial consent order with him, but I'm not signing it until after we go through custody mediation on May 3. I want shared custody at least, and if he won't agree to it, then I'll put everything on the line for the judge to decide. Finances, custody ... everything. Yes, I know the judge decided in his favor last time. Yes, I know it could happen again. Will says he does not want to go back to court because of the hurtful things my attorney says on my behalf. Of course he is hurt now in public - when I told him similar things in private, he didn't care. It's the public persona vs. private persona thing.

The things his attorney says piss me off, but I am not embarrassed. Why? Because what she says isn't true. I know the truth in my heart, and what I hear in court is not true. I am trying hard to leave it in the courtroom. What goes on in there is like a 30 second snapshot of an 18-year marriage in which no one looks good.

Well, I am embarrassed to tell people that the judge gave temporary primary custody to Will. *That* is humiliating beyond words. However, that judge's decision was *his decision*. He made it, not me. A judge, a person no better than me, made the decision, not All.

I am the best mother I know how to be. I don't deserve to parent from the sidelines of my children's lives. I am praying and listening even though All's voice sounds muted under the weight of worry and sadness I carry in my heart. All I can do is keep moving forward.

Anyway, I will not sign documents with which I do not agree, and I'm not signing anything until Will agrees to share custody. To me, shared custody means that we both live under the same set of rules. I do not have to ask him for extra time with our children and he doesn't have to ask me. Asking Will for anything, especially in relation to the boys, contributes to his ability to maintain control.

If Will won't agree to shared custody, then I won't sign anything and the judge can choose what is to become of us. I have nothing to lose. The boys are my boys no matter how much time I see them. No judge can *take them away* from me. In about five years, the judge's decision will not matter anyway.

Comments from Readers

NewDirection says - *That wish, for a happy, healthy, intact family, never truly goes away. It is the way it should be, the way it's supposed to be. The wish, however, is the thing that needs to be wrestled, caged and grieved. It is a wish for you and your children. It is the wish that every survivor of domestic violence shares. That wish is how we get here.*

We take the fantasy and hope over the reality until we are broken, bruised and mentally forced into accepting reality. Maybe we are the most stubborn hopeful women there are. Every one of us stays and goes back for that wish.

When we finally accept reality, we can let the wish go and start dreaming of a future without abuse. Replace that wish with that dream. I started a vision book to do just that. Start dreaming about what life could be for you without the chaos and emotional drain of this abusive relationship.

Write Something Good
April 20, 2010
2 months, 29 days of freedom

Tonight, a conversation occurred that I knew would come but hoped would not. Will felt angry after reading the past few days' blog entries. He feels that he is doing everything he can to provide for me, and yet I continue to drag his name through the mud. He says that he believes that I believe what I write is the truth, but says I do not tell the whole story. He insists that I have never mentioned throwing keys at him, or to saying mean things to him. He says that he has done nothing I haven't done, that we are both equally wrong. He says that I am slandering him.

Dictionary.com defines slander as "a malicious, false and

defamatory statement or report (i.e. a slander against his good name)." So I am lying, he says. He told me that I had *better write something good* about him. He has an appointment with his attorney on Wednesday and they are going to initiate the financial consent order. If I want him to be reasonable, then I'd better write something good. When I asked if he was threatening me, he said he was *promising* me.

The sad thing about his *promise* is that in the past 24 hours I spoke to two family members about the things I love about Will. Last night, I told my mother that he protected me from other men (who, after the date rape, were the enemy) and that he once felt intrigued by the ways we differed. I was an artist, a free spirit, and although he didn't understand me, I offered something to him that he must have needed. He loved me. He wanted to provide a home and financial security to our children and me, and he has done that.

Never once did I worry that my family would have no income, or that he would refuse to have or keep a job. In fact, there were times he carried the burden of two jobs on his shoulders while I remained at home, safe and sound, with our young boys.

Will re-entered the military in small part because there was no future in the company he worked for due to buyouts and the resulting seniority issues, but also because he believed that the military could offer more family time. It may sound silly to assume the military would offer more family time, but he was working second shift with no change in sight and never got to spend much time with his boys. The military offered a 9-5 job, home on the weekends; he couldn't have anticipated the number of deployments or the length of time he would be gone.

This morning, I spoke to my grandmother. I told her that Will was now the father he always wanted to be. Since his return from deployment in December, his children are his priority ... not work, not his schedule, not his commitments to friends. He is enjoying time with his boys - real and memorable time. They work together, they joke together.

I know his relationship with them is different from my relationship with them, but I sense a closeness between them that was not there before. Marc and Eddie were excited to see their dad on Sunday night; I was happy for it, happy for them - all three of them. But this post is bittersweet.

I so wish I hadn't talked to Will tonight; if I hadn't spoken to him then this post would have been better. It would have been *good* and I never would have heard his *promise* to me.

From Them
April 21, 2010
2 months, 30 days of freedom

On Sunday, the neighbors honored the boys with pallbearer duties. While they were gone, I took the opportunity to pray.

This house I stay in is so heavy. It is laden with hurtful memories; its wall bears the scar of the dresser forced into it on January 22. Sometimes when I work, I feel as if I'm suffocating under the weight of it all. There is peace here now that was not here before, but the peace is uneasy - as if at any second the walls could fall in on me. Nevertheless, the judge temporarily gave me the house. I am stuck here until Will and I sign a mutually agreeable consent order *or* the judge takes it away.

I grabbed up a bunch of sage to smolder as I went from room to room praying that All take the heaviness and the hurt away, to let me know that I was not alone. I was crying as I did this, and in the middle of my crying, praying and smudging, Will called. He asked if I'd been running and if I was all right. He sounded concerned, but I told him that I was all right (which I was) and not to worry.

Not a minute later, after I'd begun praying again, Eddie called to check in with me. I took these calls as signs that I was definitely *not* alone! But I was confused. Why had Will called at that exact time? Why had Eddie's call followed on its heels? I sat down to write in my journal about these signs. I received an answer.

This is how it went, and yes, this is how I talk to All sometimes and yes, sometimes songs start the conversations:

Me: Dear God, signs, signs, everywhere are signs...I ask to know I'm not alone and *Will* calls. Then Eddie calls. What the fuck does that mean? You know that if I could get my family back whole and intact, healthier and better than before - so much better because we two adults were doing what we needed to do to get our family back... *You know I want that!*

I don't trust Will, but he calls during a sage cleansing, a prayer? Is that You or is it me? Am I calling to him psychically or emotionally? Was that *You*?

> Them: Yes.

Me: What am I supposed to know? What am I supposed to get from that sign?

> Them: That you are never alone. That he is being honest with you. That not one of us knows how this will end.

Me: *Why*? Why can't you *do something*? Why can't you *make him wake up*? *Why*?

> Them: There is a pulling time, Kellie. It is a pulling time. We are dragging you forward and you want to

stay in dysfunctional familiarity. You do want him back, you do...but you think you must resign yourself to the old ways for it to happen. Truth be told, the only way he can come back is if things are new. We are working on him. And you. But if you won't *move* then no change can occur.

You are doing well. Your anxiety passes. You have a plan. You have goals. You will succeed. Your boys will succeed. You must concentrate on letting go of fear and doubt. Embrace love and confidence. Embrace *you*. You were not anything then that you are not now - but now you are greater than. Greater than you.

You can overcome. You can move without fear. You can You can You can.

There is a house you can physically move to. Picture it. Your own house. No bad stuff there. Nothing hurtful surrounding you. You need it, Kellie.

Me: Okay.

Them: You need to move physically and psychically from here. Return? No one knows. But you must fill your space. This house is not his or yours alone. It was "ours" and like you told him, there is no "ours" there is no "we."

You and he must see you are individuals. Must see. Then, no matter what happens, you will both know you are separate from one another. You will both know. Kellie, right now, you alone are stronger than we. You alone are stronger than he.

Quiet hero, Kellie. You will rise from these ashes and burn brighter than you can imagine right now. You are a beacon. You are the light. You Are.

Me again, with the audacity not to listen but only to demand an answer about my angel: Where is Pauline? Where are her footsteps?

Them: She is marching with you.

Conflicted
April 21, 2010
2 months, 30 days of freedom

I woke this morning with a knot spinning in my gut. It's the anxiety that comes from analyzing to death conversations with Will. It comes from thinking, loving, wanting to fix and regret.

Last Wednesday, Will and I went to custody mediation. This mediation is a free service provided to divorcing parents; the goal is to come up with a parenting agreement without attorney or court involvement. I agreed to him keeping the title of primary parent. He agreed to me seeing the boys Thursday nights through the weekend.

I wasn't happy due to the primary parent label and having to check with him for any extra overnights, and he wasn't happy because without the weekends he could not take the boys camping or four-wheeling or, in reality, have much time with them at all. On his days off, the boys would be with me.

Because neither of us was pleased with the terms of the agreement, we reached a truce and promised to return to mediation in May before our court appearance. At the last second, his attorney advised him not to sign the agreement, and he didn't.

When he first excitedly told me that his attorney advised him not to sign, I was scared and crushed. The agreement guaranteed me three overnights a week. It set precedence for future visitation.

But the agreement also set the precedence of me agreeing to his primary parent status. However, Will was excited for good reasons. He said:

- His attorney told him that the judge had set only the minimum visitation. He could allow me to see the boys Thursday night or any night I requested if he wanted. And he planned to allow the boys three nights with me per week despite what the judge ordered previously. He said that if I didn't believe him, then I could consider the fact that he wouldn't lie to his boys. He'd already told them his plan, and he wouldn't go back on it.
- But if he signed the agreement and I decided to *not* return to mediation, then changing this parenting agreement required a trial, not a court appearance. He was adamant about seeing the boys on the weekends; he didn't want to be the weekday parent.

I considered his point of view. I told him that I know he believes I flip-flopped on him initially, and although I didn't agree with his assessment, I was willing to understand his fear and willing to trust that he wouldn't go back on a promise to his boys.

We left without signing a thing, but still he allowed the boys to stay overnight with me Wednesday through Saturday last week. I allowed him time out at our house to tend to the lawn and work with the boys on Saturday. Will also fixed and repaired a hole in my car's tire. He spent a lot of time at the house on Saturday, and nothing ugly between us happened at all.

Still a Knot
April 21, 2010
2 months, 30 days of freedom

Nope. The knot in my stomach didn't go away. There's more to say.

Also on Wednesday, before his attorney advised him not to sign the parenting agreement, we had a lot of time to kill. Somehow, we decided to spend that time together, outside in front of the courthouse. It wasn't a conscious decision, and neither of us expected to spend SO LONG talking. But we did, and I left that conversation feeling better.

We talked about the primary parent status. I told him that I wanted shared status. Two more overnights a month would give it to me. He said that he wasn't going to give up any legal title until he spoke to his attorney. He said he was paying her to advise him, and he hadn't had the chance to talk to her about what shared custody (or primary, for that matter) legally meant for him.

Of course, I understood that. We are paying these attorneys money; the least they can do is advise us. I didn't like it, but I understood it. He said that he wasn't going to roll over and accept a secondary parent label because he had a penis. I also understood that thinking, and I told him I want him to see his boys. I do not want either of us to bear the primary label.

He said that he didn't know for sure, but he thought that if he didn't have a *family* (meaning the primary parent label) then the Army wouldn't pay him a housing allowance. He thinks that without a family to care for he could lose 25% of his pay. Like him, I don't know how the housing allowance would be affected if he isn't the primary parent. I agree that if he were to lose the housing allowance, then he could not afford to take care of *me* in the way he plans.

He began adding up some figures. He added together a $550 rent payment for me (he says he'd pay it initially), the $320 car payment, the $70 per month car insurance payment. He said that because I wanted to design web pages from my home, I would need cable internet and he included cable television in the figures, adding another $150 to the monthly payments. It seems that the final monthly total he came up with was about $1300, but I can't for the life of me remember what the other $200 was for - or maybe the total came to $1090 each month and I'm imagining the $1300 figure.

He said that if he kept his housing allowance, then he could afford to pay me more money. He reminded me that only his base pay determines alimony and his housing allowance income isn't figured into the equation. So in effect, what Will offered to pay me is about twice as much as the state would award based on the assumption that he keeps primary care of the children, and I pay him child support. I feel like he's trying to buy me out of my boys lives and I don't like it.

As grateful as I was to hear that he planned to *take care of me*, I am also wary. There has to be a catch. I don't trust the goodness of his heart when it comes to me, I don't. Last night on the phone, he told me that I could "go on thinking everyone is out to get you" if I wanted. I told him to hold up - I do not believe that everyone is out to get me. I don't trust *him*.

I hear a shift in his wording since our separation. When we were married, he used to yell at me for being too trusting, too naive and too out of sync with his real world. Now that we separated, he says that I think everyone is out to get me. Weird.

I told him I would consider what he proposed and do some

research on my own and consult with my attorney (if I can ever get an appointment). My no-shit main concern about him being the primary parent is the Army could move him to another post at will. If that happens, being the primary parent, he would automatically take the boys with him. If I could get it in legal writing that if he moves then the boys stay with me until he is settled (giving me time to find a place near them at their new location), then I could live with him having the primary parent title (if without it he loses his housing allowance).

Up until we separated, he believed he would remain here until he retired. We invited his father to come stay with us, built the garage and the upstairs apartment, because we were certain we wouldn't have to move from here. But now, he has a new job in a new unit. He swears that the Army will not reassign him to any other post. But again, I don't trust him.

My plan, should either of us have the primary parent title, is to move to wherever the Army re-assigns him (if that were to happen). If I am primary, then the boys and I will follow him. If he is primary, then I will follow them. I plan to keep any financial settlement money I receive in a savings account in case I have to move at some point to another state. I'm going to rent, not buy, so I don't have to sell a house in order to move. I do not want the boys to lose free access to their father. I don't want them to be without him, and I don't want them to be without me.

I told Will we needed to base the financial consent order off shared custody. I figured it would save us time in the end. I told him that I wasn't signing any financial consent order until after our May 3 custody mediation appointment. I said that if he wouldn't agree to shared custody, then I wouldn't sign the parenting agreement OR the financial consent and I'd let the judge decide our fate. I also told him that I would consult my attorney about the primary parent distinction. I told him that I would consider everything he said, and that I appreciate his willingness to go beyond the alimony payments the state would allow.

At one point, he said, "I told you before that if we ever got to this point and had to fight for the kids that it would be ugly." And it most certainly is.

Churning but Less So
April 21, 2010
2 months, 30 days of freedom

There has to be something else I must say. My belly is still churning. The anxiety is lessening, but it isn't gone.

During my conversation with Them, They told me "He is being honest with you." They said this to me before last night's horrible phone call, after Will and I had talked at the courthouse and on Saturday.

At the courthouse and here, I felt that he was being very sincere in his desire to ease my emotional burden. I feel that he means it when he says the boys will stay with me three nights a week. I believe he intends to continue to do his self-imposed duty as a financial provider for me during our transition. I even partially believe that he has considered dating me again after we get this crap sorted through; I think he doesn't want to have wasted the past 18 years we've spent together. Yet, I don't completely trust him. I wish I did, but I do not.

I understand that the day the sheriff arrested him and removed him from this stupid house, he stopped trusting me completely, too. I know that we didn't trust each other before then, either. We were working on our marriage, but it wasn't his priority. His priority was the boys (for which I was happy), our marriage and then his career (although his career felt second and our marriage a far distant third - despite his proclamations to the contrary). I know neither one of us knew what would become of our marriage.

In my mind, I was willing to work through almost anything. Then he put his hands on me again, and I had to do what I said I would do. I had to press charges. I had to get an attorney. Things fell into place like heavy bricks from that point forward.

In the past week, Will expressed genuine concern for me and to me. At not only the courthouse, but also when I told him I was going in for my first mammogram. He asked "What? Are you okay? Isn't it early for you to have mammograms? Does the doctor think something is wrong?" He expressed concern again when he called on Sunday and found me out of breath. I could tell he was curious, I thought maybe he was concerned.

Friday morning, his father had a medical episode. Will called me and told me and I went running out to his father. Will had already called 911. Everything for his father has worked out all right, so it seems for now anyway, but I know things like this bother Will emotionally. He is vulnerable when someone he loves is sick or hurt; he was vulnerable last year when his grandfather died, and there was a period of peace between us as he dealt with his grandfather passing.

I know that deep down Will must care at least a little for me. I found some peace during the past few days (before last night) in thinking that he and I may be able to work through this situation and come out better for it in the end (friends or spouses? don't know). Saturday, when he was out here mowing and fixing my car's tire, I took him aside and asked him to try to stop talking to me as if we were a couple. We'd had a conversation with his father in which he referred to the land in Texas as *ours* and that *we could* ... anyway, it was as he used to talk when we were together. We are not together. We are separate.

Staying bound to him mentally, emotionally, psychically...it is too hard. When he is vulnerable, my heart wants to hug him, to love him, to soothe him, to make it all better. I feel drawn to him in love and hope when he speaks to me in soft words, when he speaks as if we are a *we*. When he says, "Maybe we'll get back together," I want to believe him. At the courthouse, we talked about more than the custody, more than the finances. We talked about what it had felt like to be together.

We agree that we hurt each other. He wants me to take responsibility for doing exactly what he did, for being exactly like him. He wants me to stop writing online, wants me to erase all of this from my consciousness. He is asking me to erase myself.

Now my gut isn't churning so much, but the tears are flowing. It is as if me telling him that I am exactly like him somehow makes the sickness go away. If I am just like him, then I am also abusive. I get the sense that he hopes that I will say I am exactly like him, and when I do that, I will not want to face my past actions. But he is the one who abused us into pain. If I am just like him, I will change me. If I am just like him, then I don't want to be this way anymore.

Comments from Readers

Kunjii says - *You know, I've followed your blog for months now - from November before the big blow up happened. I don't understand this* we might date later *thing. What the fuck? You don't get divorced so you can date later. You get divorced so you can move on, maybe meet somebody else and make another life and so can he. You're also talking* *about* following him *wherever he goes. If you two aren't sure about getting divorced, why not put the proceedings on hold for six months until you figure out whether you can reconcile. Sounds to me you're planning to be dependent on him forever.*

Kellie Jo says - *You told me what I am not supposed to do (date later), but who gave you the right to throw your opinion about divorce onto me, and then judge me for not doing it your way (or for considering a different option)? The accusatory statement "Sounds to me you're planning on being dependent on him forever" bothers me because you are telling me what I'm thinking/planning and what I am. (Yes, I know you said, "Sounds to me" but the message is clear.)*

Kunjii, you can feel however you want, type and say whatever you want. But what you said in your comment is abusive because you assume you can put yourself into my head and heart and then tell me what I am doing, thinking and being. That is the essence of verbal abuse. "What the fuck?" lets me know that you are angry. Acting or writing in anger, in my experience, leads to bad mojo. It's better to calm down and then speak with or ask questions of whom you feel angry.

Perhaps, "I've never heard of someone reconciling after abuse, and I'm wondering if you've considered putting everything on hold for six months." Or "I think you're saying that you prefer dependency on your husband than freedom from abuse. Is that right?"

Now on to the substance of what you said. If you read closely, I am not following him. If he has primary custody, then he will take the boys with him and I will follow the boys. If I have primary custody of the boys and the Army moves him, then we (the boys and I) will follow him because he is their father. The same is true for shared custody. For the next four years at least, I will be in the same city as Will because of my children.

Ever since I started talking to my boys about sex, I've told them that they do not have to marry the baby's mother, but they must follow their child (and therefore her) around the globe if necessary, to be a father to their child. I wouldn't dream of setting a different example.

I can see the dating thing bothers you. I don't know what your situation is, but I can tell you do not understand mine. I've said it before and I'll say it again - if he admits what he did over the years and apologizes and gets some professional help, then I would consider saving this marriage. However, because I've told him this, I know (given our history) that he may use my words to attempt to manipulate me into doing something or giving up something during the separation agreement phase that puts me at a disadvantage.

I did allow myself to become financially dependent on him. Any time I stepped out on my own, life with him became increasingly difficult (and sometimes dangerous). Besides, the agreement was for me to stay with the children and for him to bring home an income. That's a valid way of life — especially when, as a young woman, I did not expect any of this to affect my life.

In addition, dependency is a two-way street. For example, an alcoholic is dependent on alcohol, but co-dependent on the people she surrounds herself with because the other people give her the excuse she needs to drink. The people who choose to continually associate with the alcoholic are also co-dependent because they make excuses to themselves to remain tied to the alcoholic and therefore make it easier for the alcoholic to continue drinking.

Abusive relationships are a two-way street whether the abuser is dependent on alcohol or not. Will is as dependent on me as I am on him, but it took time apart to see that. Moreover, remember, if a person is dependent on another that does not mean they are incapable.

Dependent
April 22, 2010
3 months of freedom

Kunjii's comment got me to thinking about my dependency on Will. Surely there is more to it than financial dependency (fear of making money on my own is a factor because I haven't done it in so long). The one area in which I did have independence most of the time was with our finances. I know how to invest and have picked solid stocks/mutual funds in the days before returning to the military. I increased the percentage of our income to our IRA every year and each time the Army promoted him. I bought an investment home a few years ago (which we sold for a huge profit). I've chosen services, balanced bank accounts, and set aside money to use in the businesses I owned and for hobbies he enjoyed. I've budgeted for groceries, gas, the kid's expenses and pleasures, et cetera based on one income - his.

There was always money for what we wanted, not always exactly when we wanted it, but for what we wanted, in part due to my money management skills but also due to his mechanical and other handy talents (everything from repairing a carburetor to building a garage). I have made mistakes, but mostly ones of small consequence. How many families with the parents pushing 40 do you know who have survived and thrived for almost two decades on one person's income? We did a good job. I did a good job.

Many of our fights were due to money. He thought we should have more. He thought I wasted it all. He disagreed with my choice of our cellular phone company. He told me to stop paying them; I wouldn't because my credit would take the hit if I defaulted. Soon after we split, he told me, "You know, I make damn good money," and I said, "I'm glad you see that." How did he not know how much money he made?

I know there must be something else, something besides financial dependency. Some good reason for hoping we'll get this family back together. There are the obvious, although increasingly idealistic reasons such as

- I love him, I love the idea of our family in the traditional sense
- I don't want our children to suffer from a broken home (despite the fact that it was *broken* when we lived together)
- Our boys would be better off if Will and I could make peace instead of war; fall back in love, show them what a good relationship looks like.
- I promised him *until death do we part*

There are things I know are *not* reasons, such as

- Fear of being alone (I've done that many times with his deployments and training)

- Fear of never loving again, fear of not being loved by another man (There were men before, there could be men again - I know I am not unlovable)

So what is the basis of my dependency on Will? My latest correspondence with the voices said, "We are dragging you forward and you want to stay in dysfunctional familiarity." I can't argue with that. I do want to cling to *something* familiar, no matter how dysfunctional my rational mind knows it to be.

Most things, the things I held dearest, are different now. My kids are spending half of their time away from me. My husband is not my husband. Nothing is ours – it is mine and his - and that change alone requires vast changes in thinking. Many thoughts that used to revolve around Will and my family are pointless now. I must cut off thoughts of Will because, technically, he is no longer my concern.

Thoughts of my family are vastly different; now family is my children and me. Period. Well, outside of the fact that Will is and always will be their father, he is no longer in my definition of my family.

I try not to care or concern myself with Will's moods or possible feelings; it is difficult because my every behavior has depended on deciphering how he feels (mostly in an attempt to avoid his anger). My attempts to disregard his feelings take up more time than caring about them. In time, this will change. I am learning how to feel what I feel, decipher what I want, after years and years of depending on Will's opinion to tell me what to do, what I should be feeling, and what to think.

He would tell me when I had a right to be angry, when I should feel ashamed, when I should respect his actions and how I should show that respect. He would let me know when it was okay to show love or to be silly (well, grown women aren't supposed to be silly in his opinion, but he would tolerate it from time to time). He told me if my behavior embarrassed him. He let me know what I should think or do to keep him happy. By comparing me to other wives (or his mom or some imaginary feminine goddess), he determined what I should be doing, feeling, saying ... and it seemed that if I wasn't behaving as he thought I should, he would explode. He told me he put me on a pedestal, and right or wrong, it was my duty as his wife to stay there.

Now, I am at a loss as to how to feel, what to think and, at times, what to do.

The voices also tell me that we must be separate in order to learn that we are individuals. I am trying. It is hard. Sometimes I long for the dysfunctional familiarity and become willing to temporarily erase my memory and substitute the dream.

When I'm with Will, he tells me what he requires of me. I suppose I miss that aspect of our old relationship. In some ways, being told who I am feels superior to determining who I am on my own. It is definitely easier in many regards, especially during the bad times when soothing his temper was merely a matter of putting on a mask. I'd put on the mask not so much to deceive him as to deceive myself into believing I *should be* what he said to be.

At the courthouse last Wednesday, he commented that I wasn't the woman he married. I agreed. But I don't yet know who I am. I've depended on him to tell me. On October 18, 1992, after six months of marriage, I wrote

> He married me to fight me, it seems. Beat me down and make me less than I am. That infuriates me. THAT is what scares me. What if he does win? Where will "I" go? Just disappear into the mold he

has laid out for me? I don't think it will come down to that. I think he'll come around before that happens. I don't want him to change, I want him to understand. Understand ME. I hope when he does understand he still loves me.

I wrote that statement 18 years ago. It is time to accept that he doesn't and cannot love me.

Comments from Readers

Fatima says - *Thank you for sharing this with me. I love your honesty ... It's almost two years that I left my abusive husband of 21 years. I have five children. I am helping myself heal and I am helping others to heal.*

> **NewDirection says** - *Kellie, I separated from my husband almost a year ago. I was where you are now in the beginning, and on lonely days when I focus on what was good, and the companionship, the feeling of family, I can still get there.*
>
> *But let me tell you what waits for you if you stand firm in your pursuit, no demand, of health for you and your family ... you learn that it is ok to love someone and not be together. You learn to see him (and yourself) in the unkind light of day and accept him and you for you who are and kindly love each of you as a separate incomplete entity. Abuse occurs in the context of a relationship, a dyad. When the relationship ends, and it is again the two of you as individuals, you can finally see who you are apart from him. You learn where he starts and you begin.*
>
> *That psychological separation is necessary for forgiveness and/or reconciliation to occur, even if it is just as co-parents. You sound like you are on your way to doing that work. That*

is the work of real love for yourself and another after you have experienced the pain of abuse. Keep up the good work!

Kunjii says - *Okay sweetie, don't get me wrong, I'm going to try to write this in a way that you won't take offense because I know you're emotionally and mentally vulnerable right now. I have been where you are. It's a scary roller coaster place: one minute you're excited about what the future possibilities could be, and the next you're terrified because ... well because sometimes it feels safer to stay with the devil you know than the devil you don't.*

I read all you blogs from the very beginning (those blogs aren't up anymore) and it brought back feelings of my own marriage where my self-esteem and self-worth was slowly grinded away by constant criticisms, analysis, comparisons and plain cruelty. My spouse knew where to hit me where it hurt: my looks, my weight, my job skills, you name it; he could be an asshole about it.

But you know what? I LOVED him. I loved him for 3 years after our divorce too. I loved him even after he remarried and somehow I would fall into bed with him when he would come over to fix the light bulb. You know why? Because I had no self-esteem.

You and Will have children and I know that makes a huge difference. But what I hear when I read your blogs is a woman who wishes it would all get fixed and you could reconcile. All I'm saying is that is still possible. I'm not telling you what to do or how I would do it - but it's always good to hear a different slant on things isn't it?

You could, if you wanted to, put a halt to the divorce proceedings and remain living apart. And you could watch him to see if he would go to counselling of his own will. If there is a possibility of a reconciliation, (the future of dating as you write) then taking a break from each other to see how it goes might be worth it.

You're right, I'm not you and so I don't know your situation. Maybe I'm reading you completely wrong. If you were my daughter, or my best friend, or my sister, this is advice I would offer. Yes, I know you didn't solicit it, but you do have a public blog and I assume you want feedback.

You could still do the things you need to do: school, work, whatever and see how stuff progresses. The court system can be a whirlwind: they're making decisions for you, telling you what to do, when you have to do it etc. Having a year apart and seeing how it progresses gives you a break - from anybody telling you how to live your life. And then if you still feel that it's not going to work, you're a little bit more prepared to all the legal wrangling and stuff that goes on..

> **Lisa says -** *Hey Kellie, I'm going to ditto Kunjii's remarks. What you told me in this blog is that you have great financial skills, organizational skills; you're smart and savvy with business. You're an independent woman waiting to happen. The emotional stuff is hard to let go of, I'm not going to kid you about that. Will is the only man you have been with for 18 years, you have two children and you have been a family. But you are also right that a family could be you and your two sons. Family is what you make it and who you want to be in it. You might always care about will as a human being because you shared so much together and that might never go away. But is that really love? And do you deserve to be loved and cherished? The answer is yes! You're not an object*

or a possession on a pedestal. You are Kellie and that's enough for anyone who truly loves you.

None of us at 40 is the girl we were at 19 or 20 - and who wants to be? I was a silly college girl who worried about stupid things and sought approval from my sorority sisters about everything. I am so much more confident of my abilities now and I am much less willing to accept anything less than what I want and deserve.

My own paycheck is sweet and I love making my own living. There's a sense of accomplishment; I'm taking off for the Outer Banks in May for two weeks and buying a new car for the drive down. It gives me power that a husband can't. There is more to dependency than the financial aspect, but the financial piece seems to bring the rest of it together. When you can truly take care of yourself financially, the rest of it starts to come together. But as long as you allow someone else to control your finances, you become dependent on them in many other ways.

Follow your bliss, Kellie. Sometimes it takes working two jobs to get there, sometimes it's hard and scary but in the end, it's worth every sacrifice.

Kellie Jo says - *Kunjii, thank you so much. You confirmed something very important for me. I read your first comments and heard only bad stuff. I told you why I heard bad stuff, and what did you do?* You understood. You realized I wasn't able to hear you, and you rephrased it. Same message, different words. *I knew it was possible for someone to do that. It may not be possible for* Will *to do it, but it is possible.*

My heart if full of thanks to you, Kunjii.

Primarily, it is my fault (request) that we do the separation agreement now instead of waiting. I've said that I wanted to get through the separation agreement first, begin living our lives secondly and then see if reconciliation is possible.

I am still of the mind that this is the best path, whirlwind and all. I knew in the beginning that we needed to physically separate, my spirit confirmed it the other day, and I do not think Will would stop now for anything. He's told me as much.

In my state, there is a required physical separation of one year. We cannot legally file for divorce until January 22, 2011. Until then, we have to work out a separation agreement attached to the divorce papers and (usually) approved by a judge at the divorce hearing. So, it's up to me to do as you and Lisa say, as my spirit says, and separate myself from Will emotionally. It's the hard part, but it is happening.

Much of the time, I write when it's the hardest. I am stronger than it seems on some days, and I will try to write more during those times.

Yes, Kunjii, I write publicly in part to hear feedback. Without it, I'd think I was truly alone. Sometimes the hard words work for me; but as you said, right now, they just hurt. Thank you for understanding. I have great respect for you.

This is Me, That is Him
April 26, 2010
3 months, 4 days of freedom

I've already texted my goodnights to the boys, but I cannot sleep despite the fact that I am pooped. Exhausted. Stress is a bitch.

Something gnaws at me, but I am not certain what that something could be. Typically, I'd write about what I thought it might be, and then narrow it down to the root cause. But I don't feel safe in doing that right now. I don't want to share yet.

Will told me the other day that I couldn't make it unless I meet certain financial conditions. He is concerned that I want the house. He can't see any other way for me to be so confident in my ability to create financial success unless I'm planning on "going for the house." Typical.

I am hopeful, and hope makes me confident. Unlike the hope I felt when I tried to force Will to see the abuse in our marriage, this hope doesn't depend on his actions. This hope depends on me. It's exhilarating to have my future in my own hands, untethered and free. The anxiety I feel facing my future alone seems distinctly different from the anxiety I once felt at the sound of his truck pulling into the drive.

I am not naive enough to think this will be easy. It would be nice if some great hand would reach down from the sky to snatch a long lost relative who left me millions. But as much fun as it is to consider that inane possibility, I do not lose myself in it. This isn't going to be easy. There is no sure-fire way to guarantee my success; but there's also no way to guarantee my failure. Will has had no faith in me for a very long time, if ever. But his insinuations no longer cause me to crawl into a hole and hide. Now, hearing him say what he says causes me to divert my attention from him and pay attention to the light in my own heart.

It feels ... strange. And good.

The most I can do is simply *start* moving away from him. I'm doing that. I'm not revealing my actions yet because they're not his business; I don't feel like giving him my secrets anymore.

Unfortunately, that means that I cannot give my secrets to *you* either.

Yes, I am slightly worried and a tad fearful. Who wouldn't be? But I know I will make this work. I have a plan.

Comments from Readers

Erin says - *I am so proud of you, Kellie! You are so strong and you encourage me through your actions. Thank you!*

> **Lisa says -** *Do it. I know you can. It's scary, but a* good *scary. You can always e-mail me if you want to get something out and don't feel safe publishing it. He knows you can do it, too. That's why he's trying to control you again. You're a strong woman, Kellie. Follow your bliss.*

Time Reports
April 27, 2013
3 months, 5 days of freedom

An article in *Time Magazine* reports:

> ...of women who said they were abused, 54% characterized their partners as very reliable, and 21% said that their partners had many positive characteristics.

There is so much to learn about abusive relationships. That statistic isn't surprising to me.

For some reason, I want to believe Will is reliable, when all evidence points to the fact that he was reliable in only one or two areas that concerned me. Mainly one - I could count on him to bring home the bacon. Now that we're divorcing, that does not concern me any longer.

Likewise, I believe Will has many positive characteristics.

Unfortunately, I'm not the one who typically gets to see them unless I watch him interact with others.

Envisioned
May 5, 2010
3 months, 13 days of freedom

I started thinking about where I wanted to live about a week after the sheriff forced Will to leave this house. I didn't want to be *here*, but where did I want to live? After shoving all the other questions out of the way, I came up with my ideal house. It looks like this:

- It's an old, probably white, farmhouse.
- There is a lot of land around it, but not much of a yard to maintain.
- It has pocket rooms - rooms in odd places, more rooms than you think by looking at it.
- It has windows and sunlight with a good place for my office, my work area.
- It's located in a safe place.
- It might have a ghost, a loving one.
- It's in the boys' current school district.
- It's affordable.

I asked the boys what they wanted in a house. They didn't care about the inside; they wanted what was outside.

- Eddie wanted trees.
- Marc wanted water, preferably a pond but a stream would be okay, too.

I added their wishes to my list, and started looking for *that* house. I've been actively looking for about six weeks, not seeing anything that I liked. There are lots of manufactured, run-down homes in my meager price range, or nicer homes in less safe areas. I thought the house I would end up with would be less than what I wanted, but thought that if it had a short lease, it would be good enough for now. I came to peace with that idea.

I started calling realtors, started calling people who put ads in the paper. I talked to more than twenty-five leads in one day, two or three leads on most days. I went back to my local realtor to remind him I was looking. Then I went back the day after. He told me I'd been on his mind, and he'd seen a friend of his working in the yard of her rental this past weekend. He called her at work, but had to leave a message.

When he told me her name, it rang a bell. Her last name if very common in these parts, but the ringing bell felt different from familiar ... it felt *hopeful*. Inspired, I decided to take a drive down some roads out by this current house, along the river. It was a beautiful day, and I thought the sun would do me good. I opened the sunroof, turned on the radio, drove and looked.

On my way back to this house, on a country road, I saw a little white farmhouse. It had a small front porch painted gray with a small red bench standing in stark but beautiful contrast to the siding. The face of the house was small, but from the side, I could tell the original house was much smaller ... the pocket rooms were added later, based on a family's needs, not aesthetics. There was no sign in the yard, so it wasn't available. Of course someone else loved it.

I thought, "No one would want to move from there!" and watched the house leave my rear view mirror.

When I got home, I sent an email to everyone I know here in town. I told them I was looking for a house and a job, and asked them to keep me in mind as they drove about town and conversed with friends. It was a tough email to send, and many of the people on the bcc: list didn't know me very well.

I left to pick up Eddie from school. We talked about finding a *good enough* house. The drive through lane at Burger King was long, so I left him to the radio while I went in to get him some slammers. When I came back out, he said, "A realtor called you." He didn't have a name, and the number on my missed calls list simply listed *unknown*.

I pressed the number and a woman answered the phone. I explained why I didn't know who I was calling, and she said, "This is [bell ringing name!], and you called in response to my ad in the paper."

My heart lifted; she was showing the house and asked if I'd like to see it. She gave me the address; it was an unfamiliar address, but she said the house was in the high school district I wanted. When she named landmarks, I knew right where she was. I had driven down that road earlier today.

I got to the house that evening. The old white farmhouse's owners had added pocket rooms over the years to contain a growing family. A little red bench accented the gray porch. I looked at this house disbelievingly. It was the same house I saw only hours before.

I spoke with the woman and her husband. I told them I had no job, but could pay several month's rent up front. I told her enough of my story so she could understand my situation, but not enough to let on *why* I left my ex-husband or the circumstances surrounding my decision. She liked me, I could tell. I definitely liked her. She wants to rent to someone who will love her family's home, who will respect and take care of it as she would. I am definitely that person.

I took Eddie to see it yesterday. He loves the trees; he loves the land behind the property that stretches all the way back to the river. He senses no foul spirits in the house, only peace (he is sensitive like that). He kept calling it *our house*.

The property owner told us all about the neighbors, her family, where she placed her Christmas Shoebox (no stockings) on Christmas Eve when she and her siblings were small.

I gave her my application, full-disclosure of course, and reminded her I could pay several months' rent upfront. Because she is the property owner, I know she wants to check my references so she stopped short of saying, "It's yours." However, when I reminded her that I wanted to move relatively soon and was wondering if I should keep looking, she cut me off and said, "Stop looking."

This is going to work. Pray for me, that I get to live in this wonderful house with my wonderful children and work with this wonderful landlord in overlooking her family home.

If you want to visualize the house, scroll to the top of this post. The description of the house in my boys' and my imaginations is the exact description of our soon-to-be home. I don't know about the ghost yet, but I'm hopeful.

Comments from Readers

PrincessLuceval says - *How wonderful! I'm so happy for you and the boys. It's great when things work out like that, you feel as if there is a higher spirit helping you.*

    Tiffany says - *It sounds perfect!*

NewDirection says - *Whether or not you get it, I truly believe God is guiding and protecting you. That is why that house and that name called to you. I hope you get it! This is* your *new life. It will be good and filled will love and peace!*

All Right
May 6, 2010
3 months, 14 days of freedom

I haven't heard back about the house yet, but I'm not expecting to hear anything until the end of this week or beginning of next. I'm not letting my hopes get too high.

Crap. Who am I kidding? I hope with all my heart. I'm hoping so much that I trust a stranger at her (almost) word that I can stop looking. In the spirit of *not looking*, I turned my attention to the other thing I need, namely a job.

I would like to have a job doing something I already love to do. But you know what? I'd be happy doing almost anything so long as I get to come home at the end of the day with enough energy to write.

I'm PMS-ing and have been for three days. Today the bomb dropped, so I should feel much better in the morning. That thought brings up something I did not notice until recently: since separating from Will, I pay attention to my period. I know about when it will happen, and I know that for the past three months, I feel overly sad three days before it starts. Looking back, this pattern *is* a pattern. I mean, it's been happening for years. But I never thought I had PMS. Ever.

Now that I'm alone, *not* thinking about what he's doing, what he's going to do, what he may do, what might make him laugh, what might make him mad - anyway, now that my mind isn't *so* preoccupied with what *might* be happening inside Will, I am able to pay attention to what is going on inside of me. Possibly, that sentiment seems insane, especially to people who haven't lived in an abusive relationship, but it is true. I spent so much time and energy focusing on *him* that I completely neglected to notice the tiniest, most natural things about *me*.

But back to Will for a second. I told him about the house and I know he is happy. (He's been living in an RV for months and can't wait to get back into this house. He wants back in almost as much as I want out! During the conversation, he even laughed at something I said (it was supposed to be funny). I couldn't remember seeing washer/dryer hook-ups at the house, and he said he would install them and maybe the landlord would take some money off the deposit. I told him if she would not let him install them, then I'd have to send my laundry back here with the boys for *him* to do (no, he didn't laugh at that)!

Despite our momentary jaunt down let's-be-friends lane, we go back to court on the 11th. I'm not looking forward to it. I have no idea what is going to happen. All I can do is forge ahead, creating a life for myself, and trust that, in the end, all will be right.

I have faith that all will be right when the dust clears, or possibly after another walk through absolute hell. I have been to Hell, and there's no guarantee I'm completely through it. Maybe I've simply passed out from emotional pain, and right now, I'm in an unconscious stupor enjoying a little peace while fiery coals burn my non-feeling backside.

I'll have to wake up for the court date though. Here is to hoping Hell is behind me!

Comments from Readers

NewDirection says - *That is so true. The best part about being out of an abusive marriage is hearing your own voice and having the energy and focus to listen! That is one of my new standards for a good man, that he support me in* *spending time and energy on me, and vice versa, without seeing it as a threat to the us.*

> **Kunjii says -** *This post reminds me of when, during the most abusive time in my partnership, I actually ran away from home so to speak and spent 3 months sitting on a beach in Southeast Asia.*
>
> *My day-to-day existence in my home was so consumed with him that I didn't even exist. His life dominated mine. Then literally within weeks of being away, I found myself happier, healthier ... I was actually laughing and enjoying life. It was easy - I was paying 300 dollars a month for a little beach hut, and getting $5 massages everyday - I was eating wonderful Thai, Chinese and Indian food for 75 cents a meal. I started wearing makeup ... and not worrying what anybody thought. It was about* me *and I was focusing on* me *because I didn't have any threat hanging over my head - whether it be verbal, emotional or physical. This sounds like what is happening to you - remember, it takes baby steps, but once you tap into your own power, then it will be strides, and then leaps. No matter what happens, remember* fear *is what always holds us back. We all die in the end, so* live *- take chances and* live.

New House New House New House New House!
May 9, 2010
3 months, 17 days of freedom

I am so grateful to the couple who decided my boys and cats and I should live in their house! I feel *free*. Then I *panic*. But then I feel free again. And then I panic. I'm hoping the panic subsides. I am sure it will as soon as I find a J-O-B.

I can't wait to transplant my lavender and sage into the front flowerbeds. The woman who owns this house has a yard style kind of like mine - if it grows and it is pretty, then it stays. A yellow flowery bush (is it wild dill?) lives in the front yard. She refused to mow it down because she thought it was pretty, but said I could take it out if I wanted. I think it is pretty too, so the wild thing stays.

I paid out the money to the property owners today, and it felt so good. I'm so willing to let the cash flow when the payback is going to be worth *so much more* than the cost.

Peace. Peace. Peace.

Happy (then anxious) happy-happy day. I cannot wait to sleep there.

Comments from Readers

PrincessLuceval says - *I'm hoping you've been using these days to move in, get settled and become one with your new home. I selfishly check back on a twice-daily basis to see if there are new posts, because your blog has helped me tremendously. I'm extremely happy for you. I'm so, so happy for you! I've been checking back for the outcome, and finally! Really, really happy for you.*

> **Kunjii says** - *Wait until you move in there! The first couple of days will feel surreal - almost like 'where am I?' and then soon it will become home. I picture miniature roses all around a little deck and a rocking chair upon it ... hee hee. You're going to be very happy there missy.*

Lisa says - *I wish you much happiness, peace, and a whole lot of wild flowers (I'm the same way, if it blooms, it stays). It's good to hear you sounding so positive. XOXO*

EagleWolfeSpirit says - *Enjoyed this series of posts. Most of all how synchronicity is so real in the dynamics of it all.*

I love seeing you develop and grow your individual independence and happiness! I truly believe when things are meant to be everything synchronizes together easily! Many blessings in your life!

Erin says - *Tears of happiness for you, Kellie! I love you so much. You deserve this more than most anything. What a beautiful house for healing. You are going into your new home in a state of unknowing not only in your future, but also in your Self. When you are ready to leave this home, you will know the person I have always known. You will know that she exists; and how strong, confident, happy, funny and bold she is. You will know that you can accomplish great feats because of all that you will have accomplished. You will be confident and excited about your future - because you will be living it.*

You keep getting stronger and braver each day. Imagine what you will unleash on the world when you are in your healing home... I know you are amazing now. You will know how amazing you are when you enter the next, next phase of your life. I love you and I am so proud of you!

Checking In
May 16, 2010
3 months, 24 days of freedom

I *finally* moved into my sweet home. I won't lie to you - this week has been an emotional roller coaster. When I started carting things from the old house to the new, I cried quite a bit. I never wanted this marriage to end. I never wanted to separate so completely, so materially. But I am glad I am the one moving from the marital home. I felt like a stranger there. I felt out of place. Feeling like a stranger in our marital home was the tough. Why would I feel like this in a home I created with items I loved?

Will let me decorate the house as I wished throughout our married life. He even let me paint colors on the walls after we moved here in 2003. He never complained about my choice of curtains, rugs, towels, etc. I furnished the house pretty much as I chose. When I moved out this week, I got to thinking about why I chose the items I was moving. Some things I didn't want to take but felt that I needed to take for now. I struggled with leaving three things:

1. A print called *La Belle Dame Sans Merci* originally painted by John William Waterhouse represented an unhealthy desire. The knight in the picture looks like Will. I had so wanted him to come home and rescue me from the pain I felt. I wanted him to be the knight in shining armor. It was an unrealistic expectation, and not one I ever want to repeat. I don't want ever to think another person can rescue me, so the picture stayed.
2. Another print called *The Kiss* originally painted by Klimt represented my dream of our future. I longed for that kind of love, from Will ... it is a wish, but my heart has no more room for wishes.
3. A family picture taken on the day he returned from the last deployment shows us smiling if not happy. It is a snapshot, but it is the last picture taken of us as a family. I have my arm across Will's shoulder. Again, I was hopeful; I didn't know what was to come. I wrestled with leaving the picture behind. I mean, we are our boys' family and that will not change. Yet I couldn't bring it here. It is too painful

to know that those four people, that family, was about to be torn apart. I couldn't take it; I couldn't bring it here.

I'm crying again. I am heartbroken. My life is new and uncertain. But I am not afraid. I don't know *how* my life will straighten itself; I only know that it will.

Things between Will and I are familiar because as always, we are fighting for the same things, but against each other. There is a kind of peace in the familiarity. He inspects and plugs my tires, tells me he hopes I find a job that I love (and I believe him). He is going through a similar hell ... but separate from my own.

I see peace in our future, working to co-parent two wonderful young men. On Monday, I'm going to social services to see if I qualify for food stamps. If they don't keep me waiting all day, I'll then go to a place a friend told me about to apply for work. When I get this new house livable, I will write more often and tell you what I've been doing in addition to transferring my life's possessions piecemeal in a car. Until then, if you think of me, think of me optimistically.

I truly know in my heart and mind that I will be okay. So many things that once mattered do not, so many things that never mattered now do. I'll be sorting through it all as I go about setting up my new life.

Comments from Readers

NewDirection says - *You made some healthy and thoughtful decisions about what you want to take with you to your new home. The first picture you have is one I have as well. Interesting how much our hopes and dreams tie in with the objects we surround ourselves with. While I stay in our old home for now, I've created a space that is brand new. A* room I can go to and be free of any of the painful memories. It helps. Sending love and prayers your way for your journey. Best wishes!

> **Lisa says** - This is what I always tell my students when they first graduate and move on to jobs and their first apartments: It's the best scary and unsettled you will ever feel. It's full of hope, challenge, and the unknown. Breathe it in, allow yourself to feel it and then let it go.
>
> Opportunity is just that; it is an opportunity and not a promise. You need to feel the scary to appreciate feeling good. I told myself this not long ago and it is still true. It does not take away the hurt and sadness, rather it allows me to accept it, feel it and then let it go. Look at the new house as the place where your life changes and begins again. Different, but as good ... if not better.
>
> Who needs a knight in shining armor when you have YOU?

Laura says - This is your Transition Zone, a place where you will find memories from the past, unsureness in the present and questions for the future. The transition zone will always feel happy and scary at the same time because it is a crossroad. It's okay ... know that this too will pass. I applaud your strength to make the difficult choices you made.

Daybreak
May 19, 2010
3 months, 27 days of freedom

Back in March, I spent a couple of days writing a story for a short story contest. I didn't win, but now I can share the story with you since the contest runner will not hold rights to it. This story did not factually happen the way I present it. I pulled it from my last night with Will and all the other times that are so vivid in my memory. Again, this story is a mash-up of times and places, a reorganization of reality, with a knife thrown in because I had only 1500 words to tell this story.

"I don't believe you," he said. "You're calm. You're calculating your next move ... I can see it in your eyes."

"What?" I asked. I felt my eyes scrunch at their lids, felt my brow knit together into the one wrinkle on my face, off-center between my eyebrows by a fraction of an inch. He used to smile at me when he saw that wrinkle appear, run his finger along it gently. Now, years later, looking into his whiskey-reddened face, I understood why he loved that wrinkle. The subtle line showed my first signs of anger. It was his clue that he was getting to me.

"I can't trust you when you're calm," he continued. I felt my wrinkle deepen. "Why won' cha you call me an asshole, a bastard? Why won' cha yell at me no more?" he said, "I'd respect that more than this calm, manipulative thing you've been doin' to me lately." He grabbed his drink from my desk. I smelled the sourness of the whiskey as he pulled the glass toward his pinched mouth. He took a sip, looked into his half-empty glass with narrowed eyes and then finally relaxed his face enough to gulp the rest.

I felt the wrinkle disappear, my face relaxed as if I were his mirror image. Calm for an instant. But then his knuckles whitened on the glass and he brought it down fast, stopping it an inch above the surface of my desk. My hand gripped the computer mouse tighter than a second before. He concentrated on his hand and banged the glass to the desk three times, seeming to need the punctuation of sound. I squeezed the mouse three times harder and felt my ribs clench together in my chest. My eyes were wide as he slowly defocused from the offending glass and settled his greener-than-sober eyes on me.

"What's that look for? What's wrong with you?" he whispered, emphasizing the "wrong."

We looked at each other for a long silent second - me wide-open and scared and him white-knuckled and angry. Was he angry because I was frightened? Was he mad because I wasn't angry? It would be wise to choose anger. Smart to give him what he wanted.

My mind shot five minutes into the future and I saw myself yelling and crying, shouting horrible things I didn't mean to placate him. I foresaw his muscles relax, envisioned him turning away toward the kitchen. He would be saying, "You're fucking irrational. I can't talk to you," with a sneer on his lips.

I would hear the ice banging into his glass, then hear the Coke fizz briefly before the whisky silenced the fuss. What he wanted was an excuse to keep drinking.

Spinning out of the vision, looking into his eyes, I realized I was stuck in a tight corner, my only exit through him. If I stood from my seat, I would have to lean into his space. Would he allow me to stand? I decided he wouldn't. I blinked my eyes, then pinched my lids together tightly for a moment. Opening them, I saw that he was leaning in closer to me, bending at his waist and eyeing me curiously. I felt like an unknown type of animal the hunter must study before killing.

"What are you doing?" I asked.

"Tryin' to figger out what you're gonna do," he said, tilting his head a little and slowly pushing his chin toward my face until he managed to look down at me even though our noses were aligned. I felt his breath on my cheek. Smelled the residual stench of alcohol mixed with sweat as if it were my own. Familiar. Threatening. Vile.

I didn't move. I thought of how a deer froze in the road as if its stillness guaranteed immunity from the car barreling down on it. The car always won. I saw my carcass in a ditch.

I snapped back in my chair. He startled. I rose up from under him and escaped the corner. I didn't go far, turning to face him as quickly as I could from a new position near the freedom of the kitchen and its exterior door. Six feet of air stood between him and me, and my purse was three feet beyond him on the table by the front door.

Could I exit the kitchen and then round to the front door, re-enter the house to grab my purse and get to the car before he could stop me? I considered his slowed and drunken state, but I doubted my ability to execute the plan. I imagined that once I was out of the house he would lock the doors, and I would be outside in my socks and the cold dark rain. Or worse, he would chase me outside to subdue me. I would run, but he would tackle me. I would fight, but he would win. What did it mean to win? What did he want from me?

"What do you want from me?" I yelled, knowing he wanted me to yell. "You are scaring the hell out of me!"

He slowly stood erect, a delayed reaction that bought time for his voice to switch to a croon. "You're scared? Come on, Woman. Have I ever hurt you before?" he said, corners of his lips lifting upward while the centers stayed straight. He slightly lowered his head like you do when you peer at your naughty child over the top of your glasses. I expected him to tsk and shake his head in disappointment.

He may have forgotten holding my face over the lit stove burner and using my neck to swing my head into the wall, but I hadn't. Five years had passed between that night and this, but I remembered it clearly.

I put my hand to my mouth partly remembering the heat and partly in shame. Why hadn't I left him then? Why was I still here?

He took a slushy step toward me and I heard the sole of his Ridge Desert Storm boot slide barely over the surface of the wooden floor. At 1 AM, he still wore his uniform and boots. That meant his knife was still attached to his belt, in its case, positioned horizontally not vertically.

I took a step backward, purposefully staring into his eyes so I wouldn't glance at the knife. He wore the knife horizontally so he could pull the 5-inch blade from his side with a smooth backward motion before giving a powerful forward thrust. He'd shown me the move, proudly, not long ago. The knife was too long to be regulation, but he'd said, "Some of us get to carry what we want," and I hadn't doubted him. He was a stellar soldier.

"Why do ya gotta be so different from me, Woman? Why d'ya havta challenge me all the time?" He took another but steadier step my way. My thighs tightened into coiled springs. He subtly rounded his back. My torso twisted slightly facilitating my right arm's creeping motion toward my own imaginary weapon. I was gonna take my knife and twist it into something raw.

"I only want you to respect me," he said. His glassy eyes filled with tears. "Why can't ya respect yur husband, Woman? Why?" He moved toward me, the toe of his boot rubbing the floor somehow wrong. He stumbled and then fell to his knees, putting his hands to his face, shamed. He sobbed. I felt the tension drain from my body. I couldn't run.

I dropped to my knees and pulled his head to my breast. My eyes welled up with tears and we cried together for a while. He cried until he passed out on my lap and I let him sleep there while my legs grew numb.

I sobbed my goodbyes to the sleeping soldier. He seemed innocent like this, on my lap, in my arms. I smoothed his thick dark hair. I wondered if he would wake to mimic my broken heart, to express grief in the same way I now mourned, realizing we would never grow old together, never see our children and never once touch one another, ever again.

It was a comforting thought, thinking he may weep for me.

I gently placed his head on the golden wood floor then straightened my legs to get the blood flowing. I uncased the knife at his side, and carried it with me to our bedroom. Packing, I would stare at the knife at times, reminding myself why I was leaving. It would be easier to pretend he hadn't wanted to stab me, that I had imagined the whole thing. I wanted to crawl into the bed and sleep away the pain. Instead, I packed.

On this side of daybreak, I stepped over the soldier on the floor. I laid his knife on the table by the front door, took up my purse and drove away.

My Job
May 28, 2010
4 months, 6 days of freedom

I love my job! I work for a woman who owns a furniture refinishing business. Her shop foreman is teaching me everything I need to know to do a professional refinishing job. I get along well with them, and they say that I am an easy learner and only need to hear something once. (We'll see how long I can keep that up - there's a lot to remember!)

It is part time, minimum wage, but the owner is expanding soon and she wanted me in on the ground floor ... this is a wonderful thing.

Will and I get along when there are witnesses, but not so much when there are none. That's okay. I can deal - especially now that I have my own home to go to at the end of the day. If I ever have the opportunity to advise someone in a similar situation, I will tell them to move away from the memories, the pain and the patterns by physically moving from the home.

Financially I am not okay. My expenses outweigh my income and will for at least another year. Well, unless I want to ruin my credit. I had to charge things to my credit card, and now I have that bill, too. The fortunate thing is that I have enough to cover my rent through the month of August, which means I have until then to make up the difference.

Nevertheless, I am happier and confident that I will be able to overcome the financial situation and move forward with grace. Too many miraculous, magical events have occurred recently for me to believe otherwise. I've worked hard. I've overcome much pain. I am able to handle the new pains that come at me as he and I separate from one another. The hardest pain to overcome pertains to our children, the fear that I will not see them as I wish. But this is simply a fear, and I cannot let it stand in my way of creating a life that is joyful, full of love, and fulfilling in every way.

He's taking me to court to change the visitation. He isn't happy that he doesn't get to be with the boys on weekends, yet he's only asked to see them on a weekend once. I want the boys to be with their dad, too; but Will is unresponsive to my requests to rotate weeks. He'd rather I see them every other weekend.

Of course.

Court next week...I hope I get what I want, but, if I don't, then I'll manage the pain. I'm a big girl, and I can take it. I do wish I didn't have to handle so much of it.

Comments from Readers

Kunjii says - *Congratulations. Remember to take* notes - *the faintest ink always outweighs the sharpest memory. When they are giving you instructions, have a legal size pad with you and write it down - you can review your notes at home. You moving on with your life might bring out some hostility in your husband - he probably wasn't expecting all this. Maybe neither were you, and isn't it a nice surprise that you did it? Again, congratulations. Power always comes from action.*

Loneliness
May 29, 2010
4 months, 7 days of freedom

In the weeks leading up to the separation day, I cried to my sister over the phone and told her that I was so fucking lonely even though Will, our boys, my friends and she were there for me. I was lonely; it was the first time I realized it, and I wondered how I could be so lonely amidst so many people.

I was looking outward for the cause of my loneliness, just as I looked outward, to other people, for a solution to end it. Isn't that what they tell us to do when we're depressed and lonely? Volunteer, make friends, fill your life full of activities and responsibilities to be happy. But that's bullshit. Those good deeds, the other people, the outward motions, they merely distract from the loneliness. They don't erase it.

When I drew the doodle I now call *Conversation with Depression*[6], I scribbled a black ball inside the solar plexus of my body. I didn't know that blackness inside of me was loneliness. I thought it was a flaw within me; that if I could find the source of the flaw, then the blackness would disappear. I was searching the blackness with a flashlight, but looking for the wrong objects. What the flashlight revealed was a great emptiness. A vast, tightly compacted, black hole. Nothing else.

I missed the blackness because I was looking for *the flaw*.

Realizing I was lonely when I was still with Will was more painful in many ways than the loneliness I now feel. I brought that pain on myself because I expected him to *make me* not lonely. I thought that if I reached out hard enough and long enough, he would eventually connect with me and ease my pain. Expecting him to make me feel something caused a flurry of secondary emotions.

Every time he did not do as I expected, I felt betrayed, hurt, unloved, crushed ... those emotions distracted me from the truth and any possible solutions.

Loneliness is realizing there is a black emptiness within myself. Loneliness is the place where I do not allow the light. I chose to keep this black hole inside me because searching the blackness with a tiny flashlight is scary; finding *nothing* when I hoped to find *the source* is terrifying. It feels like watching a horror movie when the flashlight darts from blackened corner to corner - you don't want the heroine to find the monster, but when she does see it then there is a sweet release. When she finds the monster, the heroine knows from which direction to fight or run.

I am changing course. I'm not going to search that blackness with a tiny light. I'm going to flood it with light. If my loneliness is like a black hole, a dead star, then in time, it will explode outward from the force of its own compaction. When it explodes, it will form a new universe, a new beginning. All new. All me, but re-formed and rejuvenated.

I am unaware of when my black hole's lifespan will evolve. What is the moment before the explosion going to feel like? Will I notice when it happens? Will I feel the Big Bang?

Is it possible that an infusion of intensive *light*, which is both nothing and everything on which our world depends, could hasten a black hole's end? Is light the catalyst for the Big Bang? I am going to concentrate on pushing light into the vast emptiness within me. Whenever I feel the rumblings of discomfort in my gut, I am going to imagine real love as a light source and *push* that light into that dark space. I am not looking for anything. I know there is nothing there to see because it is too densely compacted to see anything right now. But after the explosion, All will come into the light; I will *know* what I've created. Once I *know*, then I can do something about it or leave it alone to see how it develops on its own.

I will have a new universe inside of me. A new universe I will tend to, love and cherish. I can enjoy it and cease to rely on the external world for manufactured and temporary joy.

Take in the light, black hole. Your lifespan is at its end.

> Stephen Hawking thinks that once matter falls into a black hole and reaches the Singularity, this Singularity at the quantum scale may actually become a gateway or a spawning ground for a new universe which would exist in some adjacent set of space-time

dimensions. Black holes formed in our universe, according to Lee Smolin, may actually spawn universes beyond our own. - Ask the Astronomer at AstronomyCafe.net

Comments from Readers

NewDirection says - *I've felt that black hole. For me it is the gaping nothing that is where my dreams for a happy home and family were. It threatens to suck away my present joy. First, I started to hate the collapse dream, deny that I need or want it anymore. But now I know it is a space that can be filled, but maybe not the way I hoped.*

When you understand the star that collapsed making the black hole, you start to understand its properties and its gravity. Then you can keep the boundaries needed to prevent it from sucking you in.

There is a place where we merge with the divine and there we know that we are never alone and the warmth can fill us. Until we can stay there forever, we all face this existential crisis.

> **PCDee says** - *Your post reminds me of how I felt during the first year of my divorce. I can relate to your black hole analogy. You will find that you are your own constellation. Hang in there.*

Calm and Crazy
June 6, 2010
4 months, 15 days of freedom

The past few weeks with Will have gone smoothly. We have had some encouraging conversations considering what we're going through and how we're at odds over so many aspects of custody and finances. I suppose I don't know how at odds we are about the finances; we haven't moved out of the custody phase yet. He refuses to negotiate finances until I agree to his custody demands.

Whatever.

He took me to court over custody/visitation last week because "You refuse to force your attorney to respond to my consent order. When are you going to learn that your attorney works for you?"

That was his way of telling me that I was not doing this right. If I'd only tell my attorney to do it his way, we'd all be a lot happier. I didn't believe him. He likes to threaten and then not live up to his end of the deal. It works like this: First, I bow to custody, and then he rakes me over the coals financially. On the other hand, maybe he was looking out for my best interests (sarcasm).

My attorney advised that we attend financial mediation so he could understand how the financial consent order should look versus the thing he submitted to her last month. The mediation request *was* our response; but that wasn't good enough. So he demanded that visitation be changed, giving me every *other* weekend instead of every weekend.

Whatever.

He didn't get what he wanted. If I go by what Will told me on Friday, then I received one more night per month than the court guaranteed, and he receives one weekend a month. So then why did what he said tonight differ from what he said on Friday, and why did he get so angry when I asked for clarification?

Oh. Wait. I remember. I'm not supposed to question him, and I'm certainly not supposed to "always do this shit."

Despite the week's drama, Will and I held it together pretty well I thought. We are learning to co-parent more efficiently. I see that he is a better father now than he has been in the past. At least, that is what I can see. The boys smile when they see me, they smile when they see their dad. That is a very good thing.

Tomatoes for Lunch
June 8, 2010
4 months, 17 days of freedom

Today I'm eating a huge beefsteak tomato, grown locally and full of flavor. I thought about having a sandwich, but the bulk of the bread doesn't sound all that great. Sometimes, eating is a struggle. Still. But instead of stress causing me to forget to eat, I don't feel like eating. I can be STARVING and not want to eat. I kind of like the hungry feeling, but it does absolutely nothing for my mood.

But this tomato, red and cold, hits the spot. I'm glad I took the time to slice it.

I'm struggling with more than my eating habits this week. There is a change going on inside of me, and I can't quite put my finger on what it's all about. I question my habits, good and bad, past and present. I wonder which old habits I could fall back into as I create my life, and frankly, although possibly damaging, the old habits sound comforting.

Therefore, I struggle with *not* attaching myself to someone, *not* allowing my heart (or libido) to override my good sense. I miss having *someone* with me. Cats are nice, my boys are spectacular ... but I feel a void. I'm unaccustomed to being on my own, alone in this way. I know the loneliness will vanquish itself *in time*, but I don't know if I am patient enough, or good enough, to wait and grow.

When I think about finding someone to spend some time with, I wonder exactly what time I have to spend. I fear that time spent not working is wasted; I need the money work provides. I love my job refinishing furniture, but I knew when I took it that I would need something else to supplement the income.

Now I feel torn between web design and writing. Torn between sleeping and eating. Torn between dreaming and doing.

At least the tomato is delicious.

Secrets
June 9, 2010
4 months, 18 days of freedom

I was an open book when I began writing this blog. In part, I could be so open because I did not realize people other than my sister read it. I told *all*, and it felt wonderful to unload. Will desperately wanted me to shut up, to forget about it, to "stop telling lies." I could not stop telling my truth. Spilling those secrets was the best thing I ever did for myself because only by being open did I find all of you, and with you, I found the courage and power to move forward, to move away.

If I had not spilled my guts in this blog and met all of you, I never would have pressed charges against him on January 22. I would have left that night for sure; but I would have slunk back into my own home like a shamed puppy the next day. I did that before, but I could not ignore the abuse and violence again. I no longer felt ashamed of *myself* for his abusive actions.

Life here on the other side of abuse is frightening at times. Sometimes his words and behaviors still throw me for a loop, and I anxiously await the next time I must speak to him. Like always, days of calm precede the outbursts that Will orders me to consider *conversation*. And as usual, apologies will not follow the outbursts. Everything continues to be my fault in his eyes. I make him mad. I make him say the things he says and do the things he does.

I guess I have power over him, in his mind. Perhaps he thinks I feel entitled to *his* money and to get everything I want at *his* expense. Maybe he believes that I lie and manipulate my way through life, blaming him for my wrongs and taking all the credit for his success. I suppose he still considers me a cunt, to use his word.

But Will is not much of anything to me anymore. He isn't my world, he isn't my life and he isn't my other half. He is the father of my children. He is a volatile force to reckon with for sure, but because we spend so little time together now, I can better handle his eruptions. Despite the fact that I do feel anxious after an outburst, I also have a strong voice in my head that reminds me "This is the pattern. It has nothing to do with you, Kellie. Some things are his to own, whether he chooses to own them or not."

I have my own sanctuary, my house. I have my own money, my own job, my own financial plan. I have my own dreams and I am finding my place in the world. I have my own thoughts, and I can (usually) tell if my thoughts are benefitting me or hurting me. New to me are my very own secrets. I have some wonderful, heart-pounding secrets. I have secrets that shed light on my silence and I can't wait to tell them to you! But I must wait to share them.

Please don't mistake my silence for pain. Although there is still, at times, plenty of hurt, fear no longer fuels the hurt. For example, it hurts that the judge did not label me my boys' primary parent, but it is merely a flesh wound. That judge's decision injures my pride and nothing else. I tell myself that the custody situation is only temporary, but this could very well turn into the permanent custody arrangement. I could forever stay the secondary parent in the eyes of the law. Nevertheless, my boys will *never* see me as a secondary parent. I know that now, in my bones and throughout every cell in my body. I will never lose my children to their father. They will never choose one of us over the other.

Will cannot win, even if the law calls him the winner. Our boys are not a prize or a thing; our sons are feeling, thinking, loving beings who are wiser than even I gave them credit for being. They are their own people, their own men. Time will work its magic with them, too. Their broken hearts will heal, bit by bit, understanding by understanding. It probably will not happen as quickly or even how I hope, but it will happen. They will probably be angry at me, angry at dad, angry at everyone including themselves at some point. But after the anger, the healing begins.

Eventually, we will all heal. I dearly wished we would heal together, but that is not going to happen. Eventually, I will expose all my secrets. I am not worried. I am not ashamed. But I can't tell you all of them yet.

It is no secret that I am happy. I am truly, through and through, happy.

Comments from Readers

Maggie says - *My youngest talked to her college counselor a few weeks ago and disclosed to me that her counselor was angry on her behalf about how she was pulled between her two parents. I think the counselor is a clever, kind lady trying to help an unhappy young woman get her feelings out. But I felt so washed out and winded by that statement.*

I had begun to be a little bit more specific with my daughter about her father emotionally abusing her (and me) - and I suddenly I felt so guilty for putting my head above the parapet like that. However, I felt that my little one was leading me there as she is starting to notice things herself about him and his behavior. I felt it would be harder on her if I did not validate what she felt.

I so wanted to say, "I'm not the bad guy here." I had to know this quietly and get over it! She does seem a bit better now so it was worth it. As you say, they know things for themselves, and they ultimately make up their own minds.

Got a Raise
June 11, 2010
4 months, 20 days of freedom

A few days ago, my boss gave me a tape measure with my name written on it in permanent marker. I felt so darn happy - such a simple gift, yet it caused me so much joy! Go figure.

So anyway, today she gave me a raise! I was so surprised I jumped up and down and then realized I didn't have the appropriate bra on for heavy jumping and composed myself.

I don't make a lot of money, but when I'm careful, I'll make enough. I have some big dreams and hopes that need financing and *minimum wage plus a quarter per hour* isn't going to cut it. Nevertheless, I feel at home at this job. I love the people, I love the work.

In fact, I find woodworking to be very sensual. I absolutely turn myself on at work. I am wondering if it's the wood and the work, or if I'm just horny all the time! Oh well. I'll enjoy it while it lasts. But if I'm 95 years old and own my own woodworking or refinishing business, you'll know why.

Speaking of being, um, sensually minded, I am finding freedom in this area too. With Will, the sexual aspects of our relationship were stale. He is a very attractive guy, when we did have sex I could imagine better times. But now, it feels like someone tore off my blinders. I inhibited my sexuality to fit into the mold 18 years of marriage created. There was no fun, no joy... Sex's goal was to reach the end, the happy place, and the enjoyment of feeling along for the ride WITH him was lacking.

Not only his fault. It was both of our faults.

A while ago, running through my mind was the thought, "I wonder if sex would be better now, since we're separated...?" My therapist told me many people wonder how sex would be with their ex after divorce. She said that she would save me the trouble of finding out on my own: "It's *no* different." That's good to know. It saves me some grief.

One downside to being sensually oriented is that I'm single. That's a snag. If I had gone through this awakening *during the marriage*, I imagine Will and I could have pressed on. Maybe made another year of it. I'm glad that didn't happen on so many levels!

But hey, I get to work with wood all day. That's enough for now.

Some Guy off the Street
June 11, 2010
4 months, 20 days of freedom

As you may have gathered from my last post, I am entertaining the thought of having some wonderful sex in the future. While that is true, I can't seem to think about sex without also thinking about a *relationship*. Well, that is not entirely true. I very well can imagine the sex without a relationship, but I cannot imagine me having sex without also having it evolve into a relationship. Crap. That isn't entirely true either. Grabbing some guy off the street has crossed my mind.

I don't think grabbing someone up would work very well today. It may have worked when I was in high school, but today, not so much. I have a good reason for doubting it, too. The first weekend I was without my boys, a good friend took me out to a bar. (She's a brave woman!) We got completely wasted. God bless her dear husband who dropped us off and waited patiently until the wee morning hours to pick us up again.

I was not there to grab a guy off the street. I was there to drink. With my friend. And hopefully not cry. Which I didn't.

What I did experience were several conversations with several guys ranging in age from about 25 to 65. Some were creepy, some were soldiers and some were creepy soldiers. Anyhow, at one point a young soldier who hadn't found a woman his own age began talking to my friend and me. I asked how he felt about sex with strangers, and his answer was, "Well, I'd have to think about it. There are STDs and shit out there."

I wondered how long a young man would think about it today. Back in my day, the thought was probably about 15 seconds. But I digress.

His answer made me think about a hundred million diseases that are out there, and that if I did decide to have sex with some guy, then I couldn't trust a mere condom to protect me. I'd have to know him, know his history. I'd have to trust him (and the condom brand). And *trust* is a difficult feeling for me to conjure these days. Anyone I'm with, from here on out, will be someone I trust. Which takes *some guy off the street* out of the running.

On the other side of it is *the guy*. If I am looking for someone similar to me, then he's going to want to know my history, too.

He's going to want to be able to trust me. Because I do want to trust a man again in the future, then I have to make sure - completely positive - that I am being honest with any potential lover I meet. Or know. Or knew once upon a time. Or imagined and then discovered that he was real after rubbing a genie bottle.

And to be honest with *him*, I have to be honest with myself. That could very well prove to be the hardest thing to do. After all, I am getting to know myself over again. I am discovering how I've changed as well as how I've remained the same.

It's exciting, but it's also a tricky ride. Sometimes I don't know if *old Kellie* is at the wheel or if I am doing the driving. It's confusing. I don't want to default to *old Kellie's* thinking because it may not be *my* true thought. That girl *may* be long gone, but I don't think she's left the building. Some things I remember about my old self I would like to repeat. For example:

- I loved to lift weights. I loved to eat foods that allowed my muscles to show. I cheated on those diets back then but couldn't now because of slowing metabolism...but still. I liked that experience very much.
- I loved to draw and paint. I would love to do that again, but I wonder if writing best serves my creativity now.
- I loved sex. It was fun and adventurous, loving and crazy. I made mistakes with sex that I won't repeat, but I wouldn't take the experiences back for a million dollars. (Well, maybe I'd cash in on a couple.)
- I loved seeing people grow and become more of who they were. I loved it when my friends did something they thought they couldn't. I loved it when I reached a goal for myself.

- I loved being able to accept that people could freely move in and out of my life while leaving the door open for their return. Sometimes when they left they never came back, but sometimes the miracle was in their return.
- I loved being a free spirit. Things weren't always rosy; in fact, sometimes they were shitty. But my openness to life and its miraculous events created more goodness than I had imagined. Being free allowed the flow of life to continue.

And yes, back in the day I had no qualms with grabbing up some guy off the street. Now I do. So there are things *new Kellie is* not going to do:

- I used to hide my true feelings out of shame or because someone told me that I *shouldn't* feel that way. I feel the way I feel, dammit. After I express the feeling, it may change or evolve. Maybe it won't.
- I hate that I kept parts of myself secreted away because of fear. I do not want anyone in my life who judges me against him or herself. We are all different...we're all wonderful. Let me be wonderful too!
- I hate that I acted proud of some of my actions but secretly felt ashamed. I want to do things that make me proud of myself. This will require thinking before acting - a forming skill that I will develop more fully.
- I hate that I allowed someone else to absorb me. I want always to see the line of distinction between *you and me*. I want to choose what is good for *me* over what is good for *you* OR consciously choose what is better for you because that's what I want to do, not because you say it's the only way or promise me that my turn is only a little time away.

I am opening the flow once more. I closed myself off to it for long enough. I expect good things, and great things happen. Boy, some guy is going to be lucky to know me...in a few years.

Comments from Readers

Kelly says - *Today is the first day I have ever looked up anything remotely close to this subject. What scares me are all of the similarities I see when I started reading your posts. I have been married for 19 years, have two boys and my husband is very critical and controlling with us. The things you write are very close to my life. I hope that someday I have the courage to do what I need to do.*

> **Kellie Jo says** - *There is a better life for you, Kelly. No one can tell you what you should do - go or stay - but remember you always have the choice. My heart goes out to you 'cause living your life is harder than many people could imagine; whatever you decide, whenever you decide, I'm here and so are many other people who have been through or are going through the same hell.*

Luxury
June 15, 2010
4 months, 24 days of freedom

For the first time in a very long time, I'm dealing with a variety of emotions, bad and good (if I have to judge an emotion as bad or good...). In the last year(s?) of my marriage, I dealt with anger, betrayal, fear, bitterness, probably even hate. But now I find a whole world of emotion to experience that I didn't recognize, or had forgotten about or refused to feel.

I was talking to someone tonight and realized that *everything* is different now. The way I experience the world thrills me beyond reason. My microfiber chair is softer, my cat is crazier, food tastes better and music means more. Water is a need instead of a treat I may give myself if I pass a sink on the way to do something for someone else. Now I stop by the sink all the time and I love the sound of the water whooshing from the faucet, anticipating the non-taste of the cold, and quenching a deep thirst I hadn't paid attention to before.

The emotions swirling around my heart and mind excite me. Some I think I shouldn't feel, but I'm trying not to shut them off. Maybe letting them run their course, as I've allowed my anger and hate to do, will ease the intensity and mystery. Pretending not or trying not to feel something I feel is not a good thing - I know that now. It feels luxurious to be inundated with these new-found high-energy hopes (and doubts). I need it. I need this time.

Married to Will, I spent my days deciphering his emotions, his thoughts, his wants in order to avoid upsetting the balance. I didn't do it very well and beat myself up about it. I was missing my own life, my own internal workings. Outwardly focused, I forgot what it felt like to *feel* something that came from *me*.

Now I am trying very hard to stay inside my own body. I am refusing to guess what he meant by that, what she meant by that. I am trying to ask questions and accept the answer. I throw people off a little sometimes. They're not used to me asking them to clarify. I believe they appreciate it when they realize that I am truly curious, not wanting to judge their response. I've been lucky to be around people who are open to me.

Life is a luxury that I have not lived in a very long time. I'm changing that.

Comments from Readers

NewDirection says - *I couldn't relate more! Enjoy the ride. It is the journey of life and self-discovery. A journey we as women often feel too guilty to take. But once you explore the self, without fear, and allow you to flourish, you can experience more fulfilling love with another person!*

> ***Lisa says*** - *Love this post, Kellie! I've been traveling and just got to catch up;* Some Guy Off the Street *was exactly the way I feel, too. I'm doing things that I want to do, rather than what someone else wants to do. And I'm a better person for it.*

In the End
June 20, 2010
4 months, 29 days of freedom

This is a stream of consciousness writing I did on the beach some weeks back. Little punctuation, bits of clarity...I feel like sharing it with you.

> Sun Surf Freedom Coincidence and Lack. Suntans, sunburns and jumping in the waves, shaking Saltwater out of his hair. Sunshine and goodness, fisherman, vacancies. Maybe too windy. Waves drop into us as we struggle against their push. Wet and warm waves like the aftershocks of sex. The smile and sparkling eyes of a lover and the touch in intimate places feels like warm red wine not meant to be drunk but for pouring pouring pouring.
>
> Crafty and cunning is the body that longs to experience the carnal quickening of the heart, pulling hair to remind of vulnerability but not enough to threaten. I could but I won't. I trust but I watch, listen

and compare those words to the ones I've heard oft repeated in anger.

There is a difference and the difference may merely be time. Perhaps at once, time catches up to us like a freight train with no brakes, slamming into the soul. All at once, one day, one small thing is simply too much anymore to tolerate that one thing shines a bright light on the multitude of smaller harshness from the years and it is too much. Too much.

I fight back. I try to regain some knowledge of who I am and what I want. What I want. The red pouring wine. The small kisses. The shining light from his eyes as he looks at me instead of past me as if I don't exist. I miss the longing...but he cannot long for one accessible, easy. He longs for what he may not attain, not that for which he has conquered. And he conquered me. He took me. He swallowed me. And he was satiated.

I sat so long in his gut that his insides started to churn and struggle to digest me...but I wouldn't leave. And he hated me for it. Hated me. Hated him. I gave him all of me - All of me. And he hated me. I am sorry I surrendered to him and I am sorry I remember the harshness of him.

I wish I remembered what my light reflecting from his eyes felt like. What I looked like to him when I was still me. I want to see that light again. I doubt that he will be the one to see me...but perhaps someone else will.

I will see him, too. A man who is tall and thick, with laugh lines around his eyes and a leisurely pace when we're together. I'll drink him in like warm red wine and touch him along the lines most will never touch. I will see his light and soak it in, then release it back to him so I can delight in his presence instead of his shadow.

He will lift me, I will lift him. We will be as one but two distinct loving hearts. His arms will open to me a billion times, and a billion times I will rush to fill them. Strong but soft. Supporting but freeing. If I fly away, he will patiently wait and if he flies from me I will allow him freedom. Coming and going. Coming and going. Coming together in the end.

Searching
June 28, 2010
5 months, 6 days of freedom

One time an old friend said he pictured me as Peggy Hill and I about had a heart attack. Right there. On the spot. You can't forget someone comparing you to Peggy Hill. It ain't funny, y'all.

I felt like sending him a picture, but seeing that I was 200 pounds, I refrained thinking he would then picture me as Miss Piggy! Besides, it wasn't the physical aspects, I hope, but the simple fact that I now live in The South - that foreign, steamy, mystical place we Northern chicks sometimes think about, but don't want to live. Now that I live here, I find that most nights are not sultry, sit on the porch fanning and drinking tea kind of nights. They are merely frigging hot. I still feel out of place with the others who can point to their great-grandmother's house on that hill over there.

I don't transplant well, I suppose. Fourteen years of Southern living hasn't grown on me. If I were going to grow roots here, they would have sprouted by now.

I'm starting to see myself as a traveler. I'd like to visit foreign lands and stay for a while. I'd like to move to different areas of this country to see if I mesh with the natives a little better in the West, or the Southwest. Or maybe New England, although I have the feeling that like the far South, the extreme North may be foreign to me, too. I'll visit Alaska via cruise ship only - I hear it's breathtaking. Then, after the travelling, I'll pick a place, or maybe the last place I travel to will simply pick me and I'll stay because it gets me, through and through.

Part of me knows that this search for the perfect exterior place is a pipe dream. I don't believe I'll find that place until I know myself through and through AND am strong enough to not compromise what I want for myself for what someone else wants for me, or for what I want for them. The exterior world mirrors my soul; if I'm uncomfortable somewhere, it's because I do not know who I am there. It's because I'm looking for some external validation that I am okay, perfect the way I am.

I have to be very careful and remember to pay attention to my Self, my opinions, my wants and needs, before I go searching for somewhere (or someone) that *tells* me I'm okay. I want to know that I'm wonderful, beautiful, creative and strong deep inside, for me.

Comments from Readers

NewDirection says - *When you are happy within yourself, and learn to love you, your surroundings will be beautiful and your ability to love places and people will improve. If you know your value, you will learn to feel your worth. I believe when you see yourself with the love God has for you, you will know where you belong. Here's to your journey...*

I'm Not That Person...Yet
July 2, 2010
5 months, 10 days of freedom

The past month whirled around me, through me, like a red wine hurricane. I feel alive and strong, but spinning uncontrollably in my heart are questions and wishes that I'm not ready to answer or fulfill. I feel like I'm in danger of losing my vision because time isn't pacing itself with my desires - what I want to become, who I want to be is not yet centered inside of me. The person I want to be is still ahead of me on the timeline. Unfortunately, the timeline forces me to live in the present.

I am grateful beyond words that the only voice in my head is my own. After so many years of sharing space with Will's voice, I had hoped hearing only my own would end the confusion and doubt. Living free and dis-anchored from Will's reality set loose a storm of giddy emotions, loving dreams and happy thoughts within me. I've loved the time I've spent in the whirl, loved the people I've met, loved the feelings of re-connectedness to life itself. But, as all storms, it passes leaving me to deal with the thoughts and decisions I made in the spin cycle.

Despite the whirlwind of emotion, underlying it on the earthy path of my soul, I knew I was in danger of flying away into a different kind of false world. If I weren't careful, I could easily exchange Will's version of reality for another unreal reality, a possibly more dangerous one made up of my own delusion and wish-craft. A conversation with the powers-that-be warned me of the magical world of delusion and falsehood and then my flesh and bone therapist said, "It isn't *real*, Kellie. You're not yet separate from Will, from that life. You need more time."

Of course, my ego denied the gods and the therapist outright. This delusion was *fun*, it was *exciting* and it was *working*! ... Dammit. And people around me were in danger of the delusion hurting them; I was in danger of hurting, too. My boundaries blurred, my dreams for myself pushed aside, I realize I am spending too much time in the whirlwind and not enough time feeling my feet on the ground.

As I left my therapists office, I turned and asked, "How long should this last? Do I have at least another month?" I meant the storm of good-emotion fuel, the feeling of being high on living.

She said, "As long as it needs to. There's no set time." Although I told myself with forced smile that I could ride for at least another six months, inside of me, the storm began to quiet.

I denied the silencing of the storm. I forged ahead, made an emotional decision that felt good in order to re-ignite the dramatic whirl. But what I found was the drama wasn't worth the price I asked another person to pay. I know the storm is ending, and that the person I am right now is not the person I'm destined to become. I'm not the person I want to be...yet.

So now, I stand on a muddied path, feeling alive and humbled, letting the greenish overcast that fills the atmosphere after a storm flow through me. The color green heals, so I know that the coming down from the high is also part of my destiny. Although I'm saddened to know the storm has passed, it also feels good to know that I've weathered it. I haven't blown so far from my path that it is unrecognizable. My feet, firmly planted in a half-inch of mud, feels much better from the waist-deep shit I was entrenched in months ago. This mud will dry, the sky will turn blue, the birds will sing and life is good.

Life is different, again, but washed clean and humbly refreshed.

Comments from Readers

PrincessLuceval says - *Kellie, I love your term wish-craft. It is so, so true. And remember, mud is much more fertile ground for growing things than pure shit is. Bloom and grow!*

> **NewDirection says** - *In the space between who you are and who you are destined to be, I hope you find the arms of the powerful and loving God, the one who will be your husband and lover, who will show you your worth and ecstasy beyond dreams and visions. The one who will fill you with love and purpose and set your path straight to the place and person you were always meant to be...in time. You are part of a sublime romance, a divinely given love relationship which asks nothing in return but your heart. You WILL find your way. Remain playfully open to what comes next.*

Kellie Jo says - *Wish-craft is what Tabitha learned to do first as a baby witch on the old sitcom* Bewitched. *I didn't come up with it on my own - it's been around, but it fits.*

> **Erin says** - *Damn your therapist. How dare she take that from you? It's like being told there is no Santa. Who would do that? Santa Claus exists inside every one of us - and you had a blissful thing going on inside of you. You are living and doing in a way that gives you what you haven't had for many, many years. You deserve that feeling. How dare anybody give you the notion that it isn't real?*
>
> *Reality is what you make it. Each person's reality is different from another's. That is what makes us unique. That is what makes us each see the same situation in different ways. I would much rather she said, "Chances are, after you spend much needed time with yourself, your perceptions might*

change a little bit. But for now, take the ride you are on; because it is right where you need to be."

Who out there wouldn't want to live with these feelings on a daily basis: "giddy emotions, loving dreams and happy thoughts within me"? We all should be so lucky! Who cares on what those emotions are based? Who are you hurting? You are re-blossoming into a person you want to become. Like a flower through the season of warmth, you start out fresh, vibrant and green. Through the heat of summer, you must grow your roots deeper to endure the scorch of the heat and little rain. However, you remain beautiful, vibrant, and full of life ... but more stable.

No need to read into this any more than what it is. Winter doesn't have to come. But, we all experience those times when we naturally go into ourselves a little bit so we can come out more alive after the last snow. It is not a death of the flower (you), it is a time of peace to re-gather and renew. Remember though, winter comes at many different times throughout the world. There is not a set day for it. It happens when the time is right. Don't allow your therapist to force that time on you now. You have to allow your season to come when it is ready. Anything else is unnatural.

With all of this said, if your time has come to move onto deeper roots, so be it. I hope the timing is your own choice; and not a thought that somebody else planted in your mind.

Kellie Jo says - There is no cause for alarm. I would have dismissed her comment as you did if I hadn't had the same message from the higher power and felt a waning of the emotions already. Her comment simply validated externally what was already going on inside. Our lack of phone calls the past two weeks have eroded your up to the minute status, and that you need to call me so I can fill you in!

Verbal Abuse Revisited
July 3, 2010
5 months, 11 days of freedom

Lately I've not preached the gospel of what verbal abuse *is* or how it is affecting me because I'm in a new phase - the phase that exists after removing the prime abuser from the majority of life. I am reveling in the freedom, but that doesn't mean that all of *you* are reveling with me! So I'd like to share some links about abuse and where you can find help and relief.

Check online for inexpensive alternatives to traditional therapy for abuse victims. Alternative therapies are not insurance based, meaning that your abuser will not receive notice of your choice to seek therapy from any insurance approval letters that may come to your house. I've helped several women via email through free counseling sessions, too. Although some women think they're totally screwed up after leaving, only one or two encouraging conversations now and again helps immensely. We aren't as screwed up as we think we are - but the doubt and confusion relating to the abuse can sometimes make it feel that way.

Patricia Evans, author of books such as *The Verbally Abusive Man: Can He Change?*, is online and I highly recommend becoming a member of her message boards. Yes, you must call the toll free number to join the board, but she does this to ensure only abuse victims have access to this resource. No abuse perpetrators allowed. When I called, I spoke to Patricia directly, and had access to the boards within minutes.

Please call the National Domestic Violence Hotline at 800-799-7233 even if you don't know what you're going to say, and even if you haven't experienced the physically violent side of domestic violence. Domestic violence includes mental, emotional, verbal, financial, and all other sorts of abuse. If your abuser has not bloodied your lip or blackened your eye *yet*, do not mistake his past inaction for eternal restraint.

The more you know, the more powerful you become. The more power you have within yourself, the sooner you can make changes to stop the cycle of abuse. You do not have to leave your abuser right now or ever, you can stay. That is a valid choice.

I chose to stay until I'd reached a point of power within myself that did not allow me to stay any longer. But before that point, I had begun reacting differently to the abuse. Back then, there was no way to know if my ex-husband would change or not, but I hoped he would.

Hope is not a solution. It's a distraction. Stop hoping and start educating yourself.

Dear Erin
July 4, 2010
5 months, 12 days of freedom

My sister, Erin, supports me consistently and constantly. She loves me regardless of my decisions, actions and quirks. She knows my dark side and thinks it's valuable. I couldn't love her more, yet every day, I do love her more. Before I recognized the abuse in my life, she was largely quiet about it for fear of her words pushing me away from her. She knew, instinctively, that Will (probably subconsciously) wanted everyone who loved me far, far away - or at least that's how it appeared. Still, she would cry with me when I hurt in large part because there were things she wanted to say but held them inside.

One time, after realizing the abuse for myself, I asked her why she didn't *tell* me he abused me, and she said, "Would you have believed me if I had?" Of course, the answer was "No." I'll never ask that question again of her or anyone else who loves me. It's not up to them to tell us what is going on, is it? It's something we have to realize inside of ourselves. Erin is a very wise woman.

Erin wants us all to live in our own light, within our own power augmented by All (God, Goddess, Angels, Spirit or The Powers that Be). Here is an email she sent me on Facebook two days ago. She said I could share it, and I want to because you need to know that there are people in the world like her who support you, who love you, who cannot wait to help you. You may not see them until you take off the blinders abuse forced over your eyes.

Here is her email:

> I think you are overlooking something you don't want to look at again ... yet. You are a survivor. You pushed your way through a horrid time in your life when you was married, and then again pushed your way through the time of uncertainty after you left.
>
> Other women need to know they can do this. They need to know that after they leave their abusive marriages, they will come out better on the other end. I think you are not ready for it yet. You are not ready to re-visit the pain of it or face the women who are still enduring it because you *need* to keep pushing through this segment in your life.
>
> So, don't question what you should be doing to earn an income. You love your life where you are right now; and I think that is exactly where you need to be. The time will reveal itself to you when it is time to step back into the world that brought you to where

you are now... The only difference is that you will already be on the other side. Completely.

Keep doing what you are doing. You haven't been this happy, or this authentic in a long time. Own it. Live it. You will know when the time is right.

I love you, and I am so proud of you Kellie!

Hold and Release
July 5, 2010
5 months, 13 days of freedom

There must be something in the air. My mood is so serious, like a rain-filled cloud threatening to rain on my parade. Although I feel in my gut that I'm moving in the right direction, I'm getting stronger, finding out who I am and what I like (and don't), ... there's something heavily sad about this weekend.

Will and I have talked several times, amicably enough, in the past weeks. But Saturday, I found myself embroiled in a disagreement with Will, told to quit popping off at the mouth and scolded about my soap opera drama. I didn't see it that way. Said to stop telling me what I was doing and what my intentions were. He got madder. We hung up the phone. It didn't last long.

Somewhere in there, in response to him telling me he didn't trust me and that he thought I was up to no good and being dishonest, I said, "You've always thought that of me." He replied that no, he hadn't always thought it, that it's a recent thing. He got angry that I had said it, told me that he was sorry he'd tried to talk to me. I thought to myself that he wasn't talking to me, but at me.

When we hung up, I tried to shrug it off as if his words didn't bother me. They did. But what truly bothers me now is what I said: *You've always thought that of me.* Shrinks say not to use words like *always* or *never* in conversations because they are accusing words. But I used one, he felt defensive, and the rest is history. Now, writing this, I feel torn between two takes on the topic that I could write today. The first one is that it would be nice if he had only said, "I don't think it's fair to say always," and I could have corrected myself or apologized for inflammatory language.

But (and here's the second path), *I was right*. I didn't say it to accuse him of something, or "pop off" or "start some drama." I said it because it was what I was thinking, and the more I think about it, I know I was right. Although I do wish I hadn't used the word because I want to learn better ways of expressing myself that don't ignite someone's defenses, there are several reasons why *always* was the right word to describe what I felt:

- In the beginning, he called me whore often. He didn't trust me to be faithful to him.
- When I did tell him about the kiss one of his friends gave me, he told me that I was mistaken, that his friends would never betray him. Sometimes he would come home and investigate the house. He'd look for something out of place, or maybe something to give away what I was doing with my time when he was at work. Sometimes he acted as if he hit the jackpot by catching me in some imagined lie so he could go off on me. This wasn't usually about other men; it was about how I spent my time. There were times when no explanation would satisfy him. He didn't trust me to tell him the truth.
- Although the finances fell to me to handle, he constantly insinuated of my mishandling them and became angry over what I'd spent without bothering to find out what our expenses actually were. He didn't trust me with *his* money.

- When our children misbehaved, or behaved in a way he considered wrong for men to act, he claimed that it was my influence causing their *dysfunction*. If I'd only spanked them more, if I weren't so soft on them, if only I'd act more like him when he was away on deployment, they'd know better. He didn't trust me with his children.

Integrity, sex, money, children... what else was there to our marriage? I feel that I could do nothing to gain his trust in any of those areas. Everyone has weaknesses, everyone makes mistakes and I am no saint. But for crying out loud, how could I have fought this and won in any way? How do you successfully fight a fairy tale?

If he does not have trust inside of him, then how could I earn his trust? I wonder if he had any to give (to me, at least). When I would bring these things up to him, he would answer with, "I married you, didn't I?" or "I must trust you, I have to leave you with the boys when I deploy," or "You're the one who handles the money, aren't you? You could really screw me if you wanted to!" All true statements, but never truly honest.

Sigh.

But there is a silver lining to the storm cloud. It happened today. Will told me that he thinks our relationship should be only business. He wants to pull away from me. He said that he sees I'm moving on, but he's still stuck in the anger and hurt. He wants to detach, and he set clear boundaries. I listened to him without saying much at all. A big piece of me is so freaking proud of him! A big piece of me wanted to tell him that he was on the right track, that detaching from me was the right thing to do in order to find peace and health and happiness.

Yet a small piece of me is sad. The little wife inside of me wanted to hug him and tell him that it would all be all right. That I appreciate his vulnerability and that his decision is a wise one. I cried (after he left) because he is detaching from me.

You see, when I started this blog, I thought Will and I would be married forever. I thought we would have our ups and downs but solve the downs and be happy. I thought when he saw what effect his words and actions had on me that he would change them because he loved me. I thought we would heal together and never torn apart.

Now he and I are healing on our own. We will not be together when we're happy next. We will not be married forever having overcome the trials of our own humanity. We'll never sit on the porch together, rocking, gray hair blowing in the breeze. I must detach from that dream, and saying goodbye to it hurts more than any dream I've ever held and released before.

Comments from Readers

Erin says - *I wish you didn't hurt so badly about this. I wish I could say something that would help you. I wish you didn't have to feel your way through this one to come out on the other side. If there is one good thing - it's that you have done it many times before. You have come so far and this is but a hiccup. You will get over this too. I love you Kellie Jo!*

> **Kellie says -** *I am married to an abuser and have been for over 13 years. In the past two years, it has escalated to extreme verbal abuse, and he gives no thought to putting the children or me in harm's way.*
>
> *He forces me to do things that are immoral and illegal for the sake of supporting him in his business. I now visit a therapist for the first time ever. I started therapy about a*

month ago. I would walk out, but I am staying because of the thoughts you have at the end of this post. Aren't we supposed to grow old together, and enjoy that we made it through the tough times?

I cannot bear to think of growing old without him, but I'm so tired of the abuse! My thoughts go between running away and keeping the peace hour by hour. I'm terrified of what is to come. Anyway, thank you, Kellie Jo, for your blog. It has helped me realize I'm not the only one.

DreamScapes
August 1, 2010
6 months, 10 days of freedom

The dream hurt. I was at Will's house in my son's room. Beautifully decorated, I could see that he had all the things I ever wanted to give him. Professionally painted walls and trim, decorator-type bedspread and pillows, matching bedset, plush carpet - it was an oasis of his personality, soft inviting comfortable. Will provided it for him, not me. I stood there with a notebook in my hand, ready to write the emotions, willing to write the story, but lost for the words required to express the sense of utter failure I felt deep within my gut.

I pulled a book off his shelf, overladen with reading material, and opened it. In the margins were pictures of military vehicles, land and air, labeled neatly with a blurb about each one in tiny print. I felt like my tears should be wetting the pages, but the tears didn't come until I woke.

Helplessness. Defeat. Failure. Doubt. Fear. Fortunately, I was able to share the dream, and as I listened to myself talk I realized that things and appearances lie.

I know that one of my greatest faults is in thinking that I can buy my boys something to make up for the pain I imagine they feel. I was able to do it all the time when I was married to Will. Most of my married life, I didn't know what pain I was trying to make up for by purchasing the latest game console or pair of shoes. Now, in hindsight, I realize I tried to make up for the deficit I perceived in myself. Yes, I knew my boys were in pain, but they maybe didn't know it. They knew one thing all their lives ... the way things were ... they were young and didn't consider that other people may live differently. They didn't know we emotionally deprived them.

I subconsciously knew it before the word abuse entered my mind, but I consciously came to terms with it after discovering the truth. I knew their lives were lacking a mother who could give her all to them. I felt deprived of love and acceptance and projected those feelings onto them. I thought that I couldn't fully love them because the one man in the world who I wanted to love me could not. There was something wrong with me, and if purchasing them the latest toy could delay them finding out that I was a fraud, then I was willing to buy the toy. Now I cannot play anymore...I must be real. I must be myself because I have no green paper-bill Band-Aid to fill any void. Having no money literally strips me of my coping mechanism, and my guilt must be obvious to my boys. I am what I am, and I fear that who I am isn't enough.

In the dream, faced with the room Will decorated and the toys he bought for them, I came face to face with the realization that it is time to put up or shut up. No longer can I compare what I do as a mother to what he does as a father. No longer can I make up for any perceived deficits in either Will's or my character by changing who I am or what I do to mend their possibly aching heart. I cannot be the malleable wood-filler that magically fills the gaps in my boys' broken hearts.

My perception of what may go on behind their dad's closed doors haunts me. I truly hope he is the father he projects himself to be to the outside world, and the outside world now includes me. I see him nagging about homework and chores, monitoring the boys' friends, taking them to doctor appointments, and sharing horseplay and jokes with them. I see him being the father I knew he could be, and I hope I am right because I want that for Marc and Eddie. But I fear that my perception is limited. I fear that they are now experiencing what I experienced with their father, and honestly, I feel torn about it.

On the one hand, I don't want them to go through the painful voyage of realization I experienced. I want to cocoon them, protect them from finding out the truth I discovered. I pray that I am truly the only person in the world whom Will desires to be exactly like him, that I am the only person in the world expected to live on a pedestal and to sustain punishment when I fall off it.

On the other hand, I want them to see the games Will plays and the subconscious lies I feel Will tells himself. I feel that if the boys could see the manipulation and control, then they could learn to detach themselves from it. Never in a million years would I want them *not to love* their father, and I know they *could never* stop loving him. I don't want them to hate him or to avoid time with him. But I want them to be able to protect themselves.

I want them to be able to say to themselves and believe in their heart that there is nothing wrong with them, despite the tornado tearing through their heart and mind most likely created by Will's inability to allow individualism on any count. In hindsight, when I wasn't mirroring Will, then I was wrong. And I have a strong suspicion that the boys are experiencing that same tornado without the inadequate storm shelter I tried to provide. I want them to love both Will and me without limitation. I want them to be able to see each of us for all of our goodness and all of our flaws, and then choose what they want to carry with them into their own lives.

I don't want them to make subconscious choices; I want them to make conscious choices. And yet I have no control over their choices. I cannot tell them what I know, I cannot share with them the strategies they can use to protect themselves and I cannot say or do anything to help them without sounding as if I hate their father or want them to hate Will. Or at least, I haven't figured out how to do that yet. I'll search my dream for an answer.

But I already know it. I must continue to detach from Will. I must continue to accept the love and protection of the angels (living and ethereal) in my life. I must continue to shed my fears, to discover who I am, and to love my boys unconditionally even when it hurts so deep inside that I will explode into pieces.

I must rip off the Band-Aids, even when the sticky parts pull my flesh from bone.

In Isolation
September 12, 2010
7 months, 21 days of freedom

During my marriage, I lived in isolation. I knew people outside of my home and sometimes shared specific experiences concerning my ex-husband with them. But somehow, I managed to keep most of the pain and embarrassment concerning my family's truths buried deep inside. I buried them so deeply that I was able to keep them secret even from me. I could acknowledge and even vent about single incident, say an argument or behavior that annoyed or hurt me. I spread my venting comments around throughout the people I knew so none of them knew the entire truth at one time. No one had enough information to say, "Hey,

Kellie, Will's behavior sounds abusive!"

That is, until I began writing this blog. Before this blog, I lived in isolation. At that point, you readers knew more about my life than the people who saw me every day or week or month. When you validated my experience and called abuse *abuse*, I started confiding completely in some of the people I know here in town. For your anonymous support, I am eternally grateful.

From my abusive experience, I learned what it feels to be alone, separate from reality. I feel isolated again - secretive, hurting, and ashamed.

The difference is that I feel I cannot share all of my emotions and thoughts with you, my anonymous friends, because of the new and very real people now in my life. Before, during my marriage, there was no one who could hurt any more or less by the personal experiences I described. I now feel connected with people who care about me, wonder about me and maybe look for themselves in my posts. Maybe they wonder if I am going to mention them directly or indirectly, wonder if the pseudonym they see is their name in disguise.

I've been silent, for the most part, since realizing this. I don't want to hurt anyone by sharing what I've experienced the past few months with them, and because they're now a part of my life, the bits and pieces of my old marriage/current separation have merged into this life I now share with the new people I know. It's quite the conundrum...how can I be honest and open with all of you readers while allowing the friends I see every day to retain their anonymity, their privacy? How do I respect, openly and honestly, my own experience without polluting theirs?

I am going to try to update you on what's going on in my life while respecting the *all* of you and my own emotional integrity. Wish me luck. I do not wish to isolate myself anymore.

Comments from Readers

Rebecca says - Hi Kellie, I can SO relate to everything you're saying! There are minor differences in our stories (my ex and I do not have children together - he is my daughter's stepfather and my daughter is now an adult; he had already left the Army when we met) but for the most part are very similar.

I don't know if you will ever be successful in separating the old from the new. A very wise person once told me that disengaging from people such as our exes is like removing yourself from a very large piece of flypaper. You get unstuck in one place only to get stuck in another. Naturally, the drama-of-the-day is that your ex-husband effects the people around you to some degree.

In my particular situation, I separated almost a year ago, and the divorce is final. You would think I'd have my peace and quiet at this point, right? Not quite. His girlfriend of two years is also a narcissist. She chose to begin harassing me at 2 AM about a month ago. I had a Cease and Desist issued against her. This past week, he started texting as if like nothing happened asking for my help with his personal business (I'm ignoring the texts). HUGE piece of flypaper...Your blogs and posts help a lot. Any techniques I find that work I'll be happy to share.

> **Jim says** - Hello Kellie, like you I am discovering and exploring what it means to be in an emotionally destructive and abusive relationship. I am 50, married for 16 years and have two daughters, ages 12 and 14. My spouse's denial of my feelings and needs, her blaming me for everything that

is wrong in the marriage, her need to dominate and control every decision in the household, her refusal to participate in counseling to help change and her belief that it is me who is defective and must change now sadden and annoy me.

It took me years of feeling depressed and empty to begin to recognize that maybe my marriage was destructive to my emotional health. My daughters observe this dynamic and lost respect for my authority over the years. At times, I feel like an outsider in my own home and I think my spouse likes it that way. The difference between your story and mine is that I am the husband, but I can so much relate to what you describe and what you are going through.

At times, her temper is so severe I think she is on the verge of stepping toward me to hit me. Lately, through counseling, I have begun to push back and to try to force her to see that she refuses to take any responsibility for our crumbling union; she always says it's all my fault. Quick to anger and capable of leveling awful, cruel and personal attacks, often based on things she found out while searching my briefcase, my cell phone, our phone records, spying and snooping through my personal things, I have had to tell her to calm down. I am not having an affair, have not hidden money or done nothing wrong, but I do read articles on abusive marriages and keep a journal of my thoughts. I have to keep these papers at the office because she regularly searches through my things and springs her discovery on me during heated arguments. I am heartbroken and afraid of leaving and what will happen with my daughters. She says that they will not want to see me after I leave.

I admire the courage you exercised to improve your life and leave an abusive marriage. I am trying to get to the root of why I made the choices and I did. I want to own the experience so I can grow in the future. I want a partner who can love and respect me and to feel deserving of the same.

Thank you for sharing you fears, hopes, dreams and isolation.

Lisa says - *Happy to know that you're okay, Kellie. It's hard to share the feelings - mine were humiliation mostly - and that does keep you from being open and honest in new relationships with people. Hang in there, girl. This new life is going to be a good one!*

Esme says - *I guess real people who you can touch and hold and share all the delicious (and confusing) eye contact and non-verbal stuff with have to be priority don't they?*

Carolyn says - *I understand the feelings of isolation. I rarely shared my feelings with others either. I have one girlfriend that I open up to, but I am usually mute about my abuse. Mainly because I feel people do not want to hear it, they think, "If it's so bad why don't you leave?" I worry they will label me as a whiner. We all know it is not that easy to leave, or I would have, long ago.*

My husband is now very ill, and later today we might hear that he has terminal kidney cancer. I don't know how to deal with this emotionally because for so many years I suffered under his caustic tongue. Now, to think he may die and I will be alone is rather terrifying. When I look back, I can't remember any good or super times we had together because there was always arguing or his abusive comments at every turn, yet I still fear being without him. How will I ever heal and be normal once he is gone? I have never been on my own.

Fairy Tale
September 18, 2010
7 months, 27 days of freedom

Once upon a time, I lived in a world of disapproval and fear. I listened to a man who demanded I make him happy, then grew angrier when I could not. I thought something was wrong with me, so I sought to change who I was to become more pleasing to that man. But as I changed my outward self, my inner self grew angry.

I began to act out in subtle ways (like not packing his lunch as he liked - on purpose). And later, I heard my angry self yelling and screaming. One time I told that man to suck my balls. I called him a prick and raged at him. And he returned the behavior three-fold, desperately trying to re-create the princess he thought I was by intimidating the hate-filled troll, forcing her to disappear.

I didn't know *who* I was. Was I hateful or loving? Was I a princess or a troll? What exactly did I want to be? I clung to his impressions of me, his analyses of why I did what I did. I listened as he told me I hated men, I was manipulative and I was always looking for a fight. I sought to change those things about myself not realizing that he described himself, not me.

In me, he had once seen a fairy-tale princess and thought that living in a tower, isolated from the world except for him, was what I wanted. He put me on a pedestal with a tiny pinpoint place to stand. Every time I lost my balance, he became upset - his princess should know how to balance on that pedestal and never lose her footing. He saw me as weak and fragile, unable to live up to even the basest standards of the cruel world he held in his mind, and he tried to be my knight in shining armor, my only connection to the outside world of which, he imagined, I had no understanding. He tried to protect me from the world. And then he tried to protect me from myself. He tried to help in the only way he knew - by forcing me to be like him, or at least like the fairy-tale princess he imagined me to be.

And I wanted him to save me from the hate-filled troll I imagined myself to be. But no one can save me from myself. And although *myself* was horrid, it was horrid because I denied my true self. My true self fought to reclaim its place, its rightful place, by creating such an ill environment it forced me to acknowledge its presence.

But when I realized I was not hate-filled because that was *who I was* but because I was *fighting for my life*, it was the beginning of The End.

My Real World
October 5, 2010
8 months, 13 days of freedom

When I left my husband, I had no idea of the purity of life that would engulf me in these following months. I met people who said what they meant. I met people who could be upset without letting their tempers spill over into conversation with me, toward me. I met people who don't have to make someone else feel small in order to feel better about themselves. I learned that saying what I meant and meaning what I say has value.

Most people I've met respect me for being honest, whereas the man I once loved could never believe a word I said. I told myself that it was okay to believe someone when they shared a thought and to take them at face value. I learned that it is okay to trust others, that not everyone in the world will take advantage (of what he called) my inability to understand the real world. In short, many people remind me daily that it is okay to be genuine, trusting, open, honest and kind.

Yes, there are people in the world who will try to take advantage of those qualities, I suppose. I haven't met them yet. But when I do, I think there will be an aura about them, a familiar feeling will come over me and I will recognize them before it's too late. I trust that my experiences in life so far will alert me to those I must beware of before opening myself up too far. The world I find myself living in is more trustworthy than the marital relationship I am leaving behind. He was my world. He was my life. I willingly gave every part of myself to him. But I feel his view of the real world - harsh, uncaring, unjust and stereotyped - carried over into his view of me. I feel that the real world he holds in his mind destroyed us.

But it won't destroy me. I don't live in his world any longer.

Leaving But Not Free
October 6, 2010
8 months, 14 days of freedom

He and I have children together. I share a connection to him for the rest of my life, through them. Although our vow to *love, honor and cherish* fell by the wayside, *for better or worse, 'til death do we part* holds strong. I can't take back some promises.

I wish I could say I was all right with that. A part of me would like nothing better than to never ever have to see his face or hear his voice again; the other part of me knows that is impossible. By court order, we are to discuss visitation via email or text. But what about the rest of it? What about when I have to drop off the kids and he comes to the car to talk to me? What about when we're face to face and he's saved every ounce of information about our children to pass on to me at that point, verbally? How can I be pleasant to him in front of our children if I don't speak to him?

I've told him to *put that in an email* and he tells me that he's on his computer all day and doesn't have the desire to waste his time hunt and pecking emails. He says my texts are taking up so much space on his phone that he can't receive anymore and his attorney said that he can't delete them until our "bullshit drama" is over. I think he doesn't want to write because he wants to talk, face to face, and work his magic via word twists and blaming ... but who am I to assume to know what's in his head?

The other night, he sarcastically said, "Way to go, Mom!" and gave me two thumbs up because he thinks he's found out something about our son's vision that I never took the time to look into. He wants me to believe that the efforts I've made with doctors to diagnose and protect our son's vision were half-hearted (at best). He wants to go to court and prove that, on his watch, the boys are better off than they've been under mine.

My only question was "Where the hell were *you* all the time we were married?"

To which he answered, predictably, "At work! Doing my *job*!"

He doesn't seem to understand that he could have been this involved with our sons' health and welfare from the beginning. He could have taken the time at any point in their lives to do all that he's trying to make up for now. Instead, he wants to twist his frustration with how he's squandered his time with his boys into belittling me, because blaming me for how I've done MY job as a mother is far better than accepting that he hasn't been doing his.

I am a wonderful mother. I have my shortcomings as all people do, but I've raised those boys with little more than financial support despite being married to their father. He spent the past years telling me that I was twisting their minds, making them lesser men instead of taking the time to teach them his views. He's taken every opportunity to try to make me doubt my ability to parent properly, all the while seeming to undermine and poo-poo the efforts I've made. Nevertheless, when I see my boys for who they are in their hearts and minds, I see two young men who are strong, capable, smart and willing to make decisions about their own lives. I am comfortable with the people they are and I know I am raising them well.

I admire them for the way they seem to be handling their parent's divorce and how they've bounced back from living in a house where their parents fought too much and deprived them of peace and comforts of a real home. My ex-husband and I created a house full of tension and demons. Now the boys may have two homes, but at least those homes are without the anger and violence emitted by the parents who were supposed to protect them from such things.

I know my home is peaceful. I hope I am setting a positive example. I hope my boys can see the wings of freedom sprouting from my shoulder blades. I am striving to do what's right for me, and hoping that doing so spills over to them. They're capable of seeing for themselves, when they're ready, the rest of the story. The rest of my story is yet to play out. I still have four years in which a judge holds levy over who is the more capable parent. Behind the scenes, I still must practice self-control and step outside of myself to witness the twists and turns of his mindful abuses instead of feeling them as if they were true. It is difficult. Sometimes I want to revert to the old ways and scream at him "That isn't true!" But it's not worth it. I know it isn't true, and I'm learning to detach myself from his sabotage.

I'm leaving, but I'm not yet free.

Bouncy Ball
November 23, 2010
10 months, 1 day of freedom

Once upon a time, there was a very lonely woman. She had a husband, two beautiful children and friends to keep her company. She wasn't lonely because she was alone. She was lonely because a clear bouncy ball enclosed her and separated her from the world. She couldn't hug anyone. She couldn't nurture anyone. She couldn't do many things from her enclosure except complete her chores and watch the events that happened around her.

Over time, even her children knew she was of no help to them. She couldn't kiss their boo-boos, and she couldn't tuck them in at night. Their world became a lonely place too.

Of course, she was of no real use to her husband either. Their relationship suffered. There was no romance, no light touches to reassure one another. He began to see her as only the bouncy ball. What good was a bouncy ball to him?

The woman became sad. The children became lonelier, and the man pretended she wasn't inside the bouncy ball. In fact, he pretended the bouncy ball was an inconvenient object left out in the open. When he walked through the home she had made, he kicked the bouncy ball out of the way like a child's toy he had outgrown. He pretended not to see her cry. He pretended her voice could not penetrate the plastic walls of the bouncy ball.

"He's right," she thought. "I am useless to everyone; what good could I possibly be to him, my children or my friends? What use is a crying lonely woman? What use is a bouncy ball to anyone?"

Ignored by her husband except for the frequent naughty word that came along with a dismissive kick, her children began to question why she was there, too. Her children looked elsewhere for nurturing. Her friends tired of hearing only her tears. The woman found it very difficult to think of herself as anything but a ball.

One morning when her husband kicked the ball away from his path on his way to work, the woman simply sat down. She didn't look at anything, she didn't think of anything. She only sat there.

That afternoon, her husband kicked the ball out of his path upon his return from work. The woman bounced around in the ball, but it didn't hurt. She discovered that by hugging her knees, she could easily tuck in her head when he kicked her about, and it didn't hurt anymore.

She spent days marveling at how her family's attitude improved when she sat quietly in the ball, thinking nothing. She watched her husband horseplay with her children. She watched the children go to school and come home in the evening. She watched everyone smiling and watching movies after dinner. She watched them enjoy themselves, keeping her silence.

Of course, in order for her family to function this way, she found a way to do their laundry. She cooked their dinners. She cleaned up after them. She went to market to supply their home with the things that made them happy. She didn't know where the energy or the means came from to complete these tasks, but when she was alone during the day, she got them done. But when her chores were complete, she'd sit in the ball quietly because that was the only way to remain unhurt.

Thinking nothing. Doing nothing. Feeling nothing. Being nothing.

One night, her bouncy ball popped. She couldn't find the hole. The plastic slowly lost its air. It shriveled and shrank. Each breath inhaled pulled the plastic tighter around her face. She couldn't breathe anymore. That evening, the husband ranted about the unrecognizable mess someone left on the floor. He put the old toy into the garbage for the trash men to carry away.

The next morning, the children had no socks for school. The husband loudly complained to someone who wasn't there to hear. The second morning, there was no breakfast. That night there was no dinner. One of the children asked the husband why there was nothing to wear or to eat.

The husband said, "Your mother must have ran off in that fine bouncy ball I gave her. She never appreciated anything."

Comments from Readers

NewDirection says - *I like your story. A woman is an abusive and neglectful marriage often starts free and full of love, but then realizes the walls placed around her and* learns *her place* to *survive. But you are now out in the open. Sometimes it is hard to remember that the ball is gone and we carry it around in our head like a souvenir, afraid that next time it might be concrete walls or a wooden box that someone will next offer. Fear serves a purpose, but we should not serve it. Stretch your legs and feel the sun on your face. Don't rush into another cage.*

What to Say
December 11, 2010
10 months, 19 days of freedom

Life goes on; some days are wonderful, some surprising, some sad. Sometimes I wish for the happy conclusion to my marriage that I'll never have - happy in that we would die of old age after years spent peacefully and joyfully rocking on our porch. A couple of weeks ago, I visited my ex, at his request, to tell him our marriage was finished. He said he "deserves to hear it face to face" - and although I did that before - I went to his house and told him what he wanted to hear. The words I said seemed to have no effect. At least his face didn't change. He showed no sign of emotion.

Later, I told my sister that it was like he didn't hear me at all and that I wasn't surprised, but wished there had been some sort of acknowledgement that he'd heard what I'd gone over there to tell him.

Last night at 10:30, he came to my house and knocked at my door unannounced. I asked if our boys were okay (they were), and if he was okay (he was). I asked what he needed. "Nothing," he said and we stood there awkwardly. At least, I was awkward. He came over for some reason that he never told me. After a minute partly filled with questions but mostly filled with silence, I said that I had company and visiting now wasn't a good time.

"Oh, I didn't expect you to have company," he said, then turned and left. He jumped into his truck, spun quickly out of the driveway and noisily down the road.

I don't know why he came. I don't know what he expected. If it was an attempt at reconciliation then he didn't say any of the words that might have worked. He showed up at my door at 10:30 PM, unannounced. A few minutes after he'd left, he sent a text saying that I needed to tell my lawyer about this date. His text reminds me that whatever his intent had been, his anger still ruled the day.

I think sometimes that he is *only* angry. *Only* angry. I hurt for him because I don't know if he has the ability to hurt for long enough to work past the pain. If I could wish him anything, it would be the ability to feel this pain completely, past the anger, past the denial, past the past ... so he can move on to better days ahead.

As I told him at his house a couple of weeks ago, I will always love him (how could I not?), but I won't live with him anymore.

Comments from Readers

NewDirection says - *I so relate to your experience. We need help to break the attachment to him in a way that will help us heal. I think every woman who feels she was forced to divorce may have a harder than typical time healing and moving on. He may have been trying to establish a new separation date for some legal reason. Check with your lawyer. Emotionally, I find that the same men who are emotionally abusive in marriage and unable to be loving husbands, are the same men that want to maybe save their marriages but have no idea how. The same lack of loving expression before remains a lack of loving expression now.*

> **Martha says** - *It is sad, pathetic even, that his action demonstrates his continued emotional attachment, yet he can't bring himself [actually, humble himself] to acknowledge it.*

New Year says - *I recently left my husband because of emotional abuse. I relate. I feel like I am a smart woman with a beautiful 3 year old. His ability to control me is unbelievable. I wonder if he does it out of know how; or if I am weak enough to let it happen. I, like him, want a beautiful nuclear family, but his constant verbal attacks - the "I'm so sorry ... no I'm not ... it's your fault" confuses me.*

I grow then I back pedal, then I grow then I back pedal. We live separately. I have custody of our daughter. Still he controls me. What book or Band-Aid or medication could possibly help me? He abuses me in front of our daughter. He insults me and my family, friends, and job...everything. Who are we for them to abuse? It's like being punched but not as obvious to the bystander.

Last Year
December 31, 2010
11 months, 9 days of freedom

At the end of last year, before the separation, I wrote this:

> Words that once had meaning make no sense. My brain is screaming, *LOSER!* while a piece of me patiently waits for a better time. Do I need to *do* something to bring it about? 'Cause all I want to do now is sleep and keep up the appearance of caring about the house.
>
> I don't (or wouldn't) care if we ate off dirty plates. Wore dirty clothes. Neglected all our shit. I just don't care. But I *want* to care. I *want* to be productive and I *want* what I produce to replenish others' and my needs - not deplete them.
>
> Tired. Tired. Tired. Tired. Why am I so tired? *Why?*

This year is different. I know there is no loser in my brain. The words I speak to myself are so far from tired and depleted that I almost cannot remember writing that entry, almost cannot remember feeling that worthless and guilty. There is no guilt in me today. I am no longer fighting to keep the peace in my home. It never worked anyway.

This time last year, Will labeled me liar, betrayer, selfish...and that has not changed. He still tells me I have fucked up priorities, and that I don't care about my children. The difference is this year I know I am not those things and that I never was.

It is better on this side. I am stronger. I don't believe him anymore. Will's opinion is like a tiny voice that annoys me sometimes but cannot discourage me from following my heart or from being the wonderful woman I am and always have been and will become more of over all of my years. I made the right decision. I left it all behind. Even the relationships with my children, which I mistakenly thought were lost to me, return stronger every day. I was patient, and I am better off for it. I am proud of what I accomplished during this past year. I look forward to the new one with hope and peace and love. I am free.

Happy new year to all of you. Freedom isn't free, but it sure as hell is worth the fight.

The Moonlight Dance
January 11, 2011
11 months, 20 days of freedom

The subconscious dance I participated in with my ex-husband steals my thoughts today. I want to look deep inside the belly of the beast inside myself and paint a true portrait of my abusive marriage with my own blood. I don't want his blood - I cannot pretend to know what he was doing or thinking all those years. He is not fair game for analyzing. But I am.

I wrote that abuse is a cycle. Abuse does not happen in a vacuum, meaning that an abuser cannot be an abuser if there is no one to abuse. A victim cannot be a victim if there is no one to transfer authority *to*.

I transferred my authority over *me* to him a very long time ago. I gave me away. I chose to be the harmony instead of the melody. I chose to give up parts of myself in order to ... to what?

At this point, I believe I chose to give up my authenticity and authority over my *self* because I didn't trust myself to do the right thing or be the right person. I looked outward into the world for validation that I was a good person. I looked to the expressions on the faces of those who I thought loved me to gauge my worth. I used society's definition of the roles I chose to embody to determine whether I was living up to my potential.

So, when my ex-husband came along with all his assertiveness and black/white worldview, I saw in him an easy gauge of my worth. HE could tell me if I was right or good and I could trust him because he loved me. It would be easy to become the person I wanted to be with such a strong motivator on my side. I brought this problem into my marriage. I carried it with me for a very long time. It was only after I began to think that no one, not even *me*, could be as malevolent and conniving as he thought I was. No one, not even *me*, could be so thoroughly mixed-up and wrong about so many things. That is when I noticed that not only was he telling me what he thought of what I did, but he was also telling me *why* I had done such a thing. That did not sit well with the tiny flame inside.

I instinctively knew that if I acquiesced and gave myself over to the idea that he knew my motivations better than I did, then the flame inside of me would go out. I would cease to exist as a spirit and as an individual person. I would be what he told me to be and nothing more. I would be him.

I can't help but try to slip on his shoes for a moment and stand before me. I would give in my strong opinion to keep the peace. I would change my habits and actions to meet his opinion. I did my best to reflect the image he wanted to portray to the world. He says I was a good wife for the first eight years, and then something changed. From his standpoint, he had the wife he'd always wanted and didn't notice how he got her.

He didn't have to notice because I didn't challenge him; I didn't challenge myself to find my voice. I kept my fears to myself or buried them so deep I couldn't feel them. Because I deferred my presence to his, he thought I was more like him than I was. So when my differences showed, he felt betrayed. It's not that I cannot understand how he may have viewed the situation. I understand how he feels betrayed and that he feels I lied to him for years. From his point of view, I betrayed him and I lied.

But from my standpoint, I couldn't have done it any differently. I didn't know to do it differently and I didn't challenge myself to consider a different path. I feel that he did too much damage to me, and I've done too much damage to him. I feel that he and I danced so long under the shroud of moonlight that I can never dance in the sun with him. I partially have and will eventually entirely forgive him; the true test is to find it in my heart to forgive myself. I plan to dance in the sun as I discover how to look into the beast in my belly and paint with my own blood my journey to my salvation.

Comments from Readers

Laura says - *In so many ways, my experience of myself and my ex and my marriage mirrors yours. But I do not intend to forgive him; the past recedes and the pain recedes, to some extent and becomes a part of the cloth that I am, and perhaps, too, I forgive myself. But forgiving him? I don't think I could let him off; it's not that I have a kernel within that I need to stoke. It's that he has not earned my forgiveness and does not deserve it.*

> **Lisa says –** *Oh my God, Kellie, you described exactly what it is like! One day you realize that you are walking around with your head down all the time and you can't, or won't, do it*

anymore. Accepting responsibility for your own part in this is so key to moving on. The joke is that Lisa has a thing for military officers because she's had two of them. So I have to accept that I have chosen, more than once, to have this kind of relationship, and that I ignored other signs of problems (i.e. drunk women calling from bars, always taking cell phone calls outside). I accepted that it was work related because I was in a culture that put mission first. And somehow, I guess that I accepted his responsibilities, the real and the made up, were more important than my needs.

Forgiving? Until I can forgive, I still allow them to control me. Number Two and I are friends. He's a good man and a great soldier. He's committed to a culture and understands now how his actions influence what he thinks. But we can't go back. Number One I forgive and feel sorry for at times. Forgiveness is harder because the abuse escalated and I spent more time with him. But for me to be free, I have to let it go.

Shelly says - *You wrote, "He didn't have to notice because I didn't challenge him; I didn't challenge myself to find my voice."*

I too found it hard to find my voice. It took me a few years to wake up and see that his opinion of me was so ugly that it could not be true. But I kept trying to prove to him that I wasn't the ugly person he imagined me to be. Once I realized how co-dependent I was in trying to earn his love and respect (something that would never happen), I learned how to respect myself and enforce my boundaries. I didn't have to leave him - he left me. Once I would not dance with him any longer, he divorced me. It was a blessing - and more so because I don't stay in those ugly partnerships for long.

Jen says - *You describe it all very well...*

I didn't lie, I didn't know, but I sure wasn't me. We kept triggering each other, opening up wounds and hurting each other. I realized that what we were doing was not love... jealousy, control, causing pain but not love. So I moved away from what was not love, and amazingly enough found love. Thanks for sharing your story and your journey.

Part III…and the second year arrives

"Learn from yesterday, live for today, hope for tomorrow. The important thing is not to stop questioning."

~Albert Einstein

I'm Doing It!
January 25, 2011
1 year, 3 days of freedom

About a year after leaving my ex-husband, I'm in school full-time, working toward a bachelor's degree in psychology. I also found a great job helping young men straighten out their lives, so now I work on salary as a case manager.

On top of work and school, I've been tolerating my ex. Lately, Will's big deal is forcing his evaluation of why I haven't filed for divorce down my throat. I told him that even if I paid the $175 filing fee to my attorney, she would apply it to the *debt* I owe her, not toward a new motion. Or filing. Or whatever you call it.

Trust me - the papers are coming. Why can't *he* file? I don't know the answer to that. I guess I could pay another $10 to *send an email* to ask my attorney, but I'll be seeing her in court soon enough. I will pay my attorney, out of my settlement, and I will file for divorce. Nothing would make me happier.

Of course, Will doesn't believe my explanation for why I haven't filed. According to him, I want to suck on his military health insurance instead of doing the *right thing*.

He has a lot of nerve, telling me what the *right thing* to do could be. Ha.

Between you and me and the light post (and him since he reads this blog), I've done everything I could to take care of as many lingering health issues as possible this past year. The last dental appointment is tomorrow - two grand, out of pocket, to crown some teeth and get three fillings since March. If I'd known I would have been able to "suck off" his insurance past our separation date, I wouldn't have missed all those days at my *new job* - which I *love*, by the way.

Back to medical issues, the one thing I haven't needed to charge to the awesome insurance coverage his job provides is anti-depressants. So, in essence, leaving him saved his insurance company money. The best thing that ever happened to Tricare happened when I left Will.

And do I need to remind anyone that the bulk of the reason he still has his job is because I signed papers that in effect said I would like to dismiss the domestic violence charge back in March?

Good. I feel better. Now I'm going to do my freaking homework! (Yay! I have *homework*!)

Courage
January 30, 2011
1 year, 8 days of freedom

I received a comment on Facebook recently that said I was amazing and strong. I share qualities with every other person in abusive relationships.

- We're optimistic
- We sometimes suffering under the weight of depression and anxiety
- We're giving.
- We all have a bright light that other people, even our abusers, recognize; the difference is the abuser wants to absorb it all for their self and if they can't absorb it, they want it *gone*.
- We're helpful.
- We're strong. We have to be to withstand the abuse.

- We're capable of intimacy to the *detriment* of our selves within the abusive relationship and to the benefit to any other.
- We're intuitive because we know *something* is wrong in our relationship. Maybe we haven't put our finger on what *it* is, but if we haven't learned about abuse, we really can't define it as such.

In short, we're amazing human beings who embody characteristics that any person who doesn't selfishly want to steal them from us will admire and cherish.

If you look at that list the opposite way, you can see those characteristics how the abuser sees us:

- Instead of considering us optimistic, abusers think we live in idealistic and therefore unrealistic worlds and cannot understand how the world works, etc.
- Instead of seeing our depression/anxiety, the abuser thinks we look for sympathy when we should be able to solve our own problems ("get that look off your face!" or "your life is so easy!" or "what's wrong with you?" ... and on and on)
- Instead of seeing us as giving, the abuser says we're too generous, too friendly, too trusting, ...
- Instead of honoring our life and light, the abuser calls us show-offs, know-it-alls, drama queens, and holier-than-thou unappreciative women ...
- Instead of helpful, the abuser calls us nosy, looking for trouble, irresponsible, flirty, whore ...

- Instead of strong, the abuser sees us as weak. They want to believe that we look to them for *everything* and do *nothing* to further ourselves because that is the only way the abuser can remain in control of us.
- Instead of enjoying our ability to maintain intimate relationships, the abuser tells us we are too close to our family, we take other people's opinions ahead of his, we use poor judgment in relating to friends, we tell too many secrets, we complain too much ...
- Instead of appreciating our intuitiveness, the abuser tells us that we are always looking for trouble, we wouldn't know what to do with ourselves if we couldn't make up some problem, we read into things, we make mountains of molehills and think too much ...

The questions with no right answers are:

When will you decide to reject, completely and utterly, your abuser's interpretation of you?

When will you decide that YOU are the best judge of your character and capabilities?

When will you trust yourself above all others?

No one can answer those questions for you. But when the day comes where *your* answer is *today*, you will sense the seed of courage germinate and feel its roots spread to every bit of your being.

Continue learning, keep reading other people's stories, observe, see your truth, and soon the seed of courage *will* spring forth and bloom. You will overcome this mess and you will be free.

Comments from Readers

Rachel says - *I chose it to be* today! *I won't go back, and it scares the hell out of me. My three children deserve the peace that comes with feeling safe in your own home. No, he never hit me with his fists...it was worse. Some emotional wounds don't heal as easily as physical ones. And the thing you said about how the abuser sees us? Well, he has said all of those things to me more than once. Thank you. Today is the beginning of the best part of my life!*

> **PrincessLuceval says -** *Today! At least, mine was December 1. It was the last straw, and I decided I was going to have no more of it. He hit me, threatened to kill me, and I took out an order of protection against him. Kellie, your blog is one I've been reading for a long time now. You helped me realize what he's doing is wrong, and I don't have to put up with it. You are strong and tough, and it gave me strength. Thank you.*

Kellie Jo says - *I am so happy for you both! It was amazing what happened when that moment came for me. Once you know, once you really truly know what the truth is, there is no going back. I'll never ever put myself back there again. It's SO scary at times ... but SO worth it to let go of all that crap. It's so refreshing NOT to play the game. Congratulations! We should form a club.*

Anniversary Anxiety
February 1, 2011
1 year, 10 days of freedom

Last year, February 1 fell on Monday. Will and I had gone to court the Thursday before, and I had told the judge I agreed that he could see the boys. That first weekend, he wouldn't take them because he hadn't received his paperwork and was afraid that I would call the law on him after he picked up the boys.

His thinking didn't make any sense to me, but whatever. He left me to tell the boys that they wouldn't see their father that weekend because of paperwork.

Life was hell for me at that time. I was scared that Will would come back. I bought pepper spray and changed all the locks on the house. I didn't know what he was capable of doing. He told me that I betrayed him - the worst offense he could imagine.

Let's think about that for a moment. I betrayed him.

In therapy three days before he put his hands on me, I'd flat out told him that if he put his hands on me again then I would press charges. That seemed clear to me when I said it. The counselor made sure she understood what I said. Will acted like he heard me. Oh well. There must have been a gap in our communication.

Nevertheless, this time last year I was in deep mourning. I cried continually. The boys thought I was losing it. I thought I was going to die. I didn't see a future in which I would be happy.

Now, a year later, I am feeling residual effects of that week. I am anxious and nervous. I am tearful and scared. But I know why. It will pass, but I hope you'll say a little prayer for me. I have things to do, and I'm not about to let these anniversary anxieties overcome me. But it's hard.

Like last year, I'll post a little here and there to remind myself that I am going to be all right.

If I Were Married To Will Today
February 14, 2011
1 year, 23 days of freedom

Today is Valentine's Day! It is the first good one in forever which makes it impossible not to compare it to the past.

If I were married today,

...I wouldn't have received a bouquet of beautiful flowers from a man who loves me.

...I wouldn't feel special, precious or loved.

...I wouldn't be working, so I wouldn't have received Valentine's Day gifts from my Secret Pal.

...I wouldn't have wonderful people around me every day who appreciate my strengths and help me overcome my weaknesses.

...I wouldn't feel like showing appreciation for anyone except for my boys.

On the other hand, I would *be* with my boys and we would have dinner together as a family, at the table, with candles. Nevertheless, I'm taking dinner to them (heart-shaped pizza!) and will get some hugs and kisses from them tonight.

Then, I'll go to my friend's house for a movie and dinner (he's cooking!), and I'll be happy and content, hoping that my presence helps him feel wonderful too.

Life is good.

I'm so happy that this is not the same Valentine's Day as last year. This time last year, there was confusion and doubt and I wondered what to call myself ... not a victim because he was gone, not a survivor because I didn't feel strong. There is none of that this year. Today, I call myself *loved*.

Dream World
April 28, 2011
1 year, 3 months, 6 days of freedom

I wrote this some time ago:

Poe wrote, "All that we see or seem is but a dream within a dream."[7] Perhaps his statement sheds light on why abuse is so difficult to describe, so difficult to recognize, end and admit.

Living in abuse, I know that nothing is real. He labels every word I say a lie. He diminishes every emotion I feel to nothingness. But he is also unreal. He is a shadow of the bad things I tell myself, and he repeats the nonsense back to me in an effort to become real.

Abusers and victims live in an alternate world, so beyond comprehension by outsiders that the question, "Why don't you leave?" seems ridiculous to me. Asking that question shows contempt for the very real dream I live in and exposes the dream the questioner lives in, too. We all live in dreams formed by the perceptions we choose to empower.

I will not leave this marriage because you point out the benefits of doing so. I will not leave because you try to convince me I am unsafe and he is imbalanced. You ask me to leave without acknowledging the effort I've exerted to stay here, the number of times I've resurrected myself from death, or my desire to save the life of the man who kills me. You discount my belief that there is something good in Will, you tell me I am mistaken to believe he can change.

Fact is, he doesn't have to change who he is to be lovable or loving; he is, by nature, capable of loving and worthy of receiving it. I know this. Giving up on him knowing it is the very last thing I will ever do.

If you keep telling me to leave, if you keep telling me I am wrong in my assessment, then you are the last person to whom I could ever run. Your assertion that all would be well if I left is wrong. You saying it tells me you think my perception and experience is wrong. You are just like him. You live in a dream outside of me.

After a lifetime of living in my own dream, I am ready to change it. I am going to choose a different perception to empower. I have had enough of listening to the recordings of my failures, faults and sins. I have discovered that I am not fractured, not broken and not dead. I am whole and powerful enough to resurrect myself from the tomb to which you and he banished me. I have not wasted my life, for living live gave me more than it took.

Living like this allowed me to find God inside of me, a true God, a dark and light, living God who knows when it is time to expand and contract, who knows when it is time to fracture and time to become whole. God as we think of him expands and contracts across eons; I am a piece God, whole unto myself, but capable and designed to expand and contract on a shorter time-line.

Nothing you say and nothing he says will take away from me any longer. I will live as I see fit, I will monitor myself and only myself. I will decide for me when it is time to act and to be still, and I will change my mind as frequently as I like. Only I know how I will live, but I know I live.

Spiraling
May 24, 2011
1 year, 4 months, 2 days of freedom

My toilet of a brain spirals swiftly. I flush the toilet and the water spins and spins, dropping down the pipes. When my brain is working right, the spinning water leaves my mind and removes the waste. Right now however, the spinning water's exit pipe attaches to the tank where the clean water should be. The toilet is flushing, but the spinning water returns repeatedly ... the toilet doesn't stop flushing, the water doesn't stop spinning and the waste is refilling the tank.

I am spiraling in my own waste. I am depressed.

This depression tells me things like, "I'm wasting my time", "I'm not going to get out of this," and worst of all, "I don't *want* to get out of this." I feel an overwhelming desire to wallow in my own shit.

Maybe *desire* is too strong a word. I want to feel better, but I am afraid. If I feel better then maybe I'll feel forced to make choices and sacrifices I don't want to make. Choices like giving up on my dreams versus pretending they are possible. Oh wait - that is not a choice between two different thoughts! That's the same thought set up to seem like a choice. I am thinking that I will not live my dreams. Is it impossible to see clearly? Is this mind-set an illusion?

I'm feeling a lack of self-efficacy. It seems like the actions I take and have taken up to this point have put me no further along than when I started changing my situation. Will is still abusive. My children continue to feel negatively affected by the way we raised them. My brain is still malfunctioning. The money is still tight. I feel suffocated.

On top of the negativity coursing through me, I feel guilty. I feel guilty because I feel incapable of sustaining meaningful relationships with my sons and my sister. I feel myself putting up walls between those I love and my inner self. I feel myself pulling away to wallow in misery.

Erin encourages me by saying this is only temporary and that anything I want is possible. Unfortunately, no sooner does she say kind things than my brain counter-acts the statements with gloom and doom. I get pissy that she wants to cheer me up when "Can't you see that this is the end of the world dammit?" It's not the end of the world, but I'm not living in the world in which I want to live either. Imagining a better future is tough because living in the present is tougher. The toilet in my brain is heavy, and my brain's neurons are firing crap. I want to find a way to exchange the poop for fertilizer.

Poets and Knights
May 29, 2011
1 year, 4 months, 7 days of freedom

Once upon a time, there was a young woman who wanted more than anything in this world to find her *poet*, her lifetime love. She imagined long afternoons with him, sitting under shady trees and dining from picnic baskets filled with grapes and sandwiches. When he looked at her, she could see the twinkle in his eyes and knew that he, in return, could see her love for him radiating from her soul.

She imagined him in romantic fantasy and tried to find him in the young men she dated. Sometimes she found signs of him in her beaus; but the young men also held signs contrary to her imagined poet, and the relationships didn't last long.

Along the way, two of the young men she courted revealed themselves as snakes and injected their poison into her arteries. She made excuses for the snakes and allowed their poison to remain in her system, thinking that eventually it would make its way out if she ignored its potency and effect on her mind and heart. She remained quiet about both of these young men, taking on their poison as her own and allowing it to create a dark spot within her.

That dark spot eventually took on a life of its own. It began to writhe and turn and hiss lies to her. She began doubting her ability to find her poet and to succeed in the world. She feared facing herself in the mirror and felt that what she needed was a knight, not a poet. A knight could protect her at all costs and keep her from further harm.

The dark spot writhing inside of her suggested a man who would intertwine with her heart, who understood her dark, sinful soul, who knew more than she did about identifying the evils of the world. The dark spot's lies made sense. She sacrificed her desire to see the love-twinkle in her poet's eye and instead, looked for someone the others would fear.

The Knight

She found her knight and he quickly made her his own. He performed the task she set for him admirably; he whisked her away and quickly isolated her from the other poets and knights of this world. He built her a castle far away, allowing her to come and go as she wished at first. Eventually, her knight curtailed her freedoms because he seemed to see *her* as the dark plague upon his world. He thought that she purposely attracted the others, and said that the dark spot in her soul was evil and uncontrollable. He told her that if she wanted to be happy, he would have to let him protect her in *his* way.

She believed him. The dark spot in her soul crept into her consciousness. She did not remember that the dark spot inside of her was merely the poison from the others residing inside of her. She came to believe that she created the evil within her by being who she was, and thought that her knight was wise to warn her of her evil nature. She fell deeper into fear and begged her knight to tell her more about her evil nature so she could be free of it. As her knight identified the evil, the dark spot grew large, fed by the knights opinions and thoughts.

Her knight told her she had loose morals and that everyone knew she was a whore. He told her that she lacked common sense and could not see the truth. He told her that the world was black and white and the shades of gray she saw were figments of her imagination, falsely ideal versions of an evil world.

He told her that motherhood would elevate her to a higher plane in his eyes. He told her that by raising his children and staying in the castle that she could learn the truth about the world as he shared his exploits into it.

The Contract
She agreed. She remained in the castle, hidden from the world, and raised children who adored her. The knight, who was constantly out in the world having adventures, would return home and feel jealous of the bond between the young woman and his children. He told her that he didn't trust her as a mother.

He said that her children were weaker men because of her. He said that she must be like him when disciplining and speaking to her children. He criticized her ability to love his children and told her that if she did not understand his way by now then she was forever hopeless. The dark spot within her grew larger as she accepted the knight's words.

A Death
The day came when she looked at herself in the mirror and did not recognize the countenance staring back at her. The dark spot within her hissed an evil laugh. She looked into her past and realized that, once upon a time, she was vibrant and lovable; she longed for that young woman to return.

The dark spot laughed again, but this time, she took a hair pick and stabbed it deeply into her center, bright blood spilling onto the floor followed by black bile that writhed and twisted itself into a snake on the floor.

It hissed, "You worthless whore of a mother! Do you think that by ridding yourself of me that you can live freely? You don't know what it takes to make it in the world, sheltered as you've been!"

It tried to slither back into her belly, but she was too quick for it. She raised her foot and stomped on the snake's head, crushing its bones beneath her heel and grinding them into mush on the floor. The snake flopped futilely for a little while as it felt its control over her end. She felt empty and wondered what would replace the dark spot. But she didn't have to wonder for long.

Hearing the commotion, her children ran to her and their love and innocence and courage filled the hole, mending the wound, stopping the bleeding, and fusing life into her soul. She knew she only borrowed the love they gave her; eventually she must develop her own way of loving and being. For now, she could borrow their courage until forging her own. She left the castle prepared to battle with the shadow of the snake, her knight, and vowed never to allow another person's poison to fill her soul again.

Promise Me a Rose Garden
June 29, 2011
1 year, 5 months, 7 days of freedom

A few months after leaving Will, I worked through the grief stage and moved into such a euphoric state that I thought it would never end. I thought to myself, "So this is what I've been missing all these years!" and with a smile and artsy flourish of my wrist, I chucked my last eleven anti-depressants into the trash.

Here it is, almost a year later, and I feel the familiar grief settling into my joints, radiating outward. I bet you can *see* the feeling, murky and olive green, if you look hard enough. Well, in hindsight, I guess I had a good run.

Over the past year, several good things happened for me:

- Divine guidance brought me to a home I love.
- I recognized and left the employ of an abusive boss, and was fortunate to have a better paying job offered to me at the same time.
- I met a man who helps me envision a life of love instead of a life of guarded alone-ness.
- I love my no-longer-new job and get to help teenage boys set goals for their lives.
- I was able to replace the car my oldest son, Marc, flipped into the river.
- I started back to school full time.
- Marc, who had refused to stay with me, came to live with me full-time.
- Eddie, my youngest son, stays with me exactly half of the time.
- I am a paid blogger on verbal abuse at HealthyPlace.com

It is funny how life changes so slowly and so quickly at the same time. A year is not a lot of time, but it sure did seem to take forever to play out. Looking back, everything happened in its own perfect time. Once again, I find myself wishing that life would change, hoping it changes the way I want it to change, and changing *now*. I want *instant* gratification of several things!

- I want to write, full-time, with pay high enough that I can work for myself.

- I want Eddie living with me much more than half time.
- I want Marc's baby-steps toward taking responsibility for his own life to come to fruition.
- I want to replace the car I no longer appreciate – and which Marc slightly wrecked last week.
- I want to hold my bachelor's degree in my hands right *now* without feeling the frustration of working for it.
- I want to solve my co-dependent issues as if by magic instead of as part of a process.
- I want to see Marc's girlfriend Amy, who now lives with us, work through her issues and leave her controlling parent's misdeeds behind.
- I want divine guidance to lead me back to the state of peace this home brought me in the beginning.

I may be patient with my children and my boyfriend, but I am not patient with time.

Writing this, I realized that I received almost everything I wished for at this time last year! Last May, if all of those wonderful things had happened instantly, I would have been completely happy (but maybe a bit unprepared).

I said that in hindsight I saw how everything happened in its own perfect time. Maybe my depression is a result of pushing too hard (wanting to control) and wishing I had it all today while experiencing none of the difficulties it will take to achieve my goals. Is this what they mean by *enjoying the journey*? If I don't allow myself to feel happiness when I take a baby-step, then what is the point of taking that step?

Suddenly the murky olive green oppression feels a bit more translucent and spring green. I feel better. This time next year, I will have more of what I want. Wait and see.

Pride Revisited
July 9, 2011
1 year, 5 months, 17 days of freedom

Last year, I wrote a story called *Pride and Greed*[8] about how those two sins work together to create an abusive relationship. Now that I think about it, the story is not quite right. The story helped me to understand how Will and I happened, but it's off if you think Pride is a complete and utter sin.

There are philosophers whose opinions differ with the Seven Deadlies. Those philosophers' words did not make it into the Bible. Aristotle wrote,

> Pride, then, seems to be a sort of crown of the virtues; for it makes them greater, and it is not found without them. Therefore, it is hard to be truly proud; for it is impossible without nobility and goodness of character.

The idea that pride has two opposing meanings fits neatly into the idea of pride being at both ends of the expanding/contracting continuum. Pride exists in a positive way when one sets out to do something worthwhile, and in accomplishing that goal, recognizes it. All rewards humans for doing good things; pride is the result of doing good things. Why would we feel pride after doing something good if feeling prideful equated to being sinful? Knowing you did the right thing and feeling good about that is supposed to be its own reward.

The problem comes when we forget that the good things we did were for the benefit of everyone and All. The second we do good things to glorify ourselves or see our names in the papers, that is when we step into the shit side of pride. There is a fine line between pride as a virtue and pride as a sin.

When I met my husband, I exhibited pride as a virtue. He broke me down, and the pain of falling down so swiftly changed the way in which I exhibited pride. I no longer felt that I had the opportunity to do good things for All. I did them for Will or not at all. When I was able to make Will act like he was happy with me, I felt pride. At first, I was proud of myself for doing something good. As time passed, *doing something good* became exceedingly difficult. Will was never happy with me and the pride dynamic twisted into knots.

In time, I was proud of myself when I was able to *force* him to be happy. If I could outwit him at his own game, put him in a position where he *had* to be happy due to some past desire he had expressed, then I was proud of myself. He wasn't happy and I knew he wasn't happy, but goddammit he had to be nice because he said he would be if I did what I had done.

It's convoluted. I warped pride from a virtue to a sin, and then didn't understand how the same emotion (pride) could make me feel so badly now when it used to make me feel so good. I blamed Will for warping me into a sinful creature. I don't know what I could have done differently. It seems as if my life's script destined it to happen that way. It seems that I directed myself to fall, and I did. Or maybe, like in the story, Will directed me to fall but hadn't intended on me falling so far as to become unusable. The story ends:

> But now their path was dark. Neither could see where the path had gone. They stumbled about, falling hard on their faces more than once.
>
> "Dammit," Greed said, "turn on your light! I cannot see anything and we are hurting!"

"What light?" Pride asked. "You said you would protect me! You said that you would save me! I know nothing of the ways of this world, dear husband. I do not have a light."

Comments from Readers

DonnaLee says - *Ahh pride, something I have lost. I would do things for others completely from my heart. However, for my dear husband, I would do things to make him happy. He would want a boat, a motorcycle, tools and other toys. "Sure, go get them if we can afford it" I said aloud. Under my breath, I said, "If that's what makes you happy."*

Then when that did not make him happy, he would turn to me and claim he was mad because the house wasn't clean. Now, let's look at this picture: I clean everything, but I don't pick up after him anymore. I started this about a month ago. He leaves cups, glasses, clothes and tools in every room and on every surface. I pick up after myself, my daughter picks up after herself. I cook meals, but he thinks I don't because sometimes he has to barbeque.

I try to do what he tells me to do, but I'm tired of being his maid. I am off work due to being verbally abused (yes, at work too). So now I'm not bringing in enough money to afford his need for toys.

I'm a people pleaser. My first marriage ended (after 21 years) because I gave it to his needs first, tried to change that and he wouldn't have any part of it. Sadly, I ended up doing the same thing in this marriage of 5 years. I love doing things for other people, but apparently not for myself. Pride as a sin...oh yeah, that's when you don't have enough pride to take care of yourself.

Not sure if I'm making any sense as last night we had a major fight and my mind is all over the place.

I Appreciate You
July 10, 2011
1 year, 5 months, 18 days of freedom

Lately I find myself thinking about you, the readers of this blog. You readers are my core; without you, I probably would not have had the courage to continue the leaving process after it begun. Without you, I may have resigned myself to more years of abuse - maybe I would have stayed until I died.

Your encouragement, support (and in one case, your negativity) helped me to cement the idea in my head that leaving my abuser and staying gone was the right thing to do. I consider those of you who didn't contribute in writing but viewed the blog my silent army (I can see *how many* but not *who*). You were either suffering or knew someone who was, and I could not allow myself to let you down. Freedom from abuse was my only choice not only for me, but because I felt responsible to you.

During my darkest hours, I thought of you, and imagining that you were looking to me for guidance, to see what would happen if you left, allowed me to find the courage I needed. I know you are all *strangers* to me, but you are the best damn strangers anyone has ever *not* known, and I thank you for being here for me. I've never been as grateful for the prayers and thoughts from strangers as I am today, looking back.

Thank you. I appreciate you. I hope you continue forward with me.

Shutting Up
July 11, 2011
1 year, 5 months, 19 days of freedom

Last year, I tapered off writing this blog because I was afraid of what would come of it in court. Nothing came of it in court. This blog was either irrelevant or the battle didn't get nasty enough for his attorney to use it. Or maybe there was nothing to say about it. Will's real name isn't here; my name isn't here. I don't push this blog onto our children. This blog, as I always intended it to be, is mine and mine alone.

The saddish part about it is that I didn't recognize that fact. I worried that he would somehow take this piece of me away. Under the heaviness of that fear, I acted as I so often did during our marriage: I shut up. Behind the scenes, new people came into my life. I didn't know how to mention them on this blog. I didn't care what Will thought, but I worried about what the new people thought.

In my encounters with the outside world, I learned that these new people watched my blog to see if I mentioned them. "What are you going to name me?" they asked. I didn't mention them often, or I alluded to them vaguely. I didn't want the new people to be privy to my thoughts about them.

Writing this blog anonymously gave me a communication outlet I didn't have in my marriage. I became accustomed to writing of Will without telling him what I thought about him first. I thought it was unfair to tell the new people what I was thinking without telling them first, and I simply didn't know how to tell them! In the marriage, I tried to tell Will what I thought, what I felt, but he didn't (want to) hear. But these new people acted very interested in what I thought, but I couldn't bring myself to tell them intimate things face to face. So, I shut up, and I carried quietness into my new relationships.

I didn't know how to communicate intimately with people I loved. When we were face to face, I was afraid of saying the wrong thing, or blurting out an emotional statement I didn't want to say yet. I was learning to control myself. It was a scary process without Will's rules to guide me.

Slowly but surely, I'm coming out of my shell. I am challenging myself to make this promise to everyone in my life: I may speak of you on my blog, but before I do, I will tell you what I think *first*. I will use a fictitious name unless you tell me otherwise, but I won't say if it's your real name or not.

If you see someone's name here, please know that I've done the hard work before posting. I've spoken to my friends, my lover, my sister or whomever before their name ends up on this blog. This blog is mine and mine alone, and I will gladly face what other people think of me with fairness, but it may come off as a devil-may-care attitude.

Comments from Readers

Kacy says - *After reading your posts and some of the other comments, I feel like the words are my very same thoughts! I wish I had found this blog years ago. If you could see my amazon purchase list and Kindle books, you would see the amount of time and money I have spent trying to figure out if I was crazy.*

I am in my late thirties with two young boys in a very small town. My fictitious hope keeps leading me to another cycle of his rage. I keep hoping something will stop him.

I am keenly aware now how much he has stolen from me. I see the fog of despair and depression stealing my energy and time with my children. I sit near them as they play, but my mind is gone... trying to stop this pain. I guess I am most ashamed of the fact that I am unloved. I am so ashamed that I was so difficult to love. I am depressed and angry that someone could treat me this way with no remorse ... as if I don't matter at all.

I resist fully breaking the silence and fear because I am so damned afraid of what he will do. I am a stay at home mom and I am so fearful of what this will do, how I will make it, and mostly what it will do to my kids. I get the feeling that I should leave, but I can't believe that it is the right thing to do.

> ***Kellie Jo says*** *- Kacy, I wrote a post at HealthyPlace.com that you might enjoy. It talks about what life is like after leaving called* Find Freedom from the Abusive Cycle.[9] *Like you, I struggled with the right thing to do. When he hurt me physically the last time, I left. I hope you don't wait for that to happen to you. Life is too short. Trust your feeling, Kacy.*

Exorcising Demons
July 25, 2011
1 year, 6 months, 3 days of freedom

Demons worry that we will know their names (all the horror movies say so). Once we name the demon, once we recognize it, it loses its power.

For example, when I admitted to myself that the demon in my marriage was *abuse* (not Will, but an *Abuse Demon*), then Abuse held less power over me. The demon flared up in a fiery attempt to terrify me, yet, after its temper tantrum, I stood strong and continued to call it by name. Will thinks I demonized *him*, but I demonized his behavior. Will never admitted to Abuse living in our marriage. He still doesn't. The demon may keep its hold on Will, but it doesn't confine me. Once you know the demon's name, *use* it.

Call the demon out into the open. Look the demon in its face and stare it down. We are stronger than anything that cowardly hides within us.

An Exorcism...er, An Exercise
Instead of telling you what to do, I'll describe what I did. I hope that my story inspires you to terrify yourself into realizing nothing but your mind can hold power over you.

When I was very young, I watched *The Exorcist* with my parents. My dad covered my eyes at points, but he covered only his eyes when Regan, the possessed girl, spun her head completely around. Oh, my, God. My little girl brain would not let that image go. It terrified me. (What frightened you?)

Years later, separated from Will and my boys, I laid down and attempted to sleep. Instead, I fell deep into my fears of going through life alone and thought I would certainly die from the amount of terror I felt. I was so afraid that my brain (in an effort to help, I'm sure) showed me several frightening images and memories from my childhood and adult nightmares. Scary stuff. Horror movie stuff.

Suddenly, I knew Regan was outside of my bedroom door in the dark stillness where the moonlight didn't go. She was so real that I could hear her raspy breath. She wasn't standing. She was in a deep backbend, her arched back stretched so far out of position that her ribs were visible under that thin white nightgown. I decided right then that Regan was going to come into my room, and I was going to hold her hand. (Face the fear.)

I let my mind take me deeper into the vision. Regan crept slowly toward my bed in that awkward position. Her breathing sounded louder as she approached. She grunted and groaned, demon sounds interspersed with her breath. At the foot of my bed, she let out a wail so painful it hurt me to hear it. I willed myself to open my eyes, to see her in real life, and I did. I saw my imagined demon creep around the corner of the bed, flip to her stomach and slither like a snake under where I laid.

It scared me so much I closed my eyes. I knew she was lying on her back beneath the bed because I could feel her hot breath warming the mattress under my neck. I slowly moved my hand, palm upward, over the edge of the bed. I willed her to grab it, but she wouldn't. I called her name like she were my daughter, "Raaaay-gan...it's okay. Hold my hand..."

My heart beat faster. I felt movement. I felt an ice-cold finger touch my hand and almost jerked away, but she did it. She grabbed my hand. I let her.

I leaned over the edge of the bed to look into the eyes of a demon, but what I saw were the eyes of a little girl (with a nasty messed up face). She finished sliding out from under the bed. She sat on the floor, holding my hand. We breathed in and out together, raspy and soft. "Regan," I said, "we're not going to be afraid of each other anymore." I melted into sleep, holding the hand of my scary demon. (Trust, even though you are afraid, that everything is all right.)

What Did It Mean?

As weird as it was, it means that there is no fear I cannot conquer. I knew the episode was in my mind, but the terror was real! All fears are in my mind. Bringing the demons out into the light, giving them a name or a face, takes away their power over me.

Weirder still, after going through that fear purposely, I felt better about my life. I woke energized and excited for the first time in weeks. Now, all of these months later, when I am fearful of something but don't know exactly what, I conjure up Regan. We talk, face to face, and my greatest demon helps me to name my lesser ones.

Verbal Abuse Teen Style
September 18, 2011
1 year, 7 months, 27 days of freedom

Most hurtful thing I heard this week:

> I don't love you, I barely respect you and I hope the last words you hear me say are *fuck you*!

I love my son. His words did not send me into a tailspin. I didn't cry because of what he said, I cry because of the example I've allowed him to absorb. It's not my fault, but it is my problem.

Fortunately, he recognizes his temper and anger problems. He's willing to get help. Keep him in your thoughts as we regain our footing in this tumultuous post-abuse recovery.

Comments from Readers

Aimee says - *As a child raised in an abusive home and a recent escapee of my terrifying & threatening, stalking ex-husband and his new partner in crime, I called the domestic violence hotline and they referred me to books by Lundy Bancroft. The books got my attention from the very start. It was so eye opening for me and now I'm trying like crazy to spread the word.*

I usually find that many of my friends who are in controlling relationships themselves are still stuck in the denial phase and don't want anything to change. I think that's why our world is the way it is - everyone's afraid to stand up to the bullies, especially when they're family.

If you want to try to understand why your son said those things and what you can do to help the situation, please read the book titled: When Dad Hurts Mom: Helping Your Children Heal *by Lundy Bancroft. Good luck to you. Know that you're not alone!*

> ***Alison says*** *- My marriage, thank God, is not abusive, but my upbringing certainly was because of my father.*
>
> *I have seen suffering and pain in so many women I have known over the years, and I grew up in a neighborhood where it was very common. At least in my case only one of my parents was a violent drunk. Many of my contemporaries had two alcoholic, unpredictable, dangerous parents. My mum was a victim of abuse, both from her father and my father. They were drunken, violent, angry and foul-mouthed men. At this point in my life, I feel a great deal of sorrow for them both. It is a good place to be because I can think of my mum and my dad without anger now, and focus on some of the positives.*
>
> *I believe my big brother, 9 years older than me, saved me from marrying my father, as they say many people do. When I was young, my brother was my role model; he was a man to me. He was (and is) intelligent, calm and good-natured. The man I married, though far from perfect (who is?) is a reflection of my big brother and certainly not my dad, and I am so very grateful for that.*

You are so courageous to do something about this and try to rescue your children, your hostages to fortune, from this environment. My mum never did. She talked endlessly about it, and every time she said we were leaving I would feel hope, and every time she stayed, I would feel crushed. She did make my dad leave at one point, when I was about 18. What a glorious, peaceful, wonderful year that was for my younger brother and me. Even the dog was so happy and calm.

When she took him back, as I knew and dreaded in my heart that she would, I left home immediately. I remember how furious I felt and how distressed that, once again, my younger brother would have to tolerate this man. My brothers and I knew his good behavior would last no more than a few months, and we were, unfortunately, right.

For a long, long time I was so angry with my mum for not protecting us by simply leaving. It withered my feelings for her and we never had the closeness a mother and daughter should. Both my parents died a few years ago. I am glad I was able, in their last years, to be kind to them both and not berate them for what they did or didn't do. I was at least able to say the words of forgiveness that my mum needed to hear, even when I didn't always feel them. Their lives, after all, had been her punishment. I had to flee across the world from Scotland to Australia though to escape the environment, and them. I left my anger behind a long time ago, but it is sad that, when it comes to parenting, they taught me only what not *to do.*

I haven't read all your blog yet though I will over time. I wanted to say well done, you are so brave. Never doubt that you are doing the right thing to rescue your children from an abusive environment. That was a dream that never came true for me. I wish you all the very best and hope with all my heart that you and your sons can find peace, calm and happiness.

Treatment
September 19, 2011
1 year, 7 months, 28 days of freedom

I can't wait to hear back from a treatment center for my son, Marc. I found an inpatient program that allows him to continue his education without withdrawing from high school. He's three credits short of graduation, and the programs I've found in this state expect him to withdraw from school to attend. As for Amy, his girlfriend, I'm having more difficulty. The school officials are working hard to find a placement for her. I cannot do it because I'm not a legal guardian. (Oh - did I tell you that after her suicide attempt, her mom dropped her off on my doorstep?)

These two kids need help that I am unable to give. Keep us in your prayers as we (my friends, family, the school and me) look for a door that won't slam shut in the kids' faces. I guess these two aren't bad off enough to qualify for quality care.

Marijuana, DXM, alcohol dependence and a willingness to try any pill their friends give them isn't enough to qualify them for rehabilitation programs. Come on, you have to be kidding me. These kids have no *idea* what it is going to take to stay drug-free. They need help, and will need help in the future. I *hope* that rehab will teach them life skills that their abusive families weren't able to teach (my family included). Prayers, please. Thank you.

Free to Follow My Dream
October 2, 2011
1 year, 8 months, 10 days of freedom

My brain hit the ground running this morning. I tried unsuccessfully to feel the soft wind from the fan and the cozy-soft microfiber sheets. But my brain wouldn't have it. I suppose that while I slept, my brain discovered *all the answers* and couldn't wait to put me into action. Unfortunately, those answers got lost in transition from asleep to awake. I woke to find myself bombarded with noisy kids, a messy house and the other signs reminding me I am not in control of *jack shit*.

I want to have my peaceful home back, the one that I miraculously found in May of 2010 that enabled me to think to myself without interruption. I miss my safe, silent, cocoon.

On the other hand, my sons are both here all if not most of the time. Their friends are comfortable here. Friends warm my heart with their presence. The relationships in my life are intact even if this house appears turbulent. I am learning that intact, joyful relationships hold more tranquility that working alone in a neat and tidy home.

I am literally afraid of having a messy home because of what it says about me ... or rather, what a messy home caused *Will* to say about me. I despise the mess only because *he* despised the mess. When my home is messy, I hear a voice tell me that I have no sense of responsibility, I am lazy, I am letting down my family, and that if I can't keep the house clean then I am good for *nothing*.

You know what? Those words are untrue, they are *his* and it's time I let them go so I can follow my dreams. I plan to quit my day job in December. I want to begin the upcoming year with the hours I need to grow a new career. I love my job at Tarheel

ChalleNGe. I love each individual child who comes through those doors and do my best to instill a sense of hope and pride in the ones I'm able to help.

Work takes up ten and a half hours of each day, Monday through Friday, when I count shower and drive time. This leaves very little time to pursue my dream of helping abuse victims find their way out of the abusive cycle. I want to throw myself into helping to create joyful people, joyful families, and I want this work to center on abused people. I'm going to sacrifice *his* judgments so I am free to walk my path.

Taboo
October 18, 2011
1 year, 8 months, 26 days of freedom

Over the past couple of years, I've written this blog straight from my heart. When I look back over the posts, especially the ones in the beginning, I see errors in my thinking. In many posts, abuse and its effects clouded my thinking; I doubted myself at my strongest, persevered with bad decisions when I was at my weakest.

Last year I began writing a more structured blog titled *Verbal Abuse In Relationships* on HealthyPlace.com. I enjoy my blog there, but it is not like this one. Over there, people get the impression that I am an expert on the topic of verbal abuse. Unless they visit this blog, they do not know that my expertise originates from experience, not education. They do not realize that I am but one story in a sea of many.

The biggest difference between my readers (you) and me is that I put the stuff in my head and heart on the Internet. I share with you what I'm thinking although I know that I don't know everything. Every time I write this blog, I realize that next week or next year I may have to humbly reverse my actions, eat my words. Never once have I regretted writing any post or sharing any feeling. I figure you will see something helpful even when I'm wrong. I hope you sense my best intentions are sometimes flawed. I hope you act on your hunches.

When I blogged during my marriage and early separation, everything was open for discussion. I laid it out there on the line. But since breaking free of that relationship, I withdrew from blogging. I thought in the back of my mind that I had little left to offer you, especially when the judge gave primary custody of my children to *him*. I thought you would be afraid to leave your abuser knowing that it was possible to lose custody of your children.

But shit happens. And shit happens for a reason. Even the crappy stuff happens for a reason. On top of dealing with my ex during the incommunicado period, I participated in a relationship drama that I promised myself I would not revisit. I began dating an alcoholic without knowing he was an alcoholic (same mistake as with Will). I wanted to pull my brain out through my ears, punish it severely and stuff it back into my skull.

About a month after I started seeing the alcoholic, he slept with his ex-girlfriend in a drunken haze. It caused issues, to say the least. My head was screaming that I should *go* before there was more damage; but I didn't. Part of the reason I didn't sever the relationship is because I slept with him when he was still with his ex! (*What the hell? That's not who I thought I was! Definitely not the person I want to present to you!*) Finally, I began a relationship with the alcoholic when he was still my *boss* - something I swore I would never do. So there you go - my story and secrets laid bare.

I hope that I don't lose you after confessing my imperfections. I am me and proud of me - my mistakes, imperfections, goodness and successes make me who I am. After 18 years of not being me, I am so grateful that I've given myself this opportunity to find love and life in all of my relationships. Especially the relationship I have with myself. This type of freedom does not exist in an abusive relationship, and I wouldn't change one experience I've lived since I left my marriage.

Comments from Readers

Erin says - *You didn't say anything about how you laugh more now. How you are able to see things for what they are. How you and your boys have more fun together - even without as much money. How the money seems to appear for you when you need it. How you have dreams. How you are turning your dreams into goals. How you are accomplishing your goals. How proud your sister is of you... I love you Kellie. What a long and wonderful way you have come.*

> **Alistair says** - *I admire your courage and candor. I went through the same kind of process writing and I was aware of the risks I was taking when I did. I believe exposing our faults is necessary to understand our problem, and it is a way to say to the world, "I am, this is me as I am." Eliminating shame is incredibly powerful. Plus, our flaws - in a way - are what give us our credibility and authority.*

RandomlyK says - *I am grateful for your candor. I love that you are a WYSIWYG kind of person (and in case you aren't as geeky as I am, that means What You See Is What You Get). You are an inspiration for many women. I think your being real makes it easier for any of us to think though our* *own personal circumstances and try to make sense and our own decisions.*

Stranglehold
November 1, 2011
1 year, 9 months, 10 days of freedom

Writing the post on anger[10] for HealthyPlace.com yesterday brought up some bad memories. My ex-husband once terrorized my mind with his wrath. (*What will he be like tonight? Is it a good time to ask him now? What do I need to do before I run these errands so he's not angry when I return?*)

Punishment could be severe if I read his mind incorrectly. His anger intimidated me. It put me in my place - firmly beneath his heel. His face turned beet red, hazel eyes turned to green, brows knitted under his deeply lined forehead, lips alternated between a sneer and a scowl.

He leaned into me - got in my face. Stomped around. Banged his fist on the counter tops. All the while screaming in his deep resonant voice about how stupid I was, what a disappointment I'd become and how he couldn't *believe* I'd done whatever it was I'd done.

Not folding his underwear into quarters evoked this reaction. Not fixing his plate, not being a good wife. He said things like, "If you can't do what you're supposed to do, how can we expect the kids to behave?"

His words and actions made me *so mad*! I wanted to refute his every insane statement. He made no sense! He wanted me to *behave* but *he* couldn't put down the bottle, *he* acted like a raving lunatic, *he* scared the crap out of me and didn't care! Yet I was the one who must subjugate myself to *him*?

The internal torture was almost too much to bear. Fighting with him escalated the already inane situation. Sitting quietly and taking it caused me to cry in frustration and bring on further insults and degradations because he could not *stand* tears. Tears show weakness!

Trying to calmly reason with him was like trying to pet a rabid wolf.

I felt so angry and frustrated. Silenced. I felt strangled. I couldn't breathe in my own home. My every action or word held the probability of evoking his wrath.

Never a shamed look on his face. Always a hateful glare in my direction when he glanced at me over his shoulder while exhibiting his role-play smile to his friends or our boys.

I watched him manipulate them. I knew they should not trust him. I knew both sides of his face. I knew they would not see through his glamorized persona. *They* admired him. *They* thought he was charming, responsible and kind in his own rough way. *They* did not know what I knew. Yet I had no outlet for the frustration. Suck it up. Stuff it down. I was living with a maniac.

Writing about my own anger reminded me of the type of anger I once endured in my abusive marriage. I felt barely a second's worth of peace; he seemed insane.

Comments from Readers

Erin says - *Kellie, I would love to see a post about how he removed you from your family and friends. I don't remember it if you have already written one. Isolation is a very important sign for people to look for. You often overlooked it or explained it away. I only say this because by him taking you out of your own life allowed his anger to become worse,* *or at least allowed him a place where outsiders couldn't see the truth.*

> ***IdaMae says*** - *Getting flashbacks over here. I can certainly relate a whole lot more than I'm comfortable with at the moment. I'm so thankful to see you're out.*

God, I Promise You
November 3, 2011
1 year, 9 months, 12 days of freedom

Dear God,

I know what you're asking me to do. You want me to take another leap of faith. When Will put his hands on me on January 22, 2010, I left him. But I didn't want to. I cried when I filled out the ex-parte order. I cried when the judge approved it and handed me my copy over the top of her high mahogany bench. I took that leap of faith, and you readers were waiting there for me on the other side of that fear.

When I moved from my marital home into the peaceful house I now rent with the past year's tax return in my pocket, I didn't yet have a job, not even a prospect at that time. I took that leap of faith, and You were waiting there for me on the other side of my fear.

Now that You've helped me take care of my children by seeing to it that they are with me most of the time, You're reminding me that I did not leave my marriage to play it safe. You're reminding me that I have a higher purpose, and that You want me to reach for it. You want me to take another leap of faith.

Today, the director asked me if I really, truly meant to resign on the date I gave him. I said yes. I told him what You're asking of me. He said he admired my faith but worried about my timing. If I waited for the right time, it wouldn't come. I'd be sixty years old and still feel stuck. I'd be retired and wonder what I waited for.

I'm taking another leap of faith. I know You'll be there for me.

What I Want
November 7, 2011
1 year, 9 months, 16 days of freedom

About a year and a half ago, I wrote a post called *I Want to Lie to You*. I wanted to protect myself from judgment by not telling the truth. My life is different now. Other people will always judge *my* choices as they judge yours. The difference between now and then is that I let you think what you want about my choices without allowing your judgments to guide my actions. The decisions I make come from my core, my center. I cannot go wrong when I listen to All.

I am a work in progress, and I will be a better person because I willingly learn from my decisions that result in successes or mistakes. My mistakes, past and future, do not define me. My successes define me. I gave the document attached to *I Want to Lie to You* to my now ex-husband as a final attempt to save our marriage.

Weeks after receiving it, Will told me, "I will never go to counseling." His statement told me everything I needed to know. I was free. I'd done everything I could; he wasn't willing to meet me anywhere near the middle.

Today, what I want is far different from what I hoped for Will and me. The document I gave him is full of things I did NOT want to recur in our marriage, along with the few things I wanted to happen. It is a dreary document, and I'm glad he did not agree to it.

Here's my new list. It may read like a wish list, yet I feel as if it's already here with me. I feel it is my reality.

What I Want
- Healthy, solid, loving relationships with my children, my sister, mother and grandmothers.
- An old, well-preserved and refurbished home, Victorian style, in a quiet friendly neighborhood near my family from which I can both live and work conveniently and safely.
- A Dodge Charger, newest model, with a sunroof and kick-ass sound system.
- A clean-running computer set up in a room that's conducive to my work.
- A job that gives me flexibility and freedom to do what I enjoy and what I'm called to do, allows me an income of $100,000 per year or more, and places me as head of my company with employees that support my vision because they believe in it too.
- A healthy, strong body full of energy that doubles as a life-vessel from which Spirit's energy exudes and influences the world positively.
- The ability to travel and enjoy the locations I visit with time for pleasure and expanding upon Spirit's purpose for me.

Wow. What a difference 20 months can make in a former abuse victim's hopes and dreams.

Comments from Readers

Erin says - *I love your new list! Now, visualize it. See it. Create a movie in your mind that encompasses all of what you want, and play that movie at least two times per day - once in the morning and once before bed. Come up with a* *short, 1-3 word, affirmation for what you want. Say that affirmation often. Repeat it over and over. It is a way to ingrain what you want into your subconscious mind.*

We all know when your subconscious accepts an idea as true, then it will see to it that it happens! Act as if it is already happening. I know there are situations in your life right now that can make this seem almost impossible. The key is to take the time and know it is coming.

You said that you already feel it is your reality - great! Do whatever it takes to keep that thought! When you have created this shift - the one where you believe it to be yours - you are allowing it to manifest in your life. Add dates! When do you expect to have these things? The Universe, Spirit, etc. likes to know that you have a definite timeline. The key - make it a timeline that you can believe in.

You got this, Kellie! I am so proud of you!

Nurturing Myself to Death
November 11, 2011
1 year, 9 months, 20 days of freedom

Well, I've finally learned my lesson. Amy must leave my home; she is a detriment to my son's recovery. Amy's sweet demeanor helps me to love her. Her abusive past, her uncaring (unfit) parents, her drug addiction and co-dependent behavior make me want to help her grow strong and healthy.

I want to fix her. I want my *fix-it* nature to work *for* someone for a change. But it is time for me to realize that anytime I try to fix someone or their situation, I only hurt myself and all the other people I love.

I do not think my relationship to Amy was co-dependent-related in the beginning. I saw a young woman, desperate for a chance to prove herself, begging for an opportunity to flourish. I knew that she could do that in my home, and despite the odds, I gave her that chance.

I kept a hands-off attitude believing Amy would see my example and listen to what I had to say. The department of social services caseworker said Amy was thriving in my home. Hearing her say that made me wonder *what she saw* in my home. Amy did not thrive; she struggled. Yet my home was a safe place for her. It was probably the best place for her. I became unsettled. I felt pressured to create an enriching environment, but going to work each day left Amy and Marc unsupervised.

I now see that environment is impossible for me to create alone. I've tried to teach Marc and Amy how to thrive; I've exemplified it. It's not working. I gave them several chances; I've listened and empathized with their struggles. I've been tough but loving when it comes to drug addiction, and a push-over when it comes to asking them to pull their weight around the house.

In my efforts to teach, I've set impossible expectations for *myself*. I'm losing days of work and living in a terribly messy house. I now see that when my house is a mess, my mind is a mess. I have to create a cleaner environment so I can relax. I find it difficult to cultivate my strengths and talents when staring at a pile of dirty dishes and trash bags. I must take control of my home so I can regain control of my mind. Or maybe I must take control of my mind to regain control of my home.

Marc attended rehab and he is different in a good way. I feel a quiet strength in him that I want to encourage. However, I cannot encourage Marc when Amy undermines me. She is blowing off school, discouraging Marc's sobriety, lying to me and generally disregarding the rules of my home. Her actions do not line up with her words. I cannot help her any longer. I have little left to give.

Marc is my priority. It is time for me to stop blinding myself with excuses and make tough choices with tougher outcomes. Amy will leave my home by Sunday. She's going to have to fix her situation for herself.

Marc & Amy
November 11, 2011
1 year, 9 months, 20 days of freedom

I haven't shared much of Marc's story because it is his story; however, his story is and always has merged with mine. He is my son.

Monday morning, Marc and Amy sat at the table talking about withdrawing from school. Marc is severely behind in his classes due to attending rehab and his behavior prior to leaving. He said he wants to return to school next semester; his intention is to earn his high school diploma. I told him to talk to his teachers and counselors first, and then we would discuss it.

Amy wants to do online high school; I told her I did not support it. She said her parents would help her set it up. I reminded her that our deal was that she attends high school, not that she stays home all day (probably) doing nothing. I told her that she's done nothing to make me believe she would follow through with online courses. My answer was no. I sent them off to school.

The school counselor called after the first bell. She said both Marc and Amy were in her office. Marc wanted to withdraw; Amy wanted online courses. Surprise, surprise.

I asked the counselor what she would do about Marc if she were me. She said, "Well, he is too big for me to carry to class." I felt stuck. If I don't withdraw him, I face two months of forcing him to go to school with no guarantee that he would do the work. If I withdraw him, I face the possibility that he will not go back to school. I told the counselor I'd be there soon to sign the withdrawal papers. I figure we can use these two months to get his counseling and meetings aligned.

As I searched the house for Marc's psychology book, I found evidence of marijuana use. Will this ever end?

I went to the school and withdrew Marc. I confronted Marc with the paraphernalia when we got home. He attempted a weak defense, but I told him to save it.

Marc said that he didn't believe pot was a drug until he sobered up and realized that his behavior in acquiring pot was the same as when he went after any other drug. He says that he is a "bulldozer" when he's after a substance, and he realizes that pot is no different from DXM, alcohol, or any of the other drugs he's tried. I believed him.

I listened to Marc and Amy when we sat down together after work. He loves her deeply; Marc felt that removing Amy at this point would hurt too much. It appears that Marc understands his addiction better. Shoot, Marc admits he is an addict. He never did that before rehab.

Marc, Amy and I sat at the table for over an hour today. We talked about co-dependence and made a plan for relapses. Amy has bound herself so tightly to Marc that she doesn't know her own voice.

Whoomp! There It Is! Verbal Abuse Strikes Again
November 15, 2011
1 year, 9 months, 24 days of freedom

Last weekend there was a touching scene between my son and his father on my front porch. They hugged and Will said, "You look good, son!" They looked genuinely happy to see each other.

Fast forward to today when I, in my brilliance, decide to call Will. I tell him that Marc feels depressed and it is a good time to run over to my house and ask Marc if wanted to go out and get some sunshine. The scene on the porch encouraged my suggestion.

> [humming to myself] La dee da! I'm doing a good thing for my boy by communicating with my horrible ex - oops, I mean, his father! La dee da la dee da!

Hey - don't knock it. It was a nice fantasy while it lasted.

This afternoon, at work, my ex-husband called to say that he asked Eddie, our youngest, about why Marc was home from school, but Eddie was vague. I explained that Marc's grades were so low after missing so much school for rehab that he wanted to opt out of this semester and return in January. Will asked me how that would affect his GPA and I told him. Will went on to say that although he applauded Marc's decision, he did not appreciate me leaving him out of the loop.(Whoomp there it is: Loud crashing sound of my do-good fantasy collapsing around my desk followed by the thought *you knew he was a snake*...)

Oh really? I thought to myself. Paraphrasing, I said, "You didn't reach out to him in the months before he left while he was struggling. You did not support his decision to go to rehab. You didn't contact him in the days leading up to his departure although I told you when he was leaving. You didn't write him while he was at rehab. You didn't text, email or call me about Marc before or after he left. I don't think you have room to talk about being left out of the loop now."

Will became angry and exploded with a threat. I didn't listen. I hung up the phone. One of these days, I'll learn the lesson of *The Farmer and the Snake* - "Learn from my fate not to take pity on a scoundrel."[11]

One of these days, I will remember *all* the lessons I taught to me at the appropriate times. I don't like remembering important things too late.

Missing Link
November 23, 2011
1 year, 10 months, 1 day of freedom

I'm confused. I'm missing a link somewhere between where I am and where I want to be. I work from home and attend school full-time. I survive financially on a small divorce settlement in the interim, planning on it to last until I make the money I need to support myself. I do not want to go to work for anyone else (as in a *real* job) because I want to budget my own time, use my own ideas, be my own boss. I decided to use the settlement to invest in myself.

I could have invested the settlement in an IRA account. I could have hoarded it in a savings account or certificates of deposits or bonds. But I didn't. I am living on it. For now. I'm scared. I'm missing a link and I don't know what to do.

Begging for It
November 25, 2011
1 year, 10 months, 3 days of freedom

My brain muddies when I wish it would clear. I want time, more time, more time ... but time to do what? This pessimistic vibe infiltrating my outlook feels controlling and mean. I see visions of failure where visions of success once played. I feel forsaken when I'm cared for and lost although I've been found.

I think of my sister, the one who laughs and plays, always looking to today and beyond. Not worried. Encouraging everyone. I want to tell her, "It's impossible; what you say is untrue." I do not believe in joy these days. Happiness is only a dangling carrot. No, it is merely the *hologram* of a dangling carrot.

It's not okay. I'm not all right. The *good* I've done or experienced feels like fraud.

You know, twice last week I allowed thoughts of death to plod along in my mind to the point of thinking that *not being here* would be the best thing for me. But I see my children's faces in my mind's eye and I know it would never be the same for them. It wouldn't be the best thing for them. Would it?

I couldn't leave them here to experience the pain of this world alone. I feel like I'm a horribly nasty, mean, rude person who hides it well. I hate myself. It's been going on like this for a couple of weeks.

Please, All, angels, *life* ... please give me a sign that everything will work out. Something. Anything. I beg you. Please show me the way out of this lie.

Comments from Readers

Erin says - *Look in the mirror and you will see your reason to continue day after day. It is YOU. YOU are worth this patch of disappointing time.*

And, yes. Laughter, playing and hope is real. It is real if you believe it to be, so please, PLEASE believe it to be real. Think back to a time when you felt so very happy. That was real, and that is proof that it exists. You will find it again, Kellie. I promise.

Old Guilt
January 11, 2012
1 year, 11 months, 20 days of freedom

As it stands, Will doesn't communicate with Marc at all unless Marc calls him or they meet while Will drops off Eddie at my house. Marc didn't do what Will wanted him to do, so Will disowned Marc. It's a shame and a blessing all at the same time. It's a shame because I hoped that Will would become a better father after our separation. It's a blessing because Marc no longer has to be around his father's crap.

Will and Eddie get on well enough. Eddie is proud that he is his father's son and tries to imitate Will in some ways. For example, Eddie asked me to buy Irish Spring soap at the store and I told him no. I divorced Will so I wouldn't have to smell his stupid Irish Spring anymore (reminders of Will are memories I can do without). Petty, I guess, but our sense of smell attaches itself to many memories. I don't like the smell of soap triggering negative thoughts and feelings.

Anyway, Eddie makes me proud. He's a super student, responsible driver, and has the heart of a lion. He's getting his license tomorrow and he feels excited! My worry for Eddie is that one day, he's going to do something less than perfectly and suffer his father's wrath as Marc did. But, so long as Eddie fits the mold of daddy's perfect son, then he will never suffer the sting of daddy turning his back to him.

I wish that Eddie would let go a bit - be a little rotten. I worry about the stress he puts on himself for perfection. Some rebellion would be good for my boy. And for Eddie, rebellion would be calling after expected or staying out late and missing curfew. It wouldn't take much for him to spread his wings, and perhaps he'd feel better about himself for doing so. Counter-intuitive perhaps - feeling better about himself because he did something *wrong*.

I'd like Eddie to realize that he controls his world. He has the power to choose and be whomever he wants. If he grows up to show the characteristics I hope he does, then great. If he doesn't, then that's okay too - I'll love Eddie as I've loved Marc with screw-ups and shining moments and all.

Marc once controlled his world like a puppet-master. He knew the power he had, and for the most part used it for selfish reasons. After the incident with his father, Marc's ego took a hard knock. He had no control in that situation. Marc said he could have pushed his father into the open dishwasher, knives up, but he didn't do it. He did not want to injure his dad - he only wanted to get away. His father did not confine his thinking in that way at all. Will choked Marc with his forearm, spitting tobacco chew on his face.

I don't blame Marc for using his puppet master skills. He grew up watching the master manipulate and get what he wanted. Because I didn't understand what I was seeing (denial? I don't think so) and couldn't counter-act it, Marc absorbed it all like a sponge. I think Marc tries now to control what he should control (himself) and leaves others to make their own decisions. There are remnants of those old ways, but I cut him slack.

I am responsible for how I raised the boys, and old guilt dies hard. I feel guilty for many things in my past life, although I've tried to let them go. But when evidence of things I shoulda/woulda done presents itself, I shut down. In the marriage, shutting down felt like all I could do. I didn't seem to hold any control over what happened; Will held the power. The less I did the better it seemed for everyone. But when it came to our boys, Will did very little. So *we* did little for our boys, and my heart aches over it.

The old guilt leads into the denial I've felt over the past weeks. If I ignore the small stuff, then it's not happening. But it is happening - it already happened - and now I'm behind the power curve without the energy needed to fix it quickly. Denial turns me into a paper doll - faceless, flat and unable to enjoy the colors of life. Denying small problems allows them to progress into big ones.

What will happen if I continue to deny that my boys are still in peril of losing themselves to their father's unreal world where they control nothing? Or my unreal world where I sometimes purposefully blind myself to the truth?

Denial Springs Everlasting
January 12, 2012
1 year, 11 months, 21 days of freedom

Today I realized my recent depression began around the time I wrote *Whoomp! There It Is!* almost two months ago. Although I'm far away from Will emotionally, his words triggered me into feeling hopeless and despondent as I did during our marriage.

Depression saps the life from me. When I have no energy for

normal life I begin to deny the wrong or bad things happening around me. Honestly, I want to ignore my unhealthy coping mechanisms during depressions too. Changing myself under the weight of a depression calls out the unhealthy but familiar remedies from my past. Those old remedies are much easier to use than any new and healthier coping skills because I already know how to use them. When I deny knowing better than to hide alone in my room I am able to, well, *comfortably* hide in my room! Isolating myself is unhealthy, but doing the right thing seems too difficult.

Anyway, today is a good day because *realizing* I experienced a trigger will undoubtedly enable me to move past its resulting depression. I feel better already, yet I wonder how much longer emotions and behaviors from the past will haunt me. I think about how far I've come since leaving Will and feel remarkably proud of myself. I deserve to feel proud. However, knowing this process is still two steps forward and one step back causes me to feel tired of trying sometimes. I wish I was healed already!

Voicemails From the Day I Left
January 15, 2012
1 year, 11 months, 24 days of freedom

I almost chickened out the day I left Will. As I drove toward the courthouse to file for an ex-parte order, I pulled over to listen to the voice mails he left for me that morning. Honestly, I was looking for an excuse to go back home.

I was scared out of my mind, but I was not afraid of physical violence because, after all, I'd been through that before. The fear I felt concerned the future. *What would I do to survive? Would anyone hire me? What would happen to our boys? How angry would he be that I followed through on leaving the next time he put his hands on me?*

So, I listened.

He was drunk, but I already knew that. The first voice mail says,

> You gotta lotta nerve...after everything we've been through [garbled] you're gonna play me like this?

I'd left the house because of his threatening behavior and verbal onslaught (supposedly directed at a woman on television, but we know better, don't we?).

The second voicemail says,

> Thank you, Kellie, for being a traitor, and don't ever come back. This is what I've been waitin' for... Bye.

But I had gone back. The first time I'd left, he hadn't put his hands on me. It was a normal night in my abusive household. I went home after I thought he passed out, but I was wrong about the timing. He was waiting for me.

Will assaulted me. I broke free and called the cops, but they couldn't remove him from the home because I had no visible marks (yet). I chose to leave. I left the children because the department of social services told me on another occasion that if I took them with me and didn't send them to school the next day, Will could say I neglected them (turn the tables). I felt panicked, unsure about what to do next, so I left my babies there, knowing Will wasn't upset with *them*. Additionally, my youngest apparently slept through everything and I mistakenly thought my oldest had sided with his father (he cleared that up later).Besides, even after all that, part of me didn't know if I would stay away or return to the home in the morning.

After listening to his voicemails, I thought about our bank accounts. At the house, Will tried to take away my debit and credit cards, but as they had my name on them, the cops wouldn't let him do it. I checked my email and sure enough, he had tried to block me from our joint accounts by changing all the security information

He didn't know I had my own login. I used it to slip our savings out into a personal account I held. After that, I knew I wasn't going home.

I received the ex-parte order that barred him from our home. I waited to hear from the sheriff's department that they'd picked him up, but when there was no response from them by 2:30 PM, I decided to go to my youngest son's school and pick him up. When I got there, I saw both of my children getting into their dad's truck. When he saw me, he called my phone and left the third voicemail, saying,

> I talked to [Eddie], told him how I felt about how I felt it was better for him and his brother to be together, so the decision was his: he could go with you over to [my friend's house] if that's what he wanted. I'm assuming that's where you're at. And uh, he said he'd rather, well, he said he'd let me make the decision, so, with that being said, I made the decision for us to stay together tonight.
>
> So, if you have any questions or concerns, you can call me. I'm not hidin', I'm not duckin', nothin' like that, so uh, you know the phone number. Bye.

If Will wasn't duckin' or hidin', then why did he go to pull our son out of school without calling me first or stopping to speak to me in person when he saw me in the parking lot? Watching him drive away with our sons felt gut wrenching. I didn't know what was going to happen. All I knew was I wasn't going home, no matter what.

He recorded the first two voice mails drunk. If I had listened to them as he left them, I probably would have gone home despite what he said. I was upset that he blamed me for what happened ("this is how you're gonna play this" and "traitor"). What? It wasn't my fault, and I knew that. But, so you know, two years out of this mess and he still denies any responsibility.

His third voicemail sounds confident and self-assured. He's happy with himself. He presents *the facts* to me as if I have no say in the matter using his normal voice. No concern, no upset, nothing. He thinks he won. The only reason he corrected himself to say that he decided what to do was because my sons were in the car with him. If he'd been alone, he would have simply said that our sons decided to stay with him.

An Anniversary Worth Celebrating
January 22, 2012
Two years of freedom

Today, two years ago, I left my marriage. I've come so far since then; I did the right thing for my children and myself. Today, I re-read the two entries that changed the meaning of this blog forever: *My Heart is Failing* and *I Left Twice*. Soon after writing those posts, I realized my abusive marriage was over.

Today, I am fortunate to write this blog from a different perspective. The marriage was abusive, but it no longer exists. What I write now concerns how I'm moving past it and the abuse, and I am joyful that I am no longer in the marriage or embroiled in abuse.

On January 22, 2010, I left my home two times. The first time was a common event: I was scared but planned to return home after his temper had cooled or he passed out. I took a blanket and my purse. I left that time only minutes after typing the last word in the post called *My Heart is Failing*.

When I returned home, all hell broke loose. I called the police, but I had no visible bruises, so the cops would not remove him from the home (worthless!). I left because I feared what he would do after the police pulled out of the driveway and left me with Will.

It wasn't until January 24 that I had the wherewithal to write about what had happened in *I Left Twice*. By the time I wrote that entry, a judge had granted me an ex-parte order and the police had arrested Will and removed him from the home. The judge was able to do what the police could not - buy me two days of safety as Will sat in jail until Monday.

I Left Twice did not delve into my feelings so much as it reported what happened the night before. I wanted to write it out as soon as possible so I wouldn't forget. On that day, more people read my blog than on any day before that - ever. One of the people who read it commented on several other posts. Ramona Vickers obviously supported Will while saying she (or he) supported both of us. Ramona's comments inflamed me when I felt most vulnerable. I gave her (or him) more information than I would have given today.

Blessedly, in addition to my comments, two others piped in for my defense. I will never forget their words of encouragement and calm, rational thought. Well, my sister Erin may not have been calm or rational, but I appreciated her challenge to Ramona just the same.

Keep in mind what judgments you make when you hear of someone leaving his or her marriage due to abuse. It is so easy to lay blame on the victim, even when you think you're being neutral. What if I had listened to Ramona's nonsense? I wouldn't be writing this blog today, that's for sure.

Thank you for being here with me during the marriage and for this week's celebration. I am free to live my life. My new mistakes alongside greater victories remind me that although my healing is far from over, I am well on my way to being exactly who I want to be. And gosh darn it, I like who I am right now.

Appendix

About the Author

Kellie Jo Holly passionately advocates against domestic violence through her writing and mentoring service. She loves helping women cope with abuse while in the relationship and supporting them as they leave the relationship and begin to heal. Kellie began her blog titled *My Abusive Marriage...and what i'm doing in it* during the last year of her abusive marriage as a way to fight against her husband's crazy-making and gaslighting. This second book, also based on the blog, describes her healing process after leaving the abusive relationship.

Additionally, Kellie compiled the *Domestic Violence Safety Plan - A comprehensive plan that will help keep you safer whether you stay or leave*. After researching the safety plans available from several domestic violence programs across the country, Kellie recommends this *Domestic Violence Safety Plan* to counselors, crisis line volunteers, nurses and triage workers, domestic violence groups and anyone who regularly talks with victims of domestic violence and abuse.

Future planned releases include a novel and several how-to cope with abuse and how-to heal from abuse publications.

Find Kellie Jo Holly Online

Verbal Abuse Journals at http://www.VerbalAbuseJournals.com

Facebook at https://www.facebook.com/VerbalAbuseJournals

Twitter at https://twitter.com/abuse_journals

YouTube at http://www.youtube.com/user/verbalabusejournal

Amazon.com at http://www.amazon.com/Kellie-Jo-Holly/e/B009UYGMIG

Bibliography

Bancroft, L. (2002). Why does he do that?: Inside the minds of angry and controlling men. New York: Putnam's Sons.

Bancroft, L. (2004). When dad hurts mom: Helping your children heal the wounds of witnessing abuse. New York: G.P. Putnam's Sons.

Chavez, E. (n.d.). Hypnosis for Abuse Victims. Retrieved December 18, 2014, from http://www.verbalabusejournals.com/sound-files/detach-from-abuse.mp3

Could a black hole absorb enough mass to become a Big Bang? (n.d.). Retrieved December 18, 2014, from http://www.astronomycafe.net/qadir/q1355.html

Covey, S. (1989). The seven habits of highly effective people: Restoring the character ethic. New York: Simon and Schuster.

Elgin, S. (1995). You can't say that to me!: Stopping the pain of verbal abuse : An 8-step program. New York: Wiley.

Ellis, A., & Lange, A. (2005). How to keep people from pushing your buttons. New York: MJF Books.

Evans, Patricia. (2006). *The Verbally Abusive Man: Can He Change? A Woman's Guide to Deciding Whether to Stay or Go*. Avon, MA: Adams Media.

Holly, K. (2009, April 24). Effects of Verbal Abuse. Retrieved December 19, 2014, from https://www.youtube.com/watch?v=mROKUE3hyp8&list=UUina2dkBpCzmHbxMtDnRYCw

Holly, K. (2011, January 15). Verbal Abuse in Relationships - HealthyPlace.com. Retrieved December 18, 2014, from http://www.healthyplace.com/blogs/verbalabuseinrelationships

Holly, K. (2012, May 31). Conversation With Depression. Retrieved December 18, 2014, from http://verbalabusejournals.com/stories-abuse/story-of-abuse/year-2002-2007/conversation-depression/

O'Callaghan, T. (2010, April 13). Many abused women view

partners as "dependable" | TIME.com. Retrieved December 18, 2014, from http://healthland.time.com/2010/04/13/many-abused-women-view-partners-as-dependable/

Sher, B. (2006). Refuse to choose!: A revolutionary program for doing everything that you love. Emmaus, Pa.: Rodale.

The Verbal Abuse Site. (n.d.). Retrieved December 18, 2014, from http://www.VerbalAbuse.com

Verbal Abuse, Control, and Change by Patricia Evans. (n.d.). Retrieved December 15, 2014, from http://youtu.be/X4uii2KznNY

Recommended Websites

Do you recognize your relationship in these pages? If so, then it is likely your relationship is abusive. You are not alone. Many people are in your shoes, and many others want to help you.

The National Domestic Violence Hotline

800-799-7233 (SAFE) or TTY 800-787-3224
http://www.thehotline.org

This hotline is available for victims of abuse and those who love people who are victims of abuse. The hotline volunteers listen and advise, and they point you to domestic violence services in your local area.

Domestic Violence Hotline for Men & Women

888-743-5754
http://dahmw.org/

This hotline specializes in aiding abused men, but it is open to anyone needing assistance.

Verbal Abuse Journals

http://www.VerbalAbuseJournals.com

Kellie Jo Holly's website contains valuable information about all forms of domestic violence and abuse. Join a free mentoring program that provides help to abuse survivors and victims.

HealthyPlace.com

Kellie Jo Holly's blog called *Verbal Abuse In Relationships* at http://www.healthyplace.com/blogs/VerbalAbuseInRelationships

End Notes

[1] Throughout the book, I refer to God as ALL. I prefer to think of Him as a Mother and Father because the pronoun He used alone seems incomplete.

[2] You can listen to Erin's hypnosis for abuse victims at http://www.verbalabusejournals.com/sound-files/detach-from-abuse.mp3

[3] **Trick or Treat • October 31, 2008 • 1 year, 2 months, 23 days until the end**

Fight last night. I'm at a loss – I feel like I sold out.

As soon as Will seemed emotionally beat – showing wet eyes, I jumped on the chance to comfort him. Why did I do that? I felt horrible; ignoring him and staying calm took all the strength I had at the end. When he started to cry, a switch turned inside me and I ran to him to ease his mind. Am I an abuser? Am I living in a fantasy world? Am I sick?

In the beginning of the fight, when Will's dad was still in the house, Will kept baiting me with insults. I repeatedly told him that I did not want to talk. Eventually he said, "Fine, I'll sit here and just look at you then", and did so, chugging on his beer but keeping his eyes on me.

I got up and went to another room. Will decided that I could not use my computer anymore, and he unplugged everything, loudly saying, "I'm going to lock this shit up. You will have to beg me to give it back." Will's dad left to go to his apartment above the garage.

This fight went on and on and on. Will dragged our boys into it, asking them to judge whether he was verbally abusing me or if I was verbally abusing him. Those poor boys. I tried to let them know I didn't care what they said. I wanted them out of there. Marc defended me and Will almost hit him. The threat of physical violence on top of the verbal abuse – diverting and blocking plus flat out rudeness - caused me to step in to stop it. He told Marc he was a coward and for being so book smart he "sure was stupid."

I got both Marc and Eddie to my neighbor's house, but not before pushing Will out of the doorway. If Will had not drunk so much whiskey, then he wouldn't have lost his balance and the boys could not have escaped past him. That happened before 8 PM. Will kept on until 10:30. It was horrible.

Then, when he finally showed signs of wearing down, what did I do? I ran over to sit by him, comfort him and try to find a way for HIM to feel better. Toward the end, I really felt like we were getting somewhere closer to him realizing the truth. At least my idea of the truth.

Will's perspective is dreary, dark and miserable. He "sees" horrible things in the future whereas MY visions are discounted. He fears that his sons will not be capable men. He fears that I will leave him "for no reason". He fears that there will be another Great Depression, and he will lose everything he's earned. He bases his life on "fear of" this, that and the other. His fear compels him to be nice to people he hates and work for idiots instead of himself. Will says he puts in 120% every day and that he is exhausted and frustrated. Instead of putting 120% of his effort into the "two handfuls of people" he cares about, he puts all that effort into looking good to the others he claims to hate. Leaving nothing for us. Nothing.

He denies everything that concerns me. Will denies the word "abuse" in particular. My gut tells me that he will resort to physical violence before this is over. I will put the guns in the attic on Monday. He is home today and all weekend, and I do not want to take the chance of him catching me as I hide them.

I'm not sure about how helpful Will's dad could be to the boys and me. He walked out last night instead of asking the boys or me if we wanted to go with him or trying to do something to distract Will. Mr. Holly seems to be under the impression that I refuse to go to therapy with Will. I think Will told him that I am the one who wouldn't go or walked out. That is a lie. The worst part is that Will believes his own lies, so I imagine convincing his father of those lies is easy.

On the other hand, Miss Helen, our neighbor, came over earlier today. After talking for a while, she said, "How are you?" and I said, "Not good," and told her Will and I were having problems.

She grabbed me up and hugged me and said, "The minute I saw you I knew something was wrong!" and added that she knew Will had a temper and if there was anything she could ever do for me to just ask. She hugged me and that hug meant that she knew I was not a liar. It meant she believed me. I thought he had her fooled, but it looks more and more as if he is the fool.

So why do I feel so afraid to be "right" about what's going on here? What does it mean for my family if I am right?

[4] **Participant in My Own Abuse • November 26, 2008 • 1 year, 4 months, 28 days until the end**

Am I codependent? Am I an abuser? Am I an active participant in my own abuse? I am starting to believe the answer to the last question is "Yes."

I have one more strategy to try. In the book *You Can't Say That to Me* by Suzette Haden Elgin, the author describes a situation in which the verbal abuse victim participates in the cycle of abuse by using the main three natural defenses:

...pleading for the abuse to stop,

...trying to logically debate with the abuser,

...and fighting fire with fire (being abusive in return).

The author is right – those three reactions are "natural" and "common". I've used all three.

However, the abuser does not really want the answer to his questions or any other reaction besides the one he always manages to get – the victim's attention. When Will engages me in one of those horrible conversations and I actively take part by giving him the attention and reactions he's after, I am participating in my own abuse.

I know by now (after having it explained to me via the books I have read) that participating in his "conversations" always negatively affects me and the situation. There is no way to "win" but the reactions I've given lead to a "winner".

When I plead for the abuse or "conversation" to end, I "win" if it stops. If I am able to beat him at his own word game, I "win." If I am abusive to him in response, I "win" if I am able to get him to walk away and leave me alone.

I don't "win" often, and I've never considered it "winning" when I manage to get him to retreat. On the rare occasion that I do "win", I feel terrible. Conversely, when he "wins" I get more of the same treatment. He will continue to berate me because I run out of energy or he completely withdraws and ignores me for hours or days. Sometimes after "winning", he even admits that he behaved badly. Never apologizes, but admits he behaved badly.

You know what? When I "win", I typically go to him and apologize. Imagining he is hurt makes me want to fix the situation or assuage my guilt. But I am not always sure that he's hurt; perhaps he is simply plotting his revenge.

Anyway, in the book, Dr. Elgin gives alternate means of using language to diffuse the situation before it gets ugly. The abuser can get as ugly as he wants, but the theory is that if I have enough self-control to react properly to his attacks, I can leave the situation with my dignity (and his) intact.

The problem is that at this point, I am so angry that this has gone on so long, I'm not sure I even WANT to TRY her techniques. I am tired. No, exhausted. It pisses me off that I haven't figured these things out for myself, and it pisses me off that I must be the one to implement a new strategy. Maybe I need an anger management class so I can get to the point of hoping this works out and having the energy and confidence to try a new approach.

No, I don't need the class. I just need a good night's sleep and to come to terms with the fact that it is going to continue in the same manner UNLESS I change SOMETHING. I can gather my strength, overcome my anger and give it another shot. Maybe, just maybe, this approach will work to bring a little peace to my life. The author claims that it will. All I can do is summon my curiosity and TRY it.

[5] Interview with Patricia Evans at http://youtu.be/X4uii2KznNY

[6] Image available at http://verbalabusejournals.com/stories-abuse/story-of-abuse/year-2002-2007/conversation-depression/

[7] **A Dream Within a Dream • Edgar Allan Poe**

    Take this kiss upon the brow!
    And, in parting from you now,
    Thus much let me avow —
    You are not wrong, who deem
    That my days have been a dream;
    Yet if hope has flown away
    In a night, or in a day,
    In a vision, or in none,
    Is it therefore the less gone?
    All that we see or seem
    Is but a dream within a dream.

    I stand amid the roar
    Of a surf-tormented shore,
    And I hold within my hand
    Grains of the golden sand —
    How few! yet how they creep
    Through my fingers to the deep,
    While I weep — while I weep!
    O God! Can I not grasp
    Them with a tighter clasp?
    O God! can I not save
    One from the pitiless wave?
    Is all that we see or seem
    But a dream within a dream?

[8] **Pride and Greed • November 29, 2009 • 1 month, 25 days until the end**

Pride and Greed walked a darkened path. Pride spoke excitedly about the wonderful ideas floating around inside of her. She was full of promise. Her enthusiasm acted as a torch light, guiding their steps.

Pride spoke so eloquently and confidently that Greed believed her. He believed that she held the key to glory. He believed that everything she touched would turn to gold. Pride seemed to agree with him. She was sure she had all the answers, and Greed became certain he wanted them.

Suddenly, Greed wanted Pride to be his forever. He wanted to make Pride his own so she would be his helpmate. He wanted her light for himself, but she was so wonderful! He feared she would never want to be with the likes of him.

Greed sought to dim her light just enough to make her his equal, so Greed began to question Pride's statements.

Pride said, "...and the grass is green because of a photochemical-"

"Have you seen this chemical?" Greed asked.

"Well, no. I don't have to see it to know it is there."

"Yes you do. If you can't see it, you cannot be sure it's there," Greed argued.

Pride acquiesced, "You are right. If I cannot see it, then I cannot be sure it is there." Her light dimmed a little, and Greed thought he was bringing her closer to being like him.

Pride continued, "But there are ways that I can see it. I will buy a microscope and-"

Greed began laughing. "Oh my, you are funny. How will you buy a microscope on your salary? You do not have a job to support your fantasies," he said.

Pride's light dimmed a little more. "You are right," Pride said, "I cannot afford a microscope, but I can go to the library. I will bring you a book that teaches of photo-chemicals, and then even though we cannot see it, we will know it is there."

Greed said, "That is silly. Anyone can write a book and say whatever he wants to say in it. There's always some sucker willing to believe a silly lie because it is printed there."

Pride's light faded to a pale glow. "You are right. There are people like that in the world. Perhaps I don't know as much as I thought I knew about the world."

Her light dimmed lower still.

She said, "I'm worried. I'm scared that what I knew earlier is a lie and that I have no way to care for myself. I am sad that my ideas are doomed to failure." And her light went out.

Greed grabbed Pride's arm and stopped her. He saw that her torch had gone out and thought now he could have her. Now she would want him, her light would return, and it would be his.

He said, "You know, this world is a dark place. It is very dangerous for you, who will believe anything. Let me protect you. Be my wife."

Pride glanced around in the darkness and saw nothing, not even the sly smile on Greed's lips. She was scared. "Okay. I will marry you."

But now their path was dark. Neither could see where the path had gone. They stumbled about, falling hard on their faces more than once.

"Dammit," Greed said, "Turn on your light! I cannot see anything and we are hurting!"

"What light?" Pride asked. "You said you would protect me! You said that you would save me! I know nothing of the ways of this world, dear husband. I do not have a light."

[9] Find Freedom From the Abusive Cycle • July 24, 2011

Although unseen in the tumultuous immediate aftermath of *The Day I Left Him*, justice was served. Nevertheless, in my pain, I felt

- slighted by my son who ran from me
- betrayed by my husband who wouldn't admit the truth
- punished by the judge who gave custody to my abuser
- unable to see where my actions caused him any tragic feelings remotely similar to my own (I wanted him to hurt, and he didn't)

It seemed he'd won. I felt justice wasn't only blind, but also the stupidest philosophical idea ever imagined by mankind.

I was wrong, Justice was mine even then, her soft robes encircling me in a healing cocoon. I didn't see Justice because I wished her to be vengeful, but Justice decided to give me what I needed instead.

No One Can Make the Abuser Change

No one, not even Justice, could give me what I wanted because not one entity in this world or beyond can make an abuser change. Justice, in her blind wisdom, knew this.

Justice didn't bring vengeance to the fight because provoking a controller causes them to want to "win" at any cost. Controllers can act like animals forced to fight to the death; vengeance would have bled me (and our children) dry.

Balancing Between Anger and Peace

In the days after "losing" my children to him, Justice compelled me to take care of myself. There was no one else to tend to, no one else to help. Only me. I was thrown out of my comfort zone and had no other person's emotions to hide behind. Justice forced me to deal with my own.

Day by day, I found balance between anger and peace. I was so angry, yet every night, I went to sleep knowing he wasn't going to bother me tonight. Eventually, I found myself waking with a smile and hope instead of oppressive sadness. I didn't have my children with me like I wanted, yet feeling true peacefulness allowed me to believe there was a better future.

I believed my life would only get better. I believed in myself, and no longer wished he would feel anything. I didn't care what he felt. He was no longer a piece of me. We were separate, and I refused to carry the responsibility for his thoughts or emotions.

Justice prevailed. I was free.

Strength to Move Forward

I was scared, too. I realized that with freedom comes responsibility, and responsibility requires courage.

- I took classes I didn't know if I needed just to get myself out of the house.
- I made connections I didn't know if I would use just in case I needed to move in an unpredictable direction.
- I moved into a house before I had a job (only 3 months rent + deposit) just to get out of his house.
- I took a job despite the low pay just to gain experience somewhere.

My decisions at that time did not forecast where I would be now, but they pushed me in the direction I needed to go. I did what I believed would benefit me in some way at some point, and my results justified my actions.

Freedom From the Abusive Cycle

His abusive words and controlling nature still affected my emotions, but I handled them differently. I was proving to myself how wrong he was about me and how wrong I had been about myself. I am capable, prudent, intuitive and motivated.

His little nicknames (i.e. "Miss Independent" while taking his money in alimony payments) do not bother me. I am who I am; I dictate my motives, my feelings and my decisions – I am Miss Independent.

Justice, by refusing to wreak vengeance on him, taught me to feel joy and find peace through my own thoughts and actions.

Happiness underlies freedom, freedom requires responsibility and meeting those responsibilities produces happiness. That's about as far from the abusive cycle as anyone can get.

You can't always get what you want
You can't always get what you want
You can't always get what you want
But if you try sometimes well you might find
You get what you need. ~The Rolling Stones

[10] Abuse Victims & Abusive Anger • October 31, 2011

A few years ago, I promised my children that I would not yell and storm at them when it was time to do their chores. After a bit of trial and error, I successfully reigned in Mommy Mean. I felt relief when I no longer saw my boys' tear-stained faces staring at me in fear. I felt like I was a better person after taming my temper.

A couple of years later, while married to my abuser, I extended my "no yelling" policy to my husband, too. Although I wasn't quite as successful when it came to him, my participation in our once habitual yelling matches dwindled significantly. I still felt the pain and anguish, but I no longer fought fire with fire (that never worked anyway).

On the night I left, during the build-up to the main event, my husband quietly asked me, "Why don't you get mad no more?" as he traced the vertical line etched from anger between my eyebrows. I think he missed my displays of anger. I think he missed having someone to out-yell, someone to conquer, someone to reduce from hell-fire to tears.

In hindsight, I do not believe that fiery temper was ever mine. I feel I created it in reaction to his abusive anger antics. His intimidating temper worked on me; I was afraid of him. I transferred his temper's effectiveness to my innocent boys.

In the back of my mind, I thought that if the children obeyed me better, maybe my husband would respect me. My memory could be wrong after all this time, but I think that my wrath flew out of me when I was trying to accomplish something my husband wanted: a clean house, a duplicate of the mother that he remembered from childhood, a "good wife" on whom he could rely.

I take full responsibility for the damage I caused due to my actions and rage. I worked hard to remove abusive anger from my motherly repertoire and worked to replace it with something calmer, something more my style. I remember on purpose what it was like to unleash that fury onto my children because I never want to see that look of pain and betrayal on anyone's face ever again. I try so very hard to not express myself in any ugly or intimidating manner.

Please re-read that last sentence and ask yourself, "If she's got her anger under control, then why is she still trying to not be abusively angry?" If I've truly solved my anger problem, then I would not fear it boiling over, and I wouldn't have days like last Saturday.

Last Saturday I woke up seething. I was fed up with my kids seeming refusal to do any chores; sick to death of asking them to perform the simplest tasks. Fortunately, my new anger behaviors allowed me to approach them with my frustrations in a calm, collected manner.

The problem with last Saturday wasn't in how I approached the children, but in how I reacted to Max (my best friend). Max empathizes with me when I come home to a house that looks like a tornado ripped through it. He sees my frustration over my inability to completely control the household mess. Yet it was Max who endured my testiness and sharp tongue. I was angry with myself! Angry with the children! Angry with everything! I hurt Max's feelings by cutting him off mid-sentence, telling him to leave me alone, and generally acting like a caged wild animal. The more empathetic Max became, the angrier I felt.

Even so, I know what created Saturday's problem. I've overlooked a hundred little things and told myself I was controlling my temper when I was actually ignoring it. I am making the mistake of thinking that because I'm not yelling, I'm not angry. I'm wrong about that.

I'm disappointed that now, years after ending my temper tantrums, I've replaced them with comments designed to inflict damage so everyone will leave me alone. I quietly, subtly, hurt people whom I'm not angry with because I know better than to do it out loud in the faces of those with whom I am angry.

I can look at this one of two ways. 1.) I continue to have an anger problem. The only difference is that I don't yell (boo-hoo, poor me) or 2.) I realize I have an anger problem and can now work to solve it for real.

My anger issues no longer evolve around an abusive marriage. I will not hide behind a victim facade angrily screaming, "You did this to me!" Abuse did a number on me, for sure. But now that I'm free of that relationship, it's my responsibility to face my shortcomings and accept responsibility for them. My anger isn't my abuser's fault, it's mine. Fortunately, I no longer look to him to "fix" me. I am perfectly capable of fixing myself.

[11] **The Farmer and the Snake**

One winter day, a farmer found a snake by the roadside, stiff and motionless with cold. "If you put me inside your shirt," the snake said, "your body will make me warm and I won't freeze to death."

"Oh, I know your kind," replied the farmer. "If I pick you up, you will bite me."

"Oh no," the snake objected. "Why would I do such a thing, if you are good enough to help me?"

So the farmer had compassion on the snake, and taking it up, he put it inside his shirt. The warmth quickly revived the snake, and resuming its natural instincts, it bit its benefactor, inflicting on him a mortal wound.

"Oh," cried the farmer with his last breath, "why did you bite me? You promised you wouldn't."

"Ah," said the snake. "So I did. But you knew I was a snake when you picked me up."